500
Questions
—— *and* ——
Answers
on Chanukah

Also by Jeffrey M Cohen:

Understanding the Synagogue Service
A Samaritan Chronicle
Festival Adventure
Understanding the High Holyday Services
Yizkor
Horizons of Jewish Prayer
Moments of Insight
Blessed Are You
Judaism section, Penguin Encyclopedia of Religions
Prayer and Penitence
Dear Chief Rabbi (ed.)
1001 Questions and Answers on Pesach
Following the Synagogue Service
1001 Questions and Answers on Rosh Hashanah and Yom Kippur
Issues of the Day
The Abridged Haggadah for Rusty Readers
Let My people Go: Insights into Pesach and the Haggadah
The Bedside Companion for Jewish Patients
Studies and Messages for the Bar and Bat Mitzvah (In preparation)

500

Questions

—— *and* ——

Answers

on Chanukah

Jeffrey M. Cohen

VALLENTINE MITCHELL
LONDON • PORTLAND, OR

First published in 2006 in Great Britain by
VALLENTINE MITCHELL
Suite 314, Premier House,
112–114 Station Road,
Edgware, Middlesex, HA8 7BJ, UK

and in the United States of America by
VALLENTINE MITCHELL
c/o International Specialized Book Services, Inc.,
920 NE 58th Avenue, Suite 300
Portland, Oregon, 97213-3786

Website: **www.vmbooks.com**

British Library Cataloguing in Publication Data

A catalogue record for this book has been applied for

ISBN 0-85303-676-4 (cloth)
ISBN 0-85303-675-6 (paper)

Library of Congress Cataloging-in-Publication Data

A catalog record for this book has been applied for

Typeset in 10/12pt Times by FiSH Books, Enfield, Middx.
Printed in Great Britain by Creative Print and Design, Ebbw Vale, Gwent, Wales.

To Gloria
with love and gratitude

And to our children:
Harvey and Lorraine
Suzanne and Keith
Judith and Bob
Lewis and Suzanne

And to our adored grandchildren:
Joel, Phil, Alex, Eliot, Abigail,
Ariel, Charlotte, Maddy,
Sasha, Zack, Leo
and Solomon

Contents

Preface

Having already written two comprehensive works on the festivals, *1001 Questions and Answers on Pesach* and *1001 Questions and Answers on Rosh Hashanah and Yom Kippur*, friends were rather sceptical when I told them that I was continuing the series with a volume on Chanukah. 'You'll have a job to stretch it out to 200 questions!' was a typical response. And it was in that pessimistic spirit that the publishers and I decided to err on the side of caution and restrict this volume to a mere 500 questions and answers! However, Torah is an ever-expanding universe, and it was with a measure of regret that I had to condense my material and personal insights to fit the present volume. Nevertheless, I am hopeful that readers will consider that most, if not all, aspects of this festival have been touched upon, to a greater or lesser degree.

I was eager to write a volume on Chanukah for several reasons. First, because of the fascinating period of Jewish history that this festival spans. To fully appreciate Chanukah, one has to explore both the general and Jewish history of the period. And a most exciting, albeit turbulent period it was, with Jews exerting a far greater influence on events in the entire region than is generally realised, and standing out as the sole subject-state within the Greek empire to have resisted its military and cultural onslaught. The precarious geographical situation of Judea, caught between the two claws of the iron-pincer constituted by the mighty rival and ever-warring kingdoms of the Seleucids and Ptolemies, rendered her continued existence, let alone her successful rebellion and the regaining of her independence, an absolute miracle.

I had long wished to explore this phenomenon in the context of the festival that celebrates it, and to enlighten Jewish students and laymen regarding the social, religious and political background of the period. My objective is that they might better appreciate the significance of the Maccabean Struggle as well as its far-reaching ramifications for the development of Judaism. For there is no doubt that the clash, followed by the tentative steps toward interaction and accommodation between Judaism and Greek enlightenment, was not an entirely negative exercise. The effect of Judaism's vigorous promotion of monotheism, and the dignity that this doctrine conferred on all humankind, as created in God's image, coupled with the discipline, warmth and security offered by the Jewish way-of-life, cannot be overestimated as a powerful catalyst for the undermining and eventual destruction of Graeco-Roman paganism. While Christianity took the entire credit for this, it employed the distinctive armoury of the Jewish, spiritual, ethical and moral tradition.

But, conversely, it was Greek culture and enlightenment which, to a great extent, provided Jewry with the analytical prowess, philosophical sophistication, linguistic flexibility, legal principles, hermeneutic skills and economic and political theory that was to prove invaluable in the evolution of Talmudic law as one of the greatest systems of jurisprudence. It also played its part in, and provided the theoretical basis for, the cultivation of a Jewry that was passionately committed to the furtherance of education, culture, human rights, responsible citizenship and social welfare. The seeds of all those attributes were sown in the period within which the festival of Chanukah is set, and its rapid development occurred during the succeeding two centuries of independent and dynamic, albeit fraught, Jewish statehood. That Graeco-Jewish symbiosis has not received its full recognition as a remarkable example of the lion and lamb not only feeding from the same trough, but feeding each other to boot!

My second purpose in writing this volume is to fill a vacuum. I am not aware of any other book in the English language that has treated of this festival in such a detailed and comprehensive manner, covering the nature of its social and historical background, the challenge of Hellenism, a description of the Temple that was at the centre of the struggle, an analysis of the main (and conflicting) literary sources for, and traditions regarding, the festival, a detailed survey of the laws, customs and rituals governing its observance and celebration both in the synagogue and the home, as well as a section which treats philosophically and homiletically of many aspects of the festival, such as the concept of light in Jewish tradition. There is also a practical section offering guidance regarding bereavement over Chanukah, and one that chronicles the customs and exotic practices of Oriental and Occidental Jewish communities around the world. As befits a festival that especially captures the imagination of the young, the book concludes with a chapter of quiz questions and activities for the younger generation.

For whom is this book intended, and at what level is it pitched? As I wrote in the Introduction to my book on Pesach,

> I have tried to ensure that this is not a run-of-the-mill, superficial, question- and-answer manual. Every question is dealt with fully, if not exhaustively, and with reference to the sources. Where the answer could be given in a few sentences, a brief answer is employed; and where a few pages are required, they are provided. I have endeavoured to marshal my information as lucidly as possible, so that beginners as well as the more advanced reader might profit from it. I have tried to write a book for college students and their parents, for teachers and homemakers, for rabbis and laymen. (Preface to *1001 Questions & Answers on Pesach*.)

This has remained my approach in this volume, which is replete with personal insights, reasoned theories and acknowledged speculation. These are most manifest in Part Three where I analyse and attempt to unravel the mystery of the five main, and conflicting, literary sources of I and II Maccabees, Megillat Ta'anit, Talmud and liturgy. The two Books of the Maccabees, the most detailed of the historical sources (as well as being closest in time to the events of Chanukah), for example, make not a single reference to the miracle of the oil in their description of the victory celebrations, notwithstanding that it is that occurrence which lies at the very epicentre of the festival's religious ritual! Again, if the miracle of the oil had occupied centre stage at the Maccabean re-dedication ceremony in 165 BCE, how was it that the great sages, Hillel and Shammai, were in such vehement dispute, over 200 years later, regarding how the lights should be lit? This surely suggests that this ritual was of recent vintage! This problem is compounded by the fact that their contemporary, the renegade historian, Flavius Josephus, seems totally unaware of the traditional name of the festival, 'Chanukah', claiming that, from Maccabean times onward, it was called 'Lights'.

Other allied questions that call for explanation are why the Mishnah, Judaism's primary exposition of Jewish law and tradition, allocated no special volume to an exposition of the laws and rituals of this festival, such as it did in the case of Purim with its Tractate *Megillah*. Furthermore, how do we explain the fact that, although the Talmud, a late source for Chanukah, provides us with what we have come to regard as the traditional explanation for the duration of the festival, the centuries earlier source of I Maccabees offers no explanation at all? II Maccabees, on the other hand, offers the strange rationale that the re-dedication of the Temple was observed as a harvest festival, with lulav-palm and green sprigs, as compensation for the fact that, with the Temple in the hands of the gentiles two months earlier, the Jews had been unable to observe the eight day festival of Tabernacles. The 1st century *Megillat Ta'anit* source is even more ingenious, attributing the eight nights to the fact that the Jews used eight spears to improvise a Temple candelabrum for the re-dedication ceremony!

I have attempted to explain the rationale of each of those sources, and, in so doing, to trace the evolution of Chanukah from its origin, as an exclusively Temple-based festival and re-dedication celebration, to its expansion into a home ritual during the first century. I have tried to keep my exposition simple in the hope that the general reader will appreciate the fascinating exercise of linking together the literary and historical pieces that constitute the jigsaw of those apparently irreconcilable sources.

I would like to place on record my thanks to Mr Frank Cass, of Vallentine Mitchell, Publishers, for having come to the rescue of this book after the unfortunate liquidation of the original publishing company that had undertaken its publication. I also thank my nephew, Mr Michael Cohen, for his help with the compilation of the quiz questions and activities for the younger generation, and my friend, Mr Clive Boxer, for having read the proofs and for his helpful suggestions.

As always, I thank Gloria, my beloved wife of over forty years, for her infinite indulgence and patience, enabling me to lock myself away in my study for hours and months on end while working on this book, leaving her to take all the messages from our vast synagogue membership and to cajole me later to ensure that I have responded to all the accumulated matters. I also thank her for tolerating the rather distracted air that I apparently exude during the entire gestation period of a book! Above all, I thank her for her love and support, and for engendering, not only on Chanukah, but every Shabbat and festival, a unique feeling of joy, tranquillity and spirituality. I only write about it. She creates it!

JMC

I
The Historical Background

1

From Abraham to Alexander

1. Can you give us a brief overview of Jewish history until the period leading into the events of Chanukah?

It's a tall order, but I'll try. Jewish history began with Abraham and his patriarchal family who lived in Canaan (Israel) around 1900 BCE. Abraham's great grandson, Joseph, was sold into Egypt by his brothers, where he had a meteoric rise to become Viceroy of the country. His aged father and his brothers eventually came to settle there after a famine made life in Canaan very difficult. They multiplied there into a sizeable clan that came to be viewed as a threat by the indigenous population which sought to contain them by a process of oppression and enslavement. God sent Moses to negotiate their release, and, aided by heavenly plagues, they were delivered from Egypt, fulfilling to the letter every detail of the promise originally given to Abraham that his offspring would leave Egypt with great wealth to inherit the Promised land.

The ultimate conquest was a protracted exercise, spanning the period of Joshua, Moses' successor, and the Judges. The latter were tribal leaders who tried, with varying degrees of success, not only to throw off the yoke of a succession of neighbouring invaders, but also to weld the disparate Israelite tribes into a cohesive confederacy. Real national unity was ultimately (though temporarily) achieved with the establishment of the monarchy under Israel's first kings, Saul, David and Solomon. David, after neutralizing the indigenous Jebusites, made Jerusalem the nation's capital, and his son, Solomon, built the first Temple (circa 970 BCE).

At the death of Solomon, in 928 BCE, his kingdom was divided into a northern, break-away kingdom, called Israel (or Samaria), led by one Jeroboam and comprising ten of the twelve tribes, and a southern kingdom, called Judah (or Judea), loyal to Solomon's son, Rehoboam, and comprising the tribes of Judah and Benjamin, and the Temple which straddled their adjoining territory.

EXILE AND RETURN

In 721 BCE the northern kingdom was invaded by the Assyrian ruler, Sargon, who effected a mass captivity of the ten tribes of Israel. The latter quickly assimilated into the land and ways of their captors, and were 'lost' to the Jewish people and the God of Israel. The kingdom of Judah survived until 586 BCE, when it was invaded by Nebuchadnezzar, who took its entire citizenry into captivity in Babylon. However, when Cyrus the Persian, in turn, displaced the Babylonians, he gave permission for the Judeans to return and rebuild their Temple and their devastated homeland. In the year 538 BCE a group of 42,360[1] returned home under their leader, Sheshbazzar, to whom the Persians entrusted the Temple vessels originally rifled by the Babylonians.

Conditions were very difficult for the returnees. As a result of drought, failure of crops and famine, harassment by the Samaritans and the necessity of rendering heavy internal taxes for the rebuilding programme, as well as, externally, to the Persian administration, the peasants and small landowners frequently had to sell themselves into slavery. They had little time for spiritual pursuits, and, outside the Temple, there was little observance of the ancestral faith. Intermarriage was rife, and even within the gates of the Temple heathen traders turned the holy Sabbath into a market day.

So serious was the situation that two inspired religious teachers, Ezra and Nehemiah (both influential Jewish officials at the Persian court), obtained permission to return to Jerusalem to reorganize its national and religious life. Ezra returned there around 458 BCE, and was joined by Nehemiah some thirteen years later when he assumed the position of governor of Judah. They introduced some extreme measures and wide-ranging reforms, and galvanized the latent spirit into a total regeneration of civic, religious and social life.

According to tradition, the work of Ezra and Nehemiah was continued and developed by a great ecclesiastical synod, called *Anshei Knesset Ha-Gedolah*, 'the Men of the Great Assembly', the forerunner of the *Sanhedrin*, the supreme spiritual and legislative body which was created in the wake of the Maccabean victory (165 BCE). They were supported by a dynamic and creative school of *Soferim*, Scribes, so called because they disseminated copies of the Torah among the communities, thereby familiarizing the hitherto illiterate common folk with their religious heritage. They were concerned that religious expression and ritual should not be solely confined to the priests at the Temple, and, to that end, they introduced prayers and blessings to heighten the religious consciousness and experience. They also developed the Oral Law in order to supplement the Written Torah by expanding its application to changing social and economic problems and conditions.

2. Can you provide a little more detail regarding the history of the Judean community in the period between Ezra and Nehemiah and the arrival of Alexander?

Unfortunately, no! Incredible as it might sound, we have hardly any information, biblical or otherwise, regarding that community's fate during the century between Ezra and Nehemiah (444 BCE) and the coming of Alexander the Great (333 BCE). It is as if an iron curtain had descended to shut off and protect Judea from the turbulence of a period that witnessed a succession of Persian palace intrigues and assassinations, internal revolts by the satraps of the various states of the empire, the secession of Egypt, and, most fatal of all, a total misjudgement of the growing power of Philip of Macedon (359–336 BCE) who was gradually but inexorably consolidating his hold over the Greek states as a prelude to the realization of his expansionist dreams.

As regards Judea, we do not even have the names of its High Priests or civil governors, nor do we know the extent to which Ezra and Nehemiah's religious reforms continued to secure loyalty to Israel's law and traditions. We may conjecture that relations between the Judeans and the Samaritans of the north deteriorated rapidly during this century, to the extent that the latter, under Sanballat, felt compelled to signal their independence and equal political status by building their own Temple on Mount Gerizim shortly before the arrival of Alexander.

3. Is it not possible to infer, from developments subsequent to the arrival of Alexander the Great, changes that must have taken place in Judea during the previous Persian period?

We may, indeed, assume some radical developments. The Persians accorded Judea the status of a semi-autonomous commonwealth under its own High Priests. With this status came the right to strike its own coins and to levy taxes for the Temple upkeep; and archaeology has unearthed an abundance of such coins, bearing the inscription Yehud (Judea), in various locations in the western part of the Persian empire.

It is clear that this period also witnessed the gradual replacement of Hebrew by Aramaic as the language of the masses, coupled with a corresponding change in the script from the pre-Exilic, ancient Hebrew, or Assyrian, script (*ktav Ashurit*) to the square characters (*ktav meruba*) which have survived the millennia, until the present day.

ALEXANDER THE GREAT

4. What political effect on Judea did the arrival of Alexander the Great have?

In 334–333 BCE, Alexander the Great defeated the Persians at the battle of Issus, and he continued the Persian policy of non-intervention in the religious affairs of the conquered peoples. However, at his death in 323, his two generals, Ptolemy and Seleucus, did battle over the inheritance, with Ptolemy seizing control of Egypt and Phoenicia, and Seleucus controlling Syria and Mesopotamia. Israel, lying between the two powers like the filling in a sandwich, was of major strategic importance as an advance, buffer state for whichever of the two succeeded in occupying it, quite apart from its intrinsic economic attraction. It suffered greatly, therefore, throughout the Greek period, as a result of being occupied several times, alternately, by Egypt and Syria.

5. Do we have any record of the first confrontation between Alexander the Great and the Jewish community of Judea?

The Talmud preserves a tradition of such a meeting:

It was taught: The twenty-fifth of Tevet is '[The festival of] the day of Mount Gerizim', being the day when the Samaritans sought permission from Alexander of Macedonia to destroy the Temple of our God. When the report reached Simeon the Righteous he donned his High Priestly robes and took with him the most distinguished men of Jerusalem, each carrying a burning torch in his hand. Both sides [Jews and Samaritans] marched the whole night to meet Alexander. At dawn, when he caught sight of Simeon, Alexander alighted from his chariot and prostrated himself before him. When his entourage expressed amazement that he should have bowed before a Jew, Alexander explained: 'The image of this man went before me, spurring me on to victory, on every one of my battle fields.'

When he asked Simeon why he and the Jews had come to meet him, Simeon pleaded, 'How can you allow the Temple, where prayers are offered up for you and your kingdom, to be destroyed?'

Alexander then asked regarding the identity of the second group that had marched to meet him. On being told that they were the Samaritans, he turned to Simeon and pronounced, 'They are in your hands!'

The passage continues that the Jews set upon the Samaritans and dragged them back, over thorns and thistles, to their holy mountain at Gerizim, which they then proceeded to devastate.[2]

6. How historically accurate is this account?

It is a Midrashic tradition, which means that those who espouse a fundamentalist position will, in the main, take it at face value. Others might prefer to view it rather as an aetiology, that is a legend created in order to attempt to explain why Alexander established a policy of non-interference with the Jewish religion, instead of imposing the Hellenism that he revered.

In truth, Alexander adopted this benign policy in relation to all his subject peoples as a matter of political expediency to avoid fomenting rebellion until he had consolidated his holdings in the East. Nevertheless, by contrast with his Seleucid and Ptolemaic successors, who adopted a more aggressive imposition of Hellenism, Alexander's policies commended themselves as benign and righteous, and hence the creation of a Midrashic tradition to acclaim and explain his indulgence toward Judea.

7. What sort of image does Alexander the Great enjoy in Jewish tradition?

A noble one. His benign treatment of the Jews assured their eternal gratitude, to the extent that, henceforth, Jews began calling their sons after the Emperor; and the Greek name, Alexander, was elevated thereby to become an acceptable 'Jewish' name until the present day.

8. How long did those cordial relations between the Jews and their Greek invaders last?

Quite some time. After several confrontations between Ptolemy and Seleucus, culminating in the battle of Ipsos in 301 BCE, the former managed to secure Judea firmly, and it remained under Ptolemaic rule for exactly one hundred years. The

Jews were apparently submissive, and, in consequence, were allowed to organize themselves religiously under their High Priesthood. The Ptolemies further ensured that continuity was preserved in Judea by entrusting to the influential Tobiad family the same wide powers that they had enjoyed under the Persian rulers, which also involved responsibility for levying taxes and for law and order. Those wide-ranging powers made that family a veritable oligarchy, but ensured a feeling among Jews that they were enjoying a measure of independence.

THE TOBIAD FAMILY

9. But how is it that we do not hear of that influential Tobiad family after the Maccabean revolt of 168–165 BCE?

Up until the Maccabean uprising the Tobiads maintained a unified policy, offering loyal support to, and maintaining close contacts with, the Ptolemaic rulers in Alexandria, who bestowed upon them greater and greater authority, wealth and power. The Tobiads, in return, colluded in facilitating the dissemination of Hellenism within Judea. The bestowal of a Greek name, Hyrcanus, upon the third generation of the family, the son of Joseph son of Tobiah, was symptomatic of that family's cultural orientation.

Subsequently, however, they severely weakened their own position by splitting up into rival political factions, with one group, led by the High Priest and two of the Tobiad brothers, raising the banner of revolt by supporting the Syrian-based Seleucids at the outbreak of another of their battles with the Ptolemies in 246 BCE, while the other brother, Hyrcanus, led the faction which remained loyal to the latter. Through his support of the Ptolemies, Hyrcanus managed to obtain the licence for tax farming which his father, Joseph, had hitherto enjoyed. Joseph and two of his other sons went to battle against Hyrcanus on this issue, which resulted, not only in the death of two of the brothers, but also in an irrevocable breach within the family.

Two other factors contributed to the downfall of the house of Tobiah: First, Joseph ben Tobiah's slaughter of the leaders of the cities of Ashkelon and Beth Shean (Scythopolis) for refusing to help him farm the taxes of that region; and, secondly, the extreme Hellenism that he and his faction espoused and sought to impose on a reluctant Judea. To this end, he conspired to have the High Priest Jason removed and replaced by the pro-Seleucid tyrant, Menelaus. The latter despoiled the Temple treasury in order to raise funds for Antiochus IV. Inevitably, with the defeat of the latter by the Maccabees, the Tobiads, and their puppet High Priests, were swiftly and violently disposed of.

THE WIDER JEWISH DIASPORA

10. What was going on in Babylon during all this period?

The Jews who had stayed behind in Babylon after Cyrus the Persian had given permission to the Jews to return following the Babylonian captivity seem to have prospered and developed their religious life and institutions, and Babylon remained the hub of world Jewry from that time for several centuries to come. Hence the nurturing of such leaders as Ezra and Nehemiah who were distinguished in both Jewish and Persian political life (see Question 1), and the fact that, by the first century BCE, Babylon could produce an illustrious Talmudic Sage of the calibre of Hillel.

On his arrival in Judea, Hillel transformed the entire approach to the application of Jewish law by introducing its Sages to hermeneutical rules of interpretation, a system hitherto unknown to the *Bnei Beteira*, the leading scholars of the holy land, enabling the Torah Law to be applied to wider situations.

11. What was going on in the rest of the Jewish Diaspora?

The rest of the Jewish Diaspora was continually expanding during these centuries. The Book of Obadiah (verse 20) has a reference to Jews living as far off as Sefarad, which is identified with Sardis in Asia Minor, a fact corroborated by an Aramaic and Lydian inscription; and after the fall of Jerusalem (586 BCE) groups of Jews fled to Lower Egypt, on the evidence of Isaiah (19:16–25), though we have no knowledge of their subsequent fortunes.

There was also a flourishing Jewish colony at Elephantine, at the first cataract of the Nile. This began in the fifth century BCE as a base for Jewish mercenaries, and speedily developed into a settled and flourishing community, although its Temple practices included ritualistic elements derived from non-monotheistic sources.[3]

From the period of the Ptolemaic rule over Judea, Jews seeking greater commercial opportunities, or a more cultured and less religiously rigorous way of life, left Judea to settle in Egypt, which, by the first century BCE, boasted a Jewish population of one million. Although they fanned out to settle all over the country, Alexandria remained the main centre, not only for them, but, in effect, of the entire Jewish world. By this period, the number of Jews living in the Diaspora far outnumbered those of Judea.[4]

NOTES

1 See Ezra 2:64.

2 Talmud *Yoma* 69a.

3 On the community of Elephantine, see Jeffrey M. Cohen, *1001 Questions and Answers on Pesach* (NJ: Jason Aronson,1996), pp.275–6.

4 For an overview of Jewish life in Egypt down the ages, see Cohen, op. cit., pp.274–82.

2

Hellenism

12. What was Hellenism?

One of the best descriptions has been given by the historian Simon Dubnow (1860–1941), who wrote as follows:

It was a duel between 'The Eternal' on the one side, and Zeus on the other – between the Creator of the universe, the invisible spiritual Being, who had, in a miraculous way, revealed religious and ethical ideals to mankind, and the deity who resided upon Olympus, who personified the highest force of nature, consumed vast quantities of nectar and ambrosia, and led a pretty wild life upon Olympus and elsewhere. In the sphere of religion and morality, Hellene and Judean could not come close to each other. The former deified nature herself, the material universe; the latter deified the Creator of nature, the spirit informing the material universe. The Hellene paid homage, first and foremost, to external beauty and physical strength; the Judean to inner beauty and spiritual heroism. The Hellenic theory identified the moral with the beautiful and agreeable, and made life consist of an uninterrupted series of physical and mental pleasures. The Judean theory is permeated by the strictly ethical notions of duty, of purity, of holiness; it denounces licentiousness, and sets up as its ideal the controlling of the passions and the infinite improvement of the soul; not of the intellect alone, but of the feelings as well.[1]

13. But not all our readers can keep in their minds such a lengthy definition. Can you give us a more succinct definition of the difference between Judaism and Hellenism?

No problem: The Greeks believed in the holiness of beauty; the Jews in the beauty of holiness. The Greeks venerated the outer physical container; the Jews celebrated the soul within.

14. Why was the Greek system called 'Hellenism'?

Hellas was the Greek name for Greece, derived from the Hellen of Greek mythology. Hellen was the ancestor of the Hellenes, or Greeks. His sons, Dorus,

Xuthus and Aeolus, were the progenitors of the main Greek nations: the Dorians, Ionians, Achaeans, and Aeolians.

A CLASH OF OPPOSITES

15. Judaism and Hellenism have been described above as totally incompatible. In what way is this most obviously exemplified?

In their respective concepts of God. Judaism believed in a personal God Who is an absolute unity, is unseen, unknowable, all-knowing, all-powerful, and demanding of the highest standards of ethical and moral conduct from humankind.

The Greeks simply did not inhabit the same theological or moral universe. In the first place they believed in a whole panoply of gods whose mythological antics greatly influenced their art and architecture, their philosophy and literature, and even their leisure sporting activities at the gymnasia.

An axiom of mythology is that the events that occur in the celestial regions are carbon copies of what happens on earth, and the gods bear the identical variety of physical characteristics as men and women, with the sensual features being especially pronounced. The gods are susceptible, therefore, to the same desires, passions, jealousies, ambitions and moral aberrations as man. They have love affairs and marry; they go cavorting with other gods' partners; they commit incest; they are roused to anger and suffer envy; they engage in disputes and wage wars. Just as in the earthly experience there are the powerful and the privileged, the weak and the disadvantaged, so it was within the society of the gods assembled on Olympus. There were the twelve great gods and goddesses – such as Zeus, Poseidon, Apollo, Artemis and Aphrodite – and a host of lesser gods.

The Greek gods constituted the celestial counterpart and the spirit that invests every emotion, skill and activity that was employed and developed in the physical world, as well as nurturing the growth of everything required by humans for their enjoyment and survival. So there were gods of love, vengeance and war, wisdom and fortune, beauty and grace, wine and cereal, fauna and flora, fire and water, to name but a few.

When Zeus, the supreme god, wished his will to be communicated to man, he frequently charged some lesser god, often Iris or Hermes, to assume human form and fly down to earth. The gods lived on nectar and ambrosia; they enjoyed the finest luxuries. 'If the gods' daily life resembled that of men it was because, at least in appearance, their natures were not dissimilar. Their bodies were like mortal bodies, but superior in stature, strength and beauty.'[2]

Not surprisingly, therefore, Judaism could have no truck with such a mythology. For, significantly, at the very dawn of Israel's nationhood, immediately after God's revelation of the Ten Commandments at Sinai, Israel is warned, 'Do not make with Me gods of silver or gods of gold' (Exodus 20:20). Indeed, the making of the Golden Calf brought with it a swift retribution. No manifestation of deity – even of the Supreme God Himself – is permitted in Judaism. Hellenism was a heresy, therefore; a deep offence to both the Judaic intelligence and its religious sensibility.

THE JEWISH THREAT TO HELLENISM

16. One can understand, therefore, why the Jews were so offended by Hellenism, but why did the Greeks care about Jewish beliefs to the extent that they were so determined to eradicate them?

This issue is rarely raised, namely, why the mighty, conquering Greeks were so deeply troubled by the religious beliefs of one tiny subject state that they were prepared to go to such lengths to eradicate them. Later, we shall sketch in the immediate factors that brought matters to a head in the reign of Antiochus IV (see Questions 37–41), but we may assume that long before that period Hellenism must have viewed Judaism as a mortal threat. The Hellenists were especially concerned, on account of the fact that their polytheism was so inextricably interwoven with almost every facet of their civic, cultural and leisure activity. It followed, therefore, that the appeal and dissemination of Judaism's political and religious philosophy – and, in particular, its refined concept of monotheism which rendered every individual as of inestimable value in the eyes of God, and therefore in his or her own sight – carried within it the seeds of a revolution of the spirit that could, with ease, sweep away before it even the most confident and numerically powerful of civilisations. The Hellenists realized that Judaism might well be perceived not just as another competing system, but as the authentic system, the 'real thing'. It must have been feared that if ever Judaism borrowed a leaf from the Hellenists' own book, and set its sights on winning converts beyond its own borders, the Hellenized world might well be captivated in an instant.

In hindsight, the Hellenists were right to be so apprehensive, for the Graeco-Roman civilisation is the only one, other than Judaism, to have influenced the history of Western man. As Max Dimont observes, 'The Chinese, Hindu and Egyptian peoples are the only ones living today who are as old as the Jewish people. But these three civilizations had only one main cultural period, and their impact on succeeding civilizations has not been great'.[3] The Greeks recognized Judaism's unbounded potential as a world religion; and hence, for their own survival, and their pretensions to become the world culture, they determined that Judaism had to be not only stopped in its tracks, but totally eradicated.

17. But is that not a rather biased and exaggerated assessment of Judaism's appeal?

I do not believe so. Corroboration of this view may be derived from the simple fact that Judaism's value-system was borrowed, lock, stock and barrel – albeit in a modified and less rigorous form – some 400 years later, to become the basis of the Christian religion which did, indeed, exploit that potential, enabling it to become a world religion which succeeded in confronting and supplanting the legacy of Greece and Rome.

WAS HELLENISM REALLY PLAUSIBLE?

18. But how could the Greeks, who otherwise reached the acme of sophistication in their mastery of philosophy, mathematics and rational speculation, have been so gullible and irrational as to make such naïve and absurd mythological ideas the basis of a belief system?

This seems to be a valid query, but modern-day surveys of belief in the paranormal have revealed that even twenty-first century man is only slightly less committed to such phenomena than his ancient Greek antecedents! Nicholas Humphrey refers to a study he conducted of a representative cross-section of people in the fairly middle-class English town of Reading. His findings were that some 70 per cent of people believe, for example, that some houses are haunted by ghosts; and more than 50 per cent believe in transmigration, namely that we have been here before our present existence, inhabiting different bodies. The latter group also believed that some people can truly remember those past lives.[4]

Humphrey reminds us that 'the celebration of the paranormal has long been woven into the fabric of Western culture... Our most impressive buildings, from Stonehenge to Chartres Cathedral to Disney World, are monuments to paranormal ambitions and paranormal imagery... In bookshops the 'New Age' and 'Occult' sections dominate the shelves.'[5]

So, if modern day man is so gullible, why should we express incredulity that the dominant belief of Greek culture, some two and a half thousand years ago, followed such a similar inclination toward belief in such celestial beings and in their widespread influence on our world. *Plus ca change ...*

HELLENISM'S INROADS AND JEWISH RESPONSES

19. So did Hellenism fail, therefore, to make any inroads at all into the Jewish consciousness?

Quite the contrary. The Greeks succeeded quite remarkably in changing the whole complexion of life in Judea, by importing their network of educational, leisure and entertainment institutions, their language, their coinage, their dress and their art. Sadly, however, it was not the finest fruits of classical Greek thought – that of Pythagoras, Socrates, Euripides, Aristotle and Plato – that was offered to the Jews, but a debased form of Hellenism that expressed itself rather in paganism, barbarity, sensuality and immorality. This constituted an allure that many, especially of the Jewish youth, could not resist.

20. How did Greek language influence the Jews?

Until the arrival of the Greeks, the Jews spoke Aramaic. Their native language was, of course, Hebrew. But, during the Babylonian captivity, the masses had gradually assimilated Aramaic, the Eastern-Semitic *lingua franca*, into their everyday speech. The rabbis continued to employ Hebrew, especially for teaching and religious expositions, but even they found themselves resorting to the conceptual and technical vocabulary of Greek. By Mishnaic times (100 BCE–200 CE). the Greek language had gained supremacy to the extent that many Jewish religious and philosophical tracts were produced in that language. In Alexandria, which had the largest Jewish concentration of that period, a Greek translation of the Bible, the *Septuagint*, was required by the communities; and one of Alexandria's most distinguished sons, Philo (first century BCE), produced a major Bible commentary in the Greek language, saturated with Greek philosophical conceptions. Other Greek translations followed during the succeeding century, such as those by Aquila and Theodotion.

Greek was regarded as the prestige language, to the extent that public notices and inscriptions around the Temple and on its ritual objects, as well as on synagogues and epitaphs, were frequently written in that language. It is reckoned that there are some 3,000 Graeco-Roman loan words in Talmudic literature. Indeed, the Talmudic sages praised the Greek language for its beauty, and it was the only language into which they tolerated the Torah to be translated.[6]

21. But how could such a concession to a heathen culture have been justified by Israel's Sages?

The Sages were, if anything, pragmatic, and where they could not beat an enemy, they frequently joined it. Realising that the Greek language and culture had, in fact, made great inroads into Judean life, some Sages began to disseminate the quaint tradition that it actually had its roots in Israel's own native wisdom. Hence the Midrash that when Alexander the Great conquered Jerusalem he discovered there a library of Solomon's wisdom. He gave this to his teacher, Aristotle, who derived all his ideas from it. Thus, Greek wisdom is, in essence, Solomonic, and therefore totally acceptable![7]

22. Was there any attempt among the rabbis to curtail the inroads of Greek language and culture?

There were sporadic attempts to do so, as reflected in certain Talmudic statements on the subject. In the following passage, the Midrashic method is quaintly applied to the issue:

Rabbi Joshua was asked, 'May one teach one's son the Greek language?' He replied, 'Teach it him [in that split second] when it is neither day nor night, for it says, 'Thou shalt meditate in it (that is, in Torah, exclusively) by day and by night' (Joshua 1:8)!' [But one might then object that,] if so, one ought never to teach one's son a livelihood. That is no objection, said Rabbi Ishmael, since the Torah states, *Choose life* (Deuteronomy 30:19), and 'life' means a livelihood. It was also said that the prohibition of Greek was in order to avoid playing into the hands of informers.[8]

The latter were the *malshinim*, Jewish informers, who, being educated, were employed or coerced by the Greeks and Romans to inform on their fellow Jews. Presumably, the Jewish leaders would employ Greek to communicate to their colleagues sensitive information that they did not trust the masses to know, or any plans for sabotage of the invader's installations or, indeed, for armed insurrection. Those educated informers would eavesdrop and report back to their foreign masters. The above passage suggests, therefore, that there was nothing intrinsically unacceptable about the Greek language, but that it was dangerous to employ it as an elitist and confidential means of communication.

23. But are there not some Talmudic references that categorically denounce Greek culture?

A distinction was made between the Greek language, on the one hand, and Greek culture (*chokhmat yevanit*), on the other. The former was, to some extent, a necessity at that period, in order to compete and survive in the real world of commercial enterprise. The latter was an unnecessary, and, in the eyes of the Sages, a morally and spiritually harmful, preoccupation; hence such Talmudic references as 'Cursed be the man who teaches his son Greek culture'.[9] In another passage, the Talmud states that it was during the war against Titus that they forbade a man to teach his son Greek[10] This suggests that there was no blanket prohibition, but that, at times of national trauma, when Jewish nationalism was being whipped up in order to throw off the yoke of the oppressors, the religious and national leaders became more introvert, joining forces to outlaw any secularist tendency. Such a rejection of Greek culture thus came to meet the perceived spirit of the hour, but was not intended as an entrenched and universal Jewish attitude.

24. Were there any exceptions made in the Talmud to the prohibition of learning Greek?

Interestingly, in the same passage that the Talmud warns against teaching one's son Greek, it states, 'But one may teach Greek to one's daughter, because it is an adornment to her'.[11] The whole tenor of that passage seems to be suggesting that it is not treachery to study Greek; it is simply to be discouraged because it takes one's thoughts away from Torah, which ought to be our sole preoccupation when we are not earning a livelihood. Since that obligation to study Torah does not devolve upon women, the Sages were indulgent when it came to them occupying their time with such 'secular culture'.

One cannot escape the conclusion that the Talmudic Sages had a secret admiration for the wisdom of Classical Greece – its philosophy, mathematics, logic, astronomy and medicine. They might well have felt that, *for heathens*, it had the capacity to elevate the spirit, cultivate the mind and civilize the behaviour.

THE GYMNASIA

25. What was the nature of the gymnasia that the Greeks introduced into Judea?

The purpose of this institution was to promote the Greek obsession with the body beautiful and physical fitness. The *gymnasia* were built by the state, and every important city boasted at least one such leisure centre. From humble beginnings the institution grew, to the extent that it soon boasted complexes of dressing rooms, bath houses, training quarters and contest areas, employing large staffs of *gymnastae* – teachers, coaches and trainers. The athletes who competed at the *gymnasia* became the cult heroes of the age; and sport, rather than study of Torah, gradually became the main preoccupation of Jewish youth.

The literal meaning of the word *gymnasium* is 'school for naked exercise', for the youngsters who trained at those centres had to strip naked in order to run. This created considerable embarrassment for the Jewish participants whose circumcision made them particularly conspicuous, as well as the butt of racial derision and ribald jokes in the satire and theatre comedy of the age.[12]

26. But would this not have made it impossible for Jewish youth to feel at home in the gymnasia? How then were they able to continue frequenting it?

They were enabled to join in by availing themselves of an ingenious, albeit painful, surgical adjustment of the foreskin which totally disguised the circumcision. This was known as *epispasis*, or, in Hebrew, *moshekh orlah*, 'drawing forward the foreskin',[13] to cover the penis. The Talmudic sources condemn the practice in the strongest of terms – a measure of its popularity among Jewish youth.

27. Why was the gymnasium construed as such a threat to the Jewish religion?

The reason is that it was not merely a place for leisure activity, but was also a veritable Greek educational institution. It was for this reason that the name was borrowed in German-speaking countries to designate the higher-grades in secondary schools, even though they had no association with athletics or sport. Thus, those who attended the *gymnasia* were expected to reflect the highest Greek cultural values, and to develop into the finest examples of Hellenistic man. It was also a religious institution, to the extent that, at the conclusion of each programme, a special sacrifice was offered to Zeus Olympus. The Hellenistic spirit was thus so persuasive that it was impossible to enjoy the fruits of Greek modernity while at the same time remaining true to one's ancestral faith.

28. Did the Jewish religious leaders object, then, to the promotion of beauty and the pursuit of physical fitness?

In principle they did not. In itself, physical fitness does not run counter to any

Jewish principle; yet the notion of physical beauty and prowess as an end in itself certainly does. It is all a question of emphasis. After all, Joseph is described in the Torah as 'of beautiful form and exquisite appearance' (Genesis 39:6), though the whole object of that reference is merely to explain why the wife of Potiphar sought to tempt him. Saul, king of Israel is hailed for his goodly looks and physical stature – 'a head and shoulders taller than everyone else' (I Samuel 9:2). Again, these physical characteristics were not construed as ends in themselves, but as extra attributes that were beneficial in augmenting his monarchic authority and aura.

Even in the female context, beauty is perceived as inconsequential when measured against the more desirable and lofty spiritual attributes. Hence, the book of Proverbs affirms that 'Grace is false and beauty is vanity, the woman that fears the Lord, she is to be praised' (Proverbs 31:30). The verse concludes: 'Extol her for the fruit of all her toil, and let her labours bring her honour in the city gate' (v.31). In other words, 'beauty *is* as beauty *does*'. The assessment of the woman of worth is to be made not on the basis of her physical attributes, but in relation to the acts of kindness that she performs.

So Judaism did not deny the significance of physical attributes, but it insisted that they be employed and enjoyed as natural gifts, not as charms to be cultivated and exaggerated in order to allure and entice. It was the Greek exaggeration of beauty, and its worship of the god of physicality, that was so objectionable to Judaism.

29. But surely, it must have been a minute proportion of Jewish youth that was interested in such sporting activities! So why all the vehement opposition to the gymnasium?

One might have thought so, but the opposite was, in fact, the case. The gymnasium offered far more than a leisure outlet, as we have already indicated (see Questions 25 and 27). Its doors were only open to the sons of the wealthy, so that it constituted a social network – an 'Old Boys' Club' – that was essential for any Jew who had pretensions to rank and material advancement in later life. For the likes of these, it was essential to be able to speak Greek and cultivate Greek mores and Greek friends.

The *gymnasium* offered an entry to upper-class society; and the Jewish bourgeoisie, including most of the young priests – the priesthood, by that time, having formed itself into a settled oligarchy, eager to please its overlords – flocked to enrol.

The *gymnasium*, reflecting the broader Hellenistic perceptions, also encouraged gross moral corruption and decadence. We may assume that Yochanan, the High Priest, father of Mattityahu, left Jerusalem to settle in Modin as a demonstration of his distaste for such licentiousness and for the growing assimilation and Hellenization of the priesthood. And we may now understand the nature of its threat to the very fabric of the cultural, moral and social life of Jewry, and why Hellenism had to be countered on all fronts.

30. Were members of the gymnasium distinguished by any uniform?

They were, indeed. They were expected to don the fashionable dress of the Greek *epheboi*, the upper-class youth, with their broad-brimmed hats, their costly cotton or silk *chiton* and *peplos*, and their high-laced leather boots. The upper-class Jewish youth thus strutted around, emulating the superior airs and graces of the Greek occupiers, and instilling envy and a feeling of alienation into the hearts of their less well-off co-religionists. If left unchecked, an internal social schism was inevitable, with dangerous ramifications for the unity of Jewry and its ability to unite against the invader of its homeland.

31. But, notwithstanding the potent Hellenizing influence of the gymnasia, its appeal was restricted, as has been said, to the upper and youthful classes of Judean society. Surely, then, that one institution could not displace the entire nation's ancestral faith?

Maybe not in the short term, but, because it targeted the ruling classes, the trend-setters, and the future leaders, it possessed the power and potential to sow the seeds of much wider national dissolution.

WIDER GREEK ENTICEMENTS

32. So what other Hellenizing forces were at work in Judea during this period?

The honey of the Hellenic bee proved tantalizingly attractive for the Jews of both the Egyptian (Ptolemaic) and the Syrian (Seleucid) empires. This honey took several forms, notably the favourable conditions extended to all Jews by their invaders. They were allowed their own autonomy, and, because their loyalty was never in doubt, they were encouraged to enter the army, with the carrot of swift advancement and military commissions. Jewish soldiers not infrequently constituted the garrison of the royal fortresses. The army, as we know from the experience of the modern-day State of Israel, is a powerful cultural melting pot. Ethnic minority differences are soon displaced by the pervasive, overarching national spirit, and young Yemenites, Ethiopians, Libyans, Russians or Brits absorb an Israeli character and cultural complexion after only a few months under the drill-sergeant's stick. It was the same with the Jews of the Ancient Near East at that period.

A further contributory factor was the practice of creating Greek settlements in Judea. This was begun by Alexander, who brought a settlement of Macedonians to Samaria, and their offspring became a sizeable and influential element in the population. The following century witnessed the setting up of a number of new Greek cities in Judea, and the conversion of some old-established Jewish cities to become predominantly Greek.

Inevitably, these new Greek cities were launching-pads for the dissemination of Hellenism throughout the country. This was facilitated by the fact that the Greek political system was also introduced, under which single, large cities became the administrative centres for the entire surrounding country districts. These were ruled over by a *Boule*, a democratically-elected 'council', membership of which was only open to full Greek citizens, which excluded Jews unless they had renounced their religion! Nevertheless, the conviction 'that they belonged to a community much larger than their own body . . . [engendered] a wider outlook and a deeper insight into the world of their surroundings'.[14]

In short, every aspect of Greek modernity, whether expressed through education, sport, fashion, architecture, art and craft, trade, language and literature, theatre or domestic and social behaviour, was transplanted in an instant into the Judean context; and, like Western culture in the present-day State of Israel, it was soon assimilated into the essential way of life of the average Jew.

NOTES

1 S. Dubnow, *History of the Jews from the Beginning to Early Christianity* (New York: Thomas Yoseloff, 1967), vol. 1, p.453.

2 *Larousse Encyclopedia of Mythology* (edited by Robert Graves (London: Paul Hamlyn, 1959), p.103.

3 Max Dimont, Jews, *God and History* (London: W.H. Allen, 1964), p.18.

4 Nicholas Humphrey, *Soul Searching* (London: Chatto & Windus, 1995), p.4.

5 Ibid., pp.5–6.

6 Mishnah *Megillah* 1:8.

7 See L. Ginzberg, *The Legends of the Jews* (Philadelphia: The Jewish Publication Society of America, 1946), vol. VI, pp.282–3.

8 Pal. Talmud *Pe'ah* 1:1 (Krotochin ed., p. 15c).

9 Tal. *Bava Kama* 82b.

10 Mishnah *Sotah* 9:14. Another, preferred, reading refers the prohibition to 'the days of Quietus'.

11 Pal. Talmud *Pe'ah* 16b.

12 See Allen Kerkeslager, 'Maintaining Jewish identity in the Greek Gymnasium', *Journal for the Study of Judaism in the Persian, Hellenistic and Roman Period*, xxviii, 1, Feb. 1997, (Leiden, Brill), p.21; James A. Arieti, 'Nudity in Greek Athletics', *Classical World*, 68 (1975), pp.431–6.

13 See Note 11.

14 W.O.E. Oesterley, *A History of Israel* (Oxford: Clarendon Press, 1932), p.181.

3

From Alexander to Judah the Maccabee

GREECE AND JUDEA: A DETERIORATING RELATIONSHIP

33. How did the relationship between Judea and the Greek occupiers develop?

We have already referred to the peaceful relations that existed subsequent to the conquest of Judea by Alexander the Great (332 BCE), and for as long as the Ptolemies ruled Judea from their base in Egypt (see Questions 5–8). It was only after their Seleucid rivals, who ruled Syria and Mesopotamia, succeeded in seizing control of Judea (200 BCE) from the Ptolemies, that the relationship began to deteriorate.

Even then, the first Seleucid conqueror, Antiochus III, having inherited Alexander's favourable disposition towards the Jews, made a number of concessions towards them. These included non-interference with the Jewish administration of government, generous tax concessions, financial support for the refurbishment of the Temple and the provision of the sacrifices, relief from payment of the poll and crown taxes for the political leadership and Temple officiants. Most generous of all, the thousands of Jews who had been carried away into slavery as a result of the previous century's various battles for Judea, as well as their offspring, were granted their freedom.

34. Was this not rather generous of the Seleucids?

Indeed it was. The above was all contained in an official royal epistle, fully quoted by the famous historian Flavius Josephus in his *Antiquities of the Jews*.[1] But Antiochus III went even further and declared it forbidden for any gentile to come within the limits of the Temple or to breed, or cause to be brought into Jerusalem, any animal that was regarded as unclean by the Jews, or any forbidden meat.

35. So why did the relationship start to go sour?

For complex reasons, notable among which was the sudden and crushing reversal of the latter's political and financial fortunes as a result of his defeat in battle by the Romans in 188 BCE. This involved him in the loss of a vast amount of manpower, and the payment of punitive indemnities to Rome at the peace of Apamea.

Smarting under that bitter blow to his international prestige and his treasury,

Antiochus III sought to plunder the treasures of a famous Elamite temple in the hope of replenishing his empty coffers. In the mêlée of that assault, he lost his life. This planted the idea into the mind of his successors, Seleucus IV and Antiochus Epiphanes, to attempt to rifle the treasury of the Temple of the Jews in Jerusalem.

36. But, given the fate meted out to Antiochus III in his attempt to plunder a temple, why did his successors regard it as worthwhile to persevere with such an adventure?

The answer is desperation in the face of a looming financial ruin that would have deprived them of the capacity to sustain and re-equip their standing army, thus making them vulnerable to conquest, especially by Rome, the emergent world power.

It must not be thought that the Temple contained just a few valuables. Josephus reminds us of the great riches stored there:

> For he saw that there was in it a great deal of gold, and many ornaments that had been dedicated to it of very great value ... So he left the Temple bare; and took away the golden candlesticks, the golden altar [of incense], the table [of shew bread], the altar [of burnt offering] and even the fine linen and scarlet veils, as well as all its secret treasures.[2]

ANTIOCHUS IV AND REPRESSION OF THE JEWS

37. But surely the sacking of the Temple was not the only cause of the Jewish revolt?

Indeed not. As we have observed, there were more complex and far-reaching reasons, with ramifications for the continued existence of the Jewish people.

Antiochus IV, who bore the title Epiphanes, viewed Judea as of crucial strategic importance, as it constituted the southern border of his kingdom and a buffer state against his arch rivals, the Egyptian Ptolemies. He was determined to ensure, therefore, that Judea remained secure and strongly defended by an impressive Greek force, with an ample infrastructure. Judea was thus constantly under his scrutiny. He began to manipulate and interfere in every aspect of its internal affairs, including its financial, political, and subsequently, religious and cultural life.

38. But how could they affect the religious and cultural orientation of the Jews?

Very easily. We have already described the allure of Hellenism (see Questions 12–32). Antiochus vigorously encouraged and contrived the Hellenization of the entire country of Judea. He began at the centre, by replacing the High Priest, Onias III, with his brother, Jason, who had been totally won over to the Hellenistic way of life, and who had ingratiated himself with the king by intimating that, if he was given power in Judea, he could raise substantially higher taxes. He also offered to change the entire religious and cultural complexion of the country to that of a Hellenistic state, to alter the social and political status of Jerusalem to that of a Greek *polis*, and even to change its name to Antiochia, in honour of the king.

39. So how successful was Jason?

His measures met with considerable initial success, and the culture of the gymnasia and its paganistic traditions began to pervade every aspect of Jewish life, rivalling the influence of the Temple and the Torah.

Jason's personal success was eclipsed, however, by his imperial mentor, Antiochus, who, impatient for a more rapid degree of Hellenization and even greater revenue from the country, deposed Jason, in 171 BCE. Antiochus replaced him as High Priest with one Menelaus, who had made even more extravagant claims of sums he could raise in taxes from the Jews. Menelaus was not only invested with Jason's office, but was given supreme authority as Antiochus's governor in the country. The Jews were outraged by the fact that they now had, foisted upon them, a totally unacceptable and unprecedented situation of a non-priest occupying the High Priestly office, as well as virtual foreign rule by proxy, with dictatorial power.

Outrage gave way to hatred of the Greek occupation as Menelaus tightened the financial screws on the state in order to make good his promise to the king. The only way he could raise vast taxes was by a policy of cruel extortion from an already impoverished population and the stripping bare of every item and artefact of value from homes and buildings throughout the country.

This had the effect of shaking the growing number of assimilating Jews in Judea out of their complacency. They suddenly realized that not only their unique, ancestral monotheistic religion, their Hebrew language and culture, but also their very freedom was rapidly evaporating before their very eyes. While they had had no compunction about choosing to adopt appealing aspects of Greek culture, they now realized that it was quite a different matter to have the entire system imposed upon them.

40. Were there any other causes for Jewish anger?

Yes. The chief cause of Jewish anger and bitter resentment of Antiochus was an occurrence in the aftermath of one of his military forays against the Ptolemies of Egypt in 168 BCE.

During his and Menelaus's absence, a rumour spread in Jerusalem that Antiochus had been killed. The deposed high priest, Jason, gambling on the Seleucids' defeat, returned to Jerusalem and reclaimed his spiritual office. On his safe return, Antiochus determined to punish the city. He ensured that no further acts of disloyalty would be perpetrated by slaughtering tens of thousands of the inhabitants of Judea and importing into Jerusalem, on the Acra citadel, a large colony of Greek foreigners and committed, pro-Menelaus Hellenists. The foreigners brought with them a host of foreign idolatrous cults, thus changing the entire religious complexion of the city of

David. It was only a matter time before some Jewish zealot would arise to avenge his people, defend their honour and light the tinder of revolt.

41. But if the Greeks were tightening their grip so effectively, what made the Jews think that they had any prospects of throwing off the yoke of their oppression?

There were growing military signs that the Greeks were not as invincible as they had once been. Regular reports of Roman successes emboldened many to believe that the era of Hellenism was to be short-lived. This was accentuated by the reversal suffered by Antiochus in his excursion against the Ptolemies in 168 BCE. After his initial success in invading Egypt, and poised to seize Alexandria, the capital, and to overthrow the Ptolemaic dynasty, he was forced to withdraw and abandon his campaign when a vast Roman force came to the aid of the beleaguered Egyptians. When reports of the death of Antiochus – later proven to have been unfounded – reached Jerusalem, the flag of revolt was raised there and in several cities in the south. While his safe return and the punitive measures he imposed on the Jews calmed the situation, yet incalculable damage had already been done to Antiochus's prestige and the image of his invincibility. This created fertile ground for the planting of the seed of a Jewish rebellion.

AN ALTERNATIVE TO MILITARISM

42. Were there any alternative approaches to that of countering Hellenism by means of the military option?

Indeed. There were many Jews who were either pacifist by nature or who could see no permanent peace ever emerging from the tit-for-tat escalation of war between the old and the newly emerging great powers, with Judea inevitably the prime sufferer. Many of these were also possessed of a deep piety and a belief that God would confirm the words of His prophets and bring the deliverer in His own good time, and that it was useless to attempt to pre-empt that moment by force of arms.

43. So did they just sit tight and do nothing?

No, they could hardly have done that in the ferment of Judea at that period. Their piety meant that they could not expose their children to the blandishments of Hellenism, and they could hardly take a neutral position militarily without engendering great hostility from fellow Jews who were raising the flag of revolt.

Their alternative was to withdraw from city life and, seeking out kindred spirits, to create religious communes in inaccessible areas. Variant religious sects were springing up at this time in the desert areas east and southeast of Jerusalem, with some as far north as Damascus. They lived a highly disciplined, regulated and monastic way of life, and many sects practised extreme asceticism. They are generally identified as Essenes, and they spent their day in ritual immersion, prayer, agricultural labour sufficient for group subsistence, study of Torah and their own sacred texts, and with acts of benevolence and charity. Luxuries and physical pleasure were despised. As a brotherhood, women were excluded and possessions were pooled. They tended to regard themselves as the true, or ideal, Israel, and to spurn the priests of Jerusalem and their cult.

44. Do we have any detailed knowledge of the workings of those communities?

Since the discovery of the Damascus Document[3] and the Dead Sea Scrolls in the twentieth century, our knowledge of those sects has been greatly enhanced. We have their Manual of Discipline, providing detailed information regarding the structure of the communes, their initiation rules, regulations and codes of discipline, as well as their system of escatology, or theological vision of the future, as contained, for example, in the *Wars of the Sons of Light and the Sons of Darkness*. While these are the particular product of the so-called Qumran Covenanters, who lived on the northwest shore of the Dead Sea, they may be viewed as fairly representative of such groups.

45. So did they succeed in avoiding the political upheavals in Judea?

While many may have escaped the turbulence of the Maccabean uprising, the enemy clearly pursued others to their desert fastnesses. The Book of Maccabees describes how the enemy cunningly attacked those 'seekers after righteousness and justice'[4] on the Sabbath, knowing that they would not desecrate the holy day by taking up arms to defend themselves. One thousand people were mercilessly slain in cold blood.

There were allied groups of pietists who had hitherto maintained a spiritually separatist presence in towns and villages of Judea, but who may have decided, perhaps on hearing of the fate of their desert confrères, that the uprising was a *milchemet mitzvah*, a religiously-mandated exercise of defence of the faith and the Holy Land. They became convinced, therefore, of the validity of the Pharisaic view that, for the saving of life, Sabbath law is to be set aside, and, on that basis, they then went on to play a significant part in the general revolt. They are described in the Book of Maccabees as 'a community of the pious,'[5] or, simply, *Chasidim.*[6]

46. Are there any references to them outside the Book of Macabees?

If we are interested in ancient references, we may dispose of the *Megillat Antiochus* (Scroll of Antiochus), also known as *Megillat Bet Chashmonai* (Scroll of the Hasmonean Dynasty) or *Megillah Yevanit* (The Greek Scroll) – a 76-verse chronicle of the struggle. The view of Saadia Gaon (tenth century), that it is an authentic chronicle produced by the five Maccabean brothers must be discounted on the basis that it contains a reference to the destruction of the Temple in the year 70 CE, some 240 years later!

Others attribute it to the early Mishnaic sages of the first century, while the view of historians is that it was probably written around the seventh century, and, in order to achieve acceptance and status for the work, it was given a name suggestive of a contemporary Maccabean chronicle.

If we seek more contemporaneous points of contact, we might find these in some of the references to *chasidim* contained in the later psalms, such as the eulogistic verse, 'Precious in the eyes of the Lord is the death of his pious ones (*chasidav*)'[7] or the vigorous victory song of psalm 149:

> Let the *chasidim* exult in glory; let them sing for joy upon their beds.
> Let the high praises of God be in their mouth,
> And a two-edged sword in their hand;
> To execute vengeance upon the nations and chastisement upon the peoples;
> To bind their kings with chains and their nobles with fetters of iron . . .
> He is the glory of all His *chasidim*,
> *Halleluyah.*[8]

THE FINAL STRAW

47. So what was it that finally prompted the Jewish military revolt?

It was the cumulative effect of the extortion, the crippling taxation, the Hellenization that had dramatically changed the whole character of Jewish cultural and religious life and the almost total erosion of Jewish sovereignty.

The final straw, however, that galvanized the Maccabees into action was the introduction by Antiochus Epiphanes of measures designed to secure the total outlawing of the practice of the Jewish religion.

48. Do we have a record of these measures and did the Greeks actually succeed in imposing them?

We do. They are contained in a royal edict, the text of which is quoted in full in the First Book of the Maccabees. It reads thus:

> And King Antiochus wrote to his whole kingdom, that all should be one people, and that each should forsake his own laws . . . And many of Israel consented, sacrificing to the idols and profaning the Sabbath.
>
> And the king sent letters to Jerusalem and the cities of Judah, that they should adopt alien laws and abandon the cult of burnt offerings and other sacrifices in the Temple; that they should profane the Sabbaths and feasts, pollute the sacred vessels, defile those holy of status, build altars, temples and shrines for idols, sacrifice swine's flesh and other unclean beasts, leave their sons uncircumcised and make their souls abominable with all manner of uncleanness and profanation. All this, that they might forget the law and change all the ordinances. And whosoever shall not do according to the word of the king shall die.[9]

They certainly attempted to impose those measures, and they met with some initial success, especially among the unobservant who were assimilating to the Hellenistic way of life. Again the Book of Maccabees:

> And he appointed overseers over all the people, and he commanded the cities of Judah to sacrifice, city by city. And many from among those who had forsaken the law joined the Greeks [in their practices]. And they did such evil things in the land that many [Jews] attempted to flee and hide themselves in places of refuge.[10]

49. But did they succeed in infiltrating the Temple practices?

They did, indeed, as the continuation of our source testifies:

> And on the fifteenth day of Kislev in the hundred and forty-fifth year [168 BCE], they built 'an abomination of desolation' on the altar, and in the cities of Judah, on every sidewalk, they erected idolatrous sacrificial places.[11]

50. What is 'an abomination of desolation'?

Good question! This is a literal translation of the Hebrew phrase *shikkutz meshomeim* which also occurs three times in the biblical book of Daniel. The noun *shikkutz* ('detestable object') is found elsewhere in the Bible as a derogatory term for the Near Eastern cults.[12] The awkward *meshomeim* ('desolate') element is explained as a parody of the word *shamayim* ('heaven'), indicative of the fact that, instead of leading heavenwards, those cults lead to desolation and destruction.[13]

51.   Were the Greeks able to impose idolatry and the prohibition of Jewish ritual also within private homes?

They were:

> And at the doors of houses and in the streets they burnt incense. And they rent in pieces the scrolls of the Law wherever they located them, and set them on fire. And anyone found to possess a copy of the Law and to maintain loyalty to it was condemned to death by royal edict.[14]

52. What was the purpose of burning incense 'at the doors of the houses'?

This was a Greek practice, in honour of such 'gods of the street' as Hermes, Apollo, Dionysus and Artemis. Images of them were set up outside the homes, with altars for gifts and offerings to be made.[15] We may conjecture that the later, rabbinically recommended, practice of lighting the Chanukah lights in the open, at the very entrance to the forecourt of one's home, was intended not only 'to publicise the miracle', but also as a token of displacement of that idolatrous practice.

THE BOOKS OF THE MACCABEES

53. In what form have the Books of the Maccabees come down to us?

There are actually four Books of the Maccabees. The first was originally written in a pure, rich, and lucid biblical Hebrew style by a scribe who was a master of the genre. Sadly, that original was soon lost, but the work survived, primarily as a result of the popularity of the Greek, Latin and Syriac translations that were made of it. It is possible to reconstruct the quality and nature of the original, however, through the fairly literal Greek translation that was made from it.

The Second Book of the Maccabees was an original Greek production, produced by a master of the Greek language, one Jason of Cyrenaica, who employs a most sophisticated Greek style, peppered with rich vocabulary, indicating that his purpose was not only to write a history of the revolt, but also to make an impressive literary contribution. Jason was clearly a Jewish partisan, notwithstanding his thorough-going Greek education, and for that reason he frequently exaggerates the cruelty of the Greeks as well as the strength and heroism of the Jews.

As regards the opening section of the book, comprising letters sent by Judah the Maccabee and his court to the Jewish community of Alexandria, scholars have shown that it bears all the hallmarks of a Greek translation from an original Hebrew version.[16]

Jason's original version was lost in the course of time, and what has survived is an abbreviated version of it, probably made by an Egyptian-Jewish scribe who may also have been responsible for adding the opening letters.[17]

54. But why was the Hebrew original of the first Book of the Maccabees lost?

This should not surprise us, as a similar fate befell the rest of the books of the Apocrypha, referred to by later generations of Jews as *Sefarim Chitzonim*, 'external or profane literature'.[18] The original Hebrew version of the second century BCE work by Ben Sira (Ecclesiasticus), for example, was lost after the tenth century and isolated sections and pages were only discovered and identified by scholars at different times during the course of the first half of the twentieth century.

The loss of the Apocryphal books, on the other hand, was due to a different set of circumstances, primarily because they were regarded as spiritually inferior to the preserved writings of the classical prophets and the other sacred literature that was eventually accorded canonical status.

Other reasons for their exclusion may have been: (1) that their authors were not allied to the Pharisaic movement; (2) that some of the authors may have been too recent to the time of the religious leaders of Judea for their works to have been put on a par with those of the great prophets and leaders whose writings had already attracted an aura of sanctity; (3) the Greek influence that infused much of the genre; (4) the predominance of theological ideas and daring speculation regarding such matters as the last judgement, resurrection, paradise, the Kingdom of God, angelology, messianism, sin, evil, the problem of theodicy and the supremacy of the Saints. These were notions which the more conservative Pharisees did not encourage common folk to explore, believing that conflicting views on those concepts could confuse and undermine faith; (5) the result of Jewish persecution and exile, because, when Jews had to pick up their roots and flee, taking with them only their most precious belongings, they would have given priority to copies of the Torah and authorised writings, leaving behind religious literature of secondary importance, to which no sanctity was attributed; (6) the paucity of copies of the latter. Only the wealthy could afford to commission their own copies of popular books, and, in the turbulent last few centuries BCE, with Greek occupiers ransacking Jewish belongings, the survival of libraries in private possession was unlikely.[19]

55. What is the nature of the third Book of the Maccabees?

It is a work which has come down together with the first two Books of the Maccabees, but it has no direct connection with them. It is not set in that period at all, but in the reign of Ptolemy Philopater, who ruled over Egypt between 221–205 BCE – seventy years before Judah the Maccabee!

This is an example of what can happen to marginal or minor works in the course of their transmission down the ages, and the often desperate attempts of communities to save them, in the face of more widespread indifference. In the tenth century, the first three books were regarded as a unity, and referred to as the *Chronicle of the Ptolemies*, a title certainly more appropriate to the contents of this third volume.[20]

56. What is the nature of the fourth Book of the Maccabees?

Unlike the third book, this does have an intrinsic connection to the Maccabean period, though it was clearly written long afterwards and was heavily reliant on earlier sources, such as the second Book of Maccabees and the writings of Jason of Cyrenaica.

It was written by a religious Jew, living at the beginning of the first century CE. Like Philo of Alexandria, he was also immersed in Greek culture and philosophical speculation and stood for a synthesis of Torah knowledge and the allegorical method of exegesis. The author was clearly writing for a purely Greek-speaking Jewish community outside the Holy Land, though views differ as to whether this was in Egypt, Asia Minor or one of the Greek isles.

The book commences by relating the history of the Greek struggle for control of Judea, and the events leading up to the reign of Antiochus Epiphanes and his suppression of Jewish religious practices. It cites the famous story, known from II Maccabees, of the seven brothers who surrendered to martyrdom rather than submit to idolatry. Much in the spirit of the Greek school of Stoicism, it offers that as an example of pious reason being employed to conquer human passion, impulse and emotion.[21]

57. So how is it that the books of the Maccabees, and other such works, managed to survive at all, even in translation?

Ironically, it was thanks to Christianity that the books of the Maccabees, and the

Apocryphal literature in general, survived. The Church, having rejected what it dubbed 'The Old Testament', gave special status to, and produced its own expansions of, the religious and devotional writings produced in what it refers to as the 'Inter-Testamental period'. It viewed such works, especially those that treated of apocalyptic themes, as paving the way for the rise of Christianity, and accorded them, therefore, canonical status. So we are indebted to Christianity for having preserved the historical account of perhaps our greatest and most successful victory.[22]

NOTES

1. See Flavius Josephus, *Antiquities of the Jews* (London: Henry G. Bohn, 1845), pp.487–8.
2. Ibid., p.497.
3. On the Damascus Document, see *Encyclopaedia Judaica* (Jerusalem: Keter Publishing House Ltd, 1971), vol. 5, pp.1246–9.
4. See I Maccabees 2:29.
5. I Maccabees 2:41.
6. I Maccabees 7:13.
7. Psalm 116:15.
8. Psalm 149:5–9.
9. I Maccabees 1:41–50.
10. I Maccabees 1:50–53.
11. I Maccabees 1:54–55.
12. Cf. II Kings 23:13, 24; Isaiah 66:3; Jeremiah 4:1, 7:30; Ezekiel 5:11, 7:20; Daniel 9:27, 11:31; 12:11, *et al.*
13. See A. Kahane, *Ha-Sefarim Ha-Chitzonim* (Tel Aviv: Masada Publishing, 1960), II, commentary on I Maccabees 1:54.
14. I Maccabees 1:55–7
15. See commentary of Kahane, *Ha-Sefarim Ha-Chitzonim*, on I Maccabees 1:55.
16. Ibid., p.90.
17. Ibid., p.92.
18. Mishnah *Sanhedrin* 10:1.
19. Evidence for the Greek invaders' widespread destruction of scrolls and religious works is forthcoming from I Maccabees 1:56–7.
20. See Kahane, *Ha-Sefarim Ha-Chitzonim*, p.232.
21. See M. Waxman, *A History of Jewish Literature* (New York: Thomas Yoseloff, 1938), I, p.25.
22. On the process of transmission and the act of canonization of the Apocrypha, Pseudepigrapha and cognate works, see James H. Charlesworth, *The Old Testament Pseudepigrapha* (New York: Doubleday, 1983), I, pp.xxi–xxix.

4

The Maccabean Revolt

THE NAME 'MACCABEE'

58. What is the origin of the name 'Maccabee'?

It is found for the first time in I Maccabees 2:1:

> In those days, Mattityahu the son of Yochanan, son of Shimon, a priest from the line of Yehoyariv, left Jerusalem and settled in Modin. He had five sons: Yochanan, referred to as Gaddis; Shimon, referred to as Tarsi; Judah, referred to as *Maccabee*; Eleazar, referred to as Choran; and Yonatan, referred to as Chafus.

While the Hebrew names of the five sons are all traditional names, the meaning or significance of the Greek-sounding appellations is not made clear. Neither are we sure of the precise sense in which the name Maccabee was understood, and whether it was written with the Hebrew letter *kuf* or *kaf*. If the former, as generally supposed, then it may be derived from the Hebrew word *makkevet*, 'a hammer', and was probably indicative of Judah having smitten the enemy with a crushing blow. A parallel to such a designation is the name Charles Martell ('Charles the hammer'), so called because of his great victory over the Saracens in 732 CE.

A popular interpretation, found in a sixteenth century commentary on the *Machzor Roma*, has it that it was originally intended to be spelled with a *kaf*, and is reminiscent of the fact that Judah's shield bore the letters *MKBY*, the initial letters of the phrase *Miy Kamokha Ba'eilim YHWH*, 'Who is like unto Thee among the mighty, O Lord' (Ex. 15:11). However fascinating this interpretation may be, there is absolutely no historical basis for it.

59. The name Maccabee seems to have been quite well-known in Christianity. To what may this be attributed?

It is, indeed, well-known, and probably owes its origin to the impact made by the story of the martyrdom of the elderly sage, Eleazar[1] and the seven brothers,[2] as recorded in the Books of the Maccabees, which enjoyed canonical status in early Christianity. Those martyrs, encouraged by their mother,[3] submitted willingly to death rather than publicly deny their God and their religious law. They were consequently viewed by the Church as the embodiment of the quality of wholehearted sacrifice for God, to the extent that, for the past 1,300 years, in the Eastern Church, as well as in the Latin Church until the Vatican revision of the 'Catholic Calendar of Saints' in 1969, 1 August was marked as the 'Commemoration of the Sainted Maccabean Martyrs'.

60. Did the name Maccabee extend beyond its historical context?

It did. There are those who attribute the etymology of the name *Danse Macabre* ('Dance of Death') to that tragic story, believing that the word *macabre* derives from Maccabee. In the Middle Ages, the name was synonymous with valour, and various writers and historians hailed their kings and military heroes as glorious and valiant Maccabees. Richard the Lion-Heart and Robert the Bruce were especially compared by their admirers to Judah the Maccabee, and, along with Joshua and David, Judah figures as one of the 'Nine Worthies' whose figures are regularly carved above the lintels of church doors or depicted in embroidered tapestries.

JUDAS MACCABAEUS

61. Did the theme of the Maccabees extend beyond the Church and the Synagogue?

It did. Music lovers in the eighteenth century became especially acquainted with the events surrounding the life of Judah the Maccabee through the instant popularity of Georg Friedrich Handel's oratorio, 'Judas Maccabaeus', commissioned by Frederik, the Prince of Wales, in celebration of the Duke of Cumberland's military triumph at Culloden. It was first performed at Covent Garden on 1 April 1747, and was such an instant success that it was repeated seven times during its first season.

62. Were there any ramifications of the newfound popularity that Handel's oratorio provided for the story?

There were. The daring exploits of a Jewish military hero and his freedom fighters provided for the English a much-needed antidote to their ingrained image of the Jew as a grasping Shylock. This respect for Jews was heightened further when Handel added later the chorus of the Israelite maidens and youths hailing Judah's exploits in the words, 'See the Conquering Hero Comes'. This excerpt became *de rigueur* at any subsequent celebration of a military victory.

63. What is so significant about the fact that Matityahu hailed from 'the line of Yehoyariv'?

For the chronicler of the times, this established Matityahu's credentials as a priest of the most exalted lineage. The priests of the line of Yehoyariv are mentioned several times, in the books of Nehemiah[4] and Chronicles,[5] among those who returned from exile in Babylon to reconstitute the second Jewish Commonwealth.

The priests were divided into twenty-four *mishmarot*, 'duty rotas', each of which officiated at the Temple in Jerusalem twice a year, for a week at a time, supervising the sacrificial order, performing the multifarious other Temple duties and ministering to the throngs of pilgrims. The *mishmar* of Yehoyariv was regarded as the leading priestly order,[6] and this may provide a clue as to the ensuing developments and the inordinate influence Matityahu was able to exert as leader of a popular revolt.

THE NAME HASMONEAN

64. What is the origin of the name Hasmonean?

The name Hasmonean does not occur in the Books of the Maccabees, but is used by Josephus,[7] as well as by the Mishnah,[8] the Talmud[9] and the liturgy,[10] as a designation of the Maccabean dynasty.

The name derives from one Asmoneus, cited by Josephus[11] as the great grandfather of Matityahu. In the rabbinic sources the family is referred to by the Hebrew form, *Chashmona'im*, literally, 'descendants of Chashmon', though it is unclear why the glorious Maccabees should have been named after some distant and undistinguished ancestor! If the fact that our rabbinic sources never designate the dynasty by the honorific term Maccabee ('hammerer') represents a conscious attempt to disdain their militarism and the fact that, as priests, they had no right to arrogate to themselves kingship, which is reserved for the tribe of Judah,[12] then it is possible that the term *Chashmona'im* had a derogatory intention. Naming them after a non-entity was a means of showing discourtesy and displeasure.[13]

MODIN

65. Where is Modin, and why did Matityahu leave Jerusalem to settle there?

Though pronounced Modin, it should actually be transliterated as Modi'in, and it lies exactly midway between Tel Aviv and Jerusalem, and east of Lydda (Lod).

The Book of Maccabees makes it clear that Matityahu left Jerusalem to settle there on account of the violence being perpetrated against the inhabitants of Jerusalem, the deteriorating quality of religious and moral life in the capital, and Antiochus's manipulation of the High Priesthood and interference with the Temple administration and the work of the priests.[14] The plan of rebellion was clearly also germinating in Matityahu's mind, and it was far less dangerous to make his preparations in an out-of-the-way village than under the constantly vigilant eyes of the Greek soldiers in Jerusalem.

66. But why did Matityahu despair of eventual relief from the repressive measures?

Because it was clear to him that the Jews were facing an enemy whose objective was the total substitution of Olympus for heaven. This was not a normal battle wherein the victorious army becomes an occupier, imposing its rule and exacting its tributes. This was a hitherto unprecedented religious war, wherein Greece would not rest until Jews ceased to be Jews; until, in their language, their dress, their manners, their faith, their philosophy and their culture, they were indistinguishable from Greeks. This was tantamount to a total renunciation of their history, their Torah, their unique identity. This was a fight to the death. Compromise was out of the question.

67. So Antiochus must have realized then, that he was inviting a Jewish response to the death?

I would agree. One historian takes a different view, however, and maintains that Antiochus was probably unable to comprehend why his repression of the Jewish religion should have ignited such a concerted Jewish revolt. John Bright makes the strange assertion that Antiochus was not, in fact, aiming to suppress the worship of God, or replace it with the cult of another god, 'but only to bring the God of the Jews, the 'God of Heaven', into identification with the high god of the Grecian pantheon and to make the Jewish religion a vehicle of national policy'.[15]

68. On what basis does Professor Bright make that assertion?

He does not quote chapter and verse, but we may suppose that he was accepting at face value Antiochus's initial epistle to all the communities of his kingdom, summoning all citizens 'to become one people, *and that each should forsake his own laws*'.[16] How Bright could construe this, however, as a call not to abandon their own deities, but merely the cult that attached to them, beggars belief! How Bright could believe that, by outlawing basic Jewish religious laws and practices, Antiochus's objective could reasonably have been 'to make the Jewish religion a vehicle of national policy', is naïve in the extreme. There would have been no religion left to contribute to anything, let alone a national policy! Perhaps Bright has fallen into the same trap of ignorance as did Antiochus: failing to appreciate how the Jew, his Torah and his (worship of) God are inextricably interwoven.

69. But, as an historian, he must surely have provided some basis or precedence for his amazing thesis?

Bright does, in fact, quote the case of the Samaritans as a precedent for a people willingly surrendering up its temple and ritual in exchange for independence. Bright reminds us that 'the Samaritan temple was similarly dedicated to Zeus Xenius. (II Macc. 6:2). If the Samaritans objected, we do not know of it; and Josephus (Ant. XII,

V, 5), indeed says that they requested the change. Antiochus might have wondered why the Jews must be so stubborn.'[17]

We cannot accept Bright's Samaritan analogy, as it is clear from Josephus's description of the Samaritan overture to Antiochus that the Samaritans, a tiny and defenceless Galilean sect, were in such fear of the Greeks that they were prepared to barter anything for their lives. Hence their desperate attempt to conceal their national origins from Antiochus and pretend to him that they hailed originally from the stock of Medes and Persians. They added that their observance of the Jewish Sabbath should not be construed as indicative of a common national origin, but was a superstitious act on the part of their ancestors, who thought that such an observance might prove effective in warding off the effects of a devastating plague.[18] It is hardly likely, however, that Antiochus would have assumed that, just because the Samaritans had been prepared totally to merge their national and religious identity, the Jews would have been prepared to do likewise.

ANTIOCHUS: MAN AND MADMAN

70. Did Antiochus impose such destructive measures on any other countries, religions or cults that fell under Greek domination?

No he did not. And this fact remains puzzling to historians, because ancient polytheistic rulers generally adopted a fairly benign and tolerant attitude towards the cults and religious beliefs and practices of their conquered peoples. Such a thorough-going and uncompromising Hellenism was never hitherto imposed on any other nation. This also renders unacceptable John Bright's claim that there were precedents that might have convinced Antiochus that the Jews would accede to his will. No, Antiochus's action – to attempt to wipe out a religion and those who continued to adhere to it – was unprecedented in history at that time, and makes him a candidate for the title of first anti-Semite in history!

71. Is there anything in the character of Antiochus that might explain his attitude?

Well, it has to be admitted that both Jewish and Greek sources confirm that he was a truly mad individual, devoid of any ethical sensibility or moral conscience, and without so much as a tincture of compassion in his heart. In Jewish sources he is referred to as *Antiochus Ha-rasha* – 'The wicked Antiochus'. Later Greek historians, such as Polybius, Titus Livius and Diodorus, concurred, and instead of referring to him by his favoured title, Epiphanes, meaning 'divine saviour' they substituted the title Epimanes, meaning 'madman'.[19]

He may well have simply developed an irrational racist imagination that demonized Jews and sought to efface all trace of their cultural identity. That may well have been activated by the imperialistic impetus, just as some psychoanalysts have accounted for the dynamic of modern racism as emerging 'out of the socio-historical processes of Western imperialism'.[20]

72. Do we have any records detailing the specific nature of Antiochus's madness?

We do. Ancient sources relate that everything he did was calculated to draw attention to himself, to shock and to impress. He would suddenly appear in the streets, engage strangers in conversation, sit for hours with simple artisans, arrive with a troupe of musicians and gatecrash private parties. He would enter the public bath houses and throw costly myrrh over the heads of the bathers. He would behave totally irrationally towards his friends, suddenly insulting his well-tried counsellors publicly, for no reason, while lavishing costly gifts on unknown entities.

On one occasion, at a time of serious economic depression, he hosted a party lasting thirty days for 4,000 guests, with daily gladiatorial combats and athletic demonstrations, and food, wine and luxuries in abundance. He himself would organize and actively participate in the theatricals, and act as Master of Ceremonies. As the night wore on, he would frequently make a sudden appearance at a party in fancy dress. He would then shed his robes and dance naked around the hall, clearly unable to realize that he was demeaning and making a fool of himself, and blind to the looks of ridicule on the faces around him. He would also lavish huge sums on undeserving and senseless projects.

These were not the slanted and exaggerated reports of people with a grudge, whom he might have slighted, but were recorded by the most prestigious and authoritative of Greek historians.[21]

MARTYRDOM

73. What details of Jewish martyrdom are provided by the books of the Maccabees?

The Second Book of the Maccabees relates the story of the very aged scribe, Eleazar, whose mouth was forced open so that he would eat of the meat of a sacrificial swine. He took the meat into his mouth, but, approaching the instruments of torture prepared for him should he have refused, he spat the meat out contemptuously over them.

The presiding Syrians had known and respected the sage for decades, and they were most loath to take his life, as demanded by Antiochus for refusal to comply. They drew him aside, therefore, and suggested that he send for some of his own kasher meat, and publicly pretend that he was in fact eating of the meat of the sacrifice, so as to avoid death. In a powerful and eloquent speech, Eleazar refuses, telling the enemy that it was singularly inappropriate for a man of his age to adopt the guise of pretence, in consequence of which the young would believe that he was prepared to deny, in exchange for whatever little time he had left to live, the faith he had loyally followed for ninety years. He then stepped forward to the instruments of torture, and willingly submitted to the excruciating pain that ended with his death.[22]

74. What was the story of the martyrdom of the seven brothers?

This is recounted in the very next chapter of II Maccabees, and relates how a mother and her seven sons were apprehended by Greek Syrian soldiers, brought before Antiochus and subjected to torture in order to compel them to eat of swine's flesh.

One of them stepped forth, to serve as spokesmen for his brothers, and told the enemy that they were all prepared to lay down their lives for their faith, whereupon the king flew into a rage. 'He commanded that cauldrons be heated up, that the boy's tongue be ripped out, that he be scalped and have his arms and legs cut off in full sight of his mother and brothers. He then had him fried in the boiling hot cauldron'.

This act of barbarity was repeated in the case of each of the brothers in succession, after they all refused the offer of saving their lives by eating of the swine. When the last brother's turn came, however, Antiochus took him aside and promised not merely to spare his life if he complied, but to invest him with riches and high office. When he spurned the offer, Antiochus attempted to persuade his mother to intercede with him, so that she should have at least one child left alive.

The mother bent down and, with superhuman courage, urged her son to be strong in spirit: 'Fear not this butcher, but, proving thyself worthy of thy brethren, accept thy death, that in the mercy of God I may receive thee again with thy brethren.'

The youngest son was emboldened by the words of his mother to utter a powerful, condemnatory speech, damning the king and his minions to divine retribution. After he was punished with an even crueller death than the rest, the mother was also murdered.[23]

75. How true is that story?

We cannot be sure of its historicity, but it probably reflects fairly accurately the nature and intensity of such acts of barbarity and repression that succeeded in engendering a desperate rebellion of 'the few against the many and the weak against the strong'.

The present writer takes the view, however, that, in the chronicling of the episode, the writer took the opportunity to introduce and promote a basic and timely element of Pharisaic theology, namely belief in resurrection.

We quoted above the final words of the mother to her youngest son: 'That in the mercy of God I may receive thee again with thy brethren' (see Question 74). If one consults the account, one notices that, in the final speeches of defiance uttered by each son, there is a recurring reference to resurrection. Thus, the second son says: 'Thou, miscreant dost release us out of the present life, but the King of the world shall raise us up...unto an eternal renewal of life.'[24] And the third son, mockingly put out his tongue (inviting it to be cut off) and stretched out his hands, saying, 'From heaven I received these, and for his laws I shall not withhold them, for from Him I shall wait to receive them back.'[25]

76. So how are we to view these references from a literary and historical point of view?

Well, it does look as if our author had his own agenda here. Even if the account is authentic in its detail, it is highly unlikely that there could have been any Jews so close by as to be able to record *verbatim* those speeches. They could only have been the product, therefore, of a Pharisaic teacher's literary imagination that took the opportunity of promoting the concept of resurrection which was high on the agenda of that movement.

Resurrection was the Pharisees' answer to the woes that had befallen the Jewish people and the deaths of tens of thousands of righteous martyrs. It provided an assurance that their deaths were not in vain, that death was not the final end, but that there was a glorious reward in store in the hereafter for all who merited it, either through their deeds or their suffering in God's name.

Because this is not a doctrine that is found in the Torah, it was rejected, therefore, by the Sadducees, who only accepted what was explicitly written. Our Pharisaic author of II Maccabees clearly protests too much, therefore, and, by interposing the doctrine into the speech of each son, it is clear that he had a polemical purpose in mind, to promote and publicize it in the face of those many Jews who rejected it. We may thus trace the date of the wider dissemination of this doctrine to the Maccabean period

77. Did the inclusion of this doctrine have any effect on the way the book was received?

We may conjecture that one of the reasons the Book of the Maccabees was revered and preserved by the Church, in addition to the fact that the story of the martyrs provided an inspirational paradigm of wholehearted service to God (see Question 59), was precisely because of its promotion of the doctrine of resurrection. This was one of the cardinal tenets of the new faith, especially the resurrection of Jesus three days after his martyrdom. Thus, the Book of Maccabees provided the Church with an inspirational precedence of martyrdom and the promise of resurrection.

HANNAH?

78. Why, in your account, above, of the martyrdom of the mother and her sons, did you not refer to her by her name, 'Hannah'?

Surprisingly, although she is universally known by that name, it is not actually found either in the Book of Maccabees or in the Talmudic reference to the episode,[26] both of which are content to leave her in her anonymity. Curiously, those two sources do not place the circumstances of that martydom against the backcloth of the Maccabean period, but in that of the Hadrianic persecutions, some 300 years later!

79. So, how did the name Hannah come to be so famously identified with that mother?

The name Hannah was not attributed to the heroine of that episode until the appearance of a Spanish version of the popular (tenth-century) work, Josippon, published in Constantinople in 1510. The writer was probably influenced by the story of the biblical Hannah – a sad and heroic figure – who refers to herself as 'a barren woman who bore seven'.[27] This is problematic, however, in that verse 21 of that chapter relates that, in addition to Samuel, she bore three sons and two daughters, which amounts to six children, not seven![28]

THE BEGINNING OF THE REVOLT

80. Did the Maccabees have any expectation of outside help before they embarked upon their revolt against Antiochus?

We have already referred to the Roman intervention against Antiochus in 168 BCE, forcing him to withdraw just when he was poised to overrun Egypt (see Question 41).

II Maccabees Chapter 11 refers to a letter sent by two Roman ambassadors to the Jews in 164 BCE. According to the First Book of the Maccabees, a treaty with Rome was arranged by Judah in 161 BCE. There must have been an antecedent relationship leading up to such a treaty. We may infer, therefore, that such a relationship was in the making, between the Jews and the Romans, possibly going back to the very beginning of the Maccabean revolt against Antiochus in 168 BCE. And this may hold the key to the confidence with which the Jews embarked on an otherwise most dangerous escapade.[29]

81. Was Antiochus's antipathy to the Jewish faith shared by the surrounding Hellenistic civilization?

No it was not. In fact, relations between Jews and pagans were generally quite cordial. 'There is no anti-Jewish passage in Greek literature before the Maccabean struggle, nor any recorded anti-Jewish action.'[30] Quite the contrary: large numbers of Greek pagans were being won over to the worship of Israel's God. These tended to be the well-educated inhabitants of the Greek cities of the Near East, rather than the dwellers in the countryside; and their status, at first, was that of semi-proselytes. Hence the references to them in Jewish sources such as *Sebomenoi* or *Yir'ei Hashem* (God-fearers). Many of them accepted monotheism, though held back from many other basic ritual precepts. It was left to their offspring either to slip back into paganism or to become full converts. The victory of the Maccabees made the latter a popular alternative.

And these latter two considerations may also have emboldened the Maccabees into taking on Antiochus, believing with justification that the surrounding population had no feelings of antipathy towards them, and that, given his unstable nature and widespread unpopularity, they might well be able to count on assistance, when necessary, from the general population. It should not be forgotten that the Greeks were occupiers of Asia Minor, and the attempt by the Jews to throw off the Greek yoke might well have inspired the surrounding peoples to throw in their lot with them.

82. What was it that ultimately sparked off the rebellion?

The tinder was eventually ignited by an occurrence in Modin when all the townspeople, Matityahu and his sons included, were summoned to attend a public sacrifice to the Greek gods. Matityahu was singled out, as the most honoured citizen, and asked to lead the sacrifice. Like the youngest of the seven martyrs, he was offered an inducement of wealth and rank. In a voice quaking with emotion, Matityahu proclaimed:

> If all the nations that are in the king's dominion obey his command, to reject each his ancestral faith in favour of the king's edict, yet will I and my sons and my brethren walk in the covenant of our fathers. Heaven forbid that we should forsake the law and the commandments. We shall not obey the king's commands, to turn aside from our worship, either to the right or to the left.[31]

83. So was Matityahu seized and scourged at that point, like the previous martyrs?

No he was not. For, before the guards had time to react, a Hellenized Jew stepped forward, and, ascending the high altar, volunteered to perform the act of sacrifice and obeisance.

Matityahu's anger, shame and zeal for his God knew no bounds. He pursued the Jew and ran him through with his sword, 'as did his ancestor Pinchas, unto Zimri the son of Salu'.[32] He then proclaimed aloud, 'Whomsoever is zealous for the Law and clings firm to the covenant, let him follow me!'

According to the account in the Book of Maccabees, Matityahu and his sons, and his new followers, overwhelmed the Greek guards and slew Apelles,[33] the King's representative, in order to make good their escape into the desert, 'leaving behind all the possessions they had in the city'.[34]

THE BOOK OF DANIEL: A SPIRITUAL CALL TO ARMS

84. Was any encouragement of the revolt forthcoming from the religious leaders of the day?

According to H.H. Rowley, the book of Daniel was written by a religious visionary of the period who wrote that apocalyptic tract with a view to encouraging his people to hold fast to their faith, intensify rather than abandon their religious practices, fight the Lord's battle with zeal and courage, and await His intervention to secure the imminent downfall of their enemies.

85. What is meant by the above reference to the Book of Daniel as an 'apocalyptic' work?

Apocalypse means, literally, 'revelation', but is applied specifically to a prophetic revelation of the future or the end of time. The Apocalyptic Literature is the name given to an entire post-Biblical genre that dealt, unsystematically, with that theme, though often employing esoteric phraseology which is open to variant interpretation and which frequently obscured more than it revealed!

The age of prophecy was by that time regarded as at an end, and the writers or preachers of apocalypse were obsessed by the notion that the period referred to by the classical prophets as 'the end of days', when God's purpose was to be revealed, was imminent. They believed that the political events of their own time – with empires such as the Assyrian, Babylonian, Persian and Greek, achieving ascendancy only to collapse in fairly rapid succession – provided portents, for those who knew how to read the signs, of the unfolding of the cosmic struggle between God and the ungodly forces.

Their vision of the approaching denouement was couched in bizarre terms, employing the imagery of grotesque and violent beasts: of a two-horned ram, standing before a stream and 'pushing westward, northward and southward, with no other beast able to stand before him or deliver out of his hand',[35] until the arrival of a flying he-goat, with a conspicuous horn emerging from between his eyes, which smashed and trampled the invincible two-horned ram and beat it into the ground.

Numerology also figures prominently in this system, and, by juggling with numbers, the exponents attempted to pin-point precisely when the 'end' could be expected, followed by the arrival of the Final Judgement, the vindication of the saints and the establishment of God's kingdom on earth.

The Book of Daniel is unique as the only work of that genre that was included in the canon of the Bible. It is construed by scholars as a contemporary attempt to convince the faithful that the current struggle against the Satanic Greek force that was attempting to destroy the saints and banish Torah, the source of light and goodness, from the world, was a precursor to the glorious period that would be not just 'a turning point in history, however dramatic, but a new world (age) beyond history'.[36]

MACCABEES ON THE WAR PATH

86. What details do we possess of the military training and planning undertaken by the Maccabees in preparation for their battles with the Greeks?

Regretfully, neither the Book of Maccabees nor Josephus supply us with much information on that score. We may suppose that the Jews' superior knowledge of the terrain gave them the opportunity of engaging in guerrilla warfare and launching lightning night-time raids, thus preventing the Greek forces from fighting the face-to-face battles for which they were trained. Unable to group themselves into their traditional battle formations, and pursue the generally accepted procedures and norms of engagement, Greek casualties were very heavy.

87. For how long did Matityahu lead the freedom-fighters?

He was already well-advanced in years when he raised the standard of revolt, and his act of zeal in assassinating the renegade Hellenized Jew, and the subsequent need to flee in haste into the desert, must have taken its toll on his health. Within a few months, in the 146th year of the Seleucid Era (166 BCE), he died, having issued instructions that his third son, Judah (the Maccabee) should succeed as military commander, but that they should always look to Simeon for counsel and political guidance.[37]

88. Who led the Greek offensive, and where did the main opening clashes occur?

Antiochus, who was engaged elsewhere in the empire, assumed that the Greek forces based in Judea would be able to contain the uprising. To be on the safe side, he dispatched Apollonius, a leading general, from Samaria, together with a large detachment of extra troops. Judah and his men overwhelmed them and the Greeks suffered heavy casualties, including the death of their commander. We are told that Judah took the sword of Apollonius, and used it throughout his subsequent adventures.

The account in the Book of Maccabees omits any mention of where that great victory was won![38] It tells us, however, that a second, heavily-augmented, Greek force, under the command of Seron, who had been serving in Syria, was despatched against Judah, who engaged it, with a numerically much inferior force, at the ascent to Bet-Horon. The mighty Maccabees, with the advantage of the upper slopes, overran the enemy and slew some 800 men. The rest fled before the Jews in the direction of Philistia.

89. Confronted with such resolute Jewish resistance, why did Antiochus not assume personal command, in order to bring a swift end to the revolt?

He was unable personally to take charge of operations, nor was he able to send his main army against Judea, because he was preoccupied with fighting the Parthians. He also discovered that he did not have sufficient money in his treasury to pay salary to his soldiers,[39] a situation that was certain to create half-hearted, and therefore ineffectual, fighters. He determined, therefore, that he would lead an expedition to his eastern territories and attempt to levy huge taxes to finance the war against the Jews, leaving his deputy, Lysias, in charge of operations in Judea until his return.

90. What resources did Antiochus put at Lysias's disposal to confront the plucky Maccabees?

In fairness to him, Antiochus gave Lysias all the support he could reasonably have expected, including an augmented force of some 47,000 men – half the entire Greek army in the East – under the command of three experienced generals, Ptolemy, Nicanor and Georgias.[40] This number is regarded as rather exaggerated by commentators, as it does not harmonise with parallel numbers quoted in other parts of Maccabees. We may nevertheless assume that Lysias now had a force that he regarded as adequate to confront the enemy. Antiochus also left him his entire force of elephants[41] – a formidable fighting machine for any enemy to confront.

91. So where did Lysias choose to engage the Maccabees?

His vast force made their camp at Emmaus, at the boundary between the central mountain range and the Shephelah area, 33 kilometres north-west of Jerusalem and about five hours marching time. So unequal were the forces that merchants from all the surrounding areas, Philistia, Syria, and so on, followed the Greek army, bringing with them vast sums of money, in expectation of there being innumerable captive Jews available for purchase as slaves at very competitive prices![42]

91.Have we any information regarding what preparations the Maccabees made for this particular engagement?

We have the account of the Book of Maccabees, which relates that the Maccabees' preparation did not take the form of last-minute military training or briefing, but, rather, of spiritual engagement.

They assembled together at Mizpeh, opposite Jerusalem, for in Mizpeh there had existed, from time immemorial, a place of prayer for Israel. They fasted and put on sackcloth, and ashes on their heads. They rent their clothing and spread out the scrolls of the Torah upon which the Gentiles had sought to draw images of their idols. They also brought out the priests' robes and the first fruits and tithes, and paraded the Nazarites who had completed the period (of their vow).

They then cried out to heaven, saying, 'What shall we do with these [first fruits and tithes, seeing that we have no Temple]? And where shall we direct these [Nazarites, seeing that, without a Temple, they cannot bring their sin-offering of resumption before they can return to normal life]? Your holy place is trodden down and profaned, and your priests are in mourning and depression. See how the Gentiles have assembled together to destroy us. You know what they have planned for us. How can we withstand them without Your assistance?'

They then sounded the rams' horns and cried out in a loud voice [for divine help].[41]

93. But did not Judah direct any final personal message to his forces?

He did. It was a very direct and concise one which they could carry with them verbatim into battle:

> Gird yourselves and be valiant and ready for tomorrow, to fight against the Gentiles who have assembled to destroy us and our holy place. For it is better to die in battle than to look upon the evil that has been visited upon our nation and our sanctuary. Whatever is God's will, that He will do.[44]

94. Presumably, with such a smaller group of fighters to call upon, the Maccabees must have drafted every single person they could possibly muster, irrespective of age and situation?

The assumption is, in fact, quite erroneous. Surprising as it may seem, the Maccabees were meticulous to follow the regulations of warfare found in the Torah. Hence we are told that, after allocating captains of thousands, hundreds, fifties and tens, Judah directed that, in accordance with Deuteronomic law, 'those who were [still in the process of] building their houses, betrothing their wives and planting their vineyards, as well as those who were faint-hearted, should return home and attend to their own needs, according to the law'.[45]

95. What was the Greek's opening strategy?

We shall never know! The Maccabees did not wait for their enemies to make the first move. That night, Judah was informed that the Greek general, Georgias, had taken 6,000 of his troops, and had left the main camp in order to try and locate the Maccabean centre of operations.

Judah immediately withdrew his soldiers from Mizpeh that night and journeyed to place themselves in a south-west position for an unexpected attack on the main Greek force at Emmaus. When Georgias finally located and entered the camp at Mizpeh, he found it abandoned. In vain he searched all around the surrounding hills, and immediately concluded that the Maccabees had fled in panic.

At dawn, the well-trained, well-armed Greek army, supported by cavalry divisions, found themselves in formation facing in the wrong direction when the poorly armed, Jewish freedom fighters, numbering a mere 3,000 men, prepared to attack.

96. But still, how could the out-numbered, amateur Maccabees possibly face such a formidable adversary?

This was truly one of the great miracles of Israel's history. We are told not to rely on miracles, but it seems as if Judah's faith was so strong, and his courage so unshakeable, that he was in no doubt that God would, once again, reveal 'His great hand' and repeat for Israel the miracle of the Red Sea. Indeed, after giving his men another rousing call to arms, telling them not to be afraid of the enemy's vastly superior numbers, he reminds them 'how our fathers were saved in the Red sea, when Pharaoh pursued them with a vast army'. He told them, therefore, to cry out to heaven for God to remember the covenant with their forefathers and to destroy this present enemy.

The Maccabees took the initiative and launched an attack on the Greeks before the latter could turn around, sounding shofars (rams' horns) as they charged. Having probably expected the Maccabees to retreat in disarray at the very sight of their vast army, the Greeks were thrown into panic at the sudden charge of the Maccabees, combined with the terrifying sound of the horns which may have made the Greeks think that they were being attacked by an additional force on another side. They broke their formations, turned around in every direction, and were set upon by the valiant Maccabees and routed, with those who could, fleeing into the surrounding plain.

97. Did the Maccabees pursue them?

Most definitely. They could not possibly give their enemies the opportunity to re-group and launch another assault. A miracle may happen once; to expect it twice is quite audacious – even on the part of Jews!

Elements of the Greek army attempted to flee to Gezer, an important strategic and well-fortified town nearby. The Maccabees knew how important it was to frustrate their ability to occupy that town, and they therefore pursued them with lightning speed and cut them down. Others attempted to flee to 'the fields of Edom, Ashdod and Yavneh'.[46] The fact that Edom was a two-day journey to the east of the battle field, and Ashdod and Yavneh were two nearby towns to the west, is in itself indicative of the panic that had gripped the enemy and the confusion that characterized their flight. The Maccabees pursued, and killed some 3,000 men

98. But surely there were other, relief divisions of the Greek army that could have been mustered to return and confront the Maccabees?

There were, indeed. The general, Lysias, was disconsolate when he received news of the rout of the Greek forces, and the following year he assembled a force of 60,000 foot soldiers and 5,000 cavalrymen to subdue the Jews. He encamped at Bet Zur, south of Jerusalem, on the way to Hebron, a fortification on the border with Idumea (Edom). This was a new strategy, of attempting to attack the Jews from the south, and may have been suggested by Georgias who was Commander of the Idumean region.[47]

This time, Judah's forces had swelled to 10,000 men, and the respite had undoubtedly provided them with plenty of time to train in the Maccabeans' preferred type of warfare. Judah and his men attacked the forces of Lysias, and destroyed 5,000 of his men in the initial foray. When Lysias saw this unprecedented Jewish heroism, and the ease with which they had overwhelmed his men, he retreated and moved the rest of his forces to Antioch. This was the signal for the Jews to reassert their independence and to reoccupy the Temple in Jerusalem that had been polluted by the Greeks and their worship.

99. But, surely, this was also not a total Jewish victory, but rather just a show of strength. What emboldened the Jews, therefore, to think that they could now assert their independence?

Good point. To answer this we have to turn to the Second Book of the Maccabees which fills in the background to the fate of Antiochus Epiphanes at the same time as the aforementioned battles were in progress.

From that source we learn that Antiochus embarked upon a raid on the Persian city of Persepolis, and proceeded to attempt to rob one of the temples of its treasures. He did not anticipate the multitudes that suddenly appeared and set upon his forces, who fled to Ecbatana in disarray and ignominy. While there, he received news of a crushing defeat, and the loss of some 9,000 men, suffered by his most able general, Nicanor. He was so inflamed with anger that he determined 'to make Jerusalem the collective graveyard of the Jews'.[48] But, no sooner were the words out of his mouth when he collapsed with excruciating bowel pain.

His hatred of the Jews was so all-consuming that, ignoring his pain, he determined to undertake the journey to punish the Jews. As his chariot gathered speed it hit a pot hole, and Antiochus was pitched out, falling heavily and compounding his terrible pain. He was unable to proceed in his chariot, as he suffered agonies with every jolt, and he had to continue his journey being carried in a litter. To make matters much worse, there suddenly appeared the manifestation of some horrendous and consumptive disease of the internal organs, such as riddled his flesh with worms, causing it to emit a most unbearable stench.

According to our source, a shaft of uncharacteristic insight made him realize that all this had come upon him as a punishment from the Jewish God for what he had done to the Jews and their sacred Temple, and a tincture of remorse set in. He determined to reverse his policies, to withdraw his troops from Jerusalem, declare it a free city, grant the Jews citizenship 'on a par with the Jews of Athens', make multiple restitution of what he had stolen from the Temple, defray the costs of the sacrificial system and – wait for it! – become a convert to, and travelling missionary for, Judaism![49] He was mighty scared of dying!

Thus, given the growing numerical and military strength of the Maccabees, and the growing impotence of the opposition, it is understandable that the former should have felt that the moment was opportune to seize back Jerusalem and the Temple and reassert Jewish independence in their land.

100. But, does not Antiochus's volte face sound rather like a traveller's tale?

It does, indeed. However, the next chapter of Maccabees goes on to relate the contents of a letter that he subsequently sent to 'his loyal Jewish subjects', wishing them happiness and informing them of his illness and his hopes for recovery, and stating that, should he not recover, he was appointing his son Antiochus (V) as his successor, and that, in return for their good will toward him, 'he, in gentleness and kindness, will follow my purpose and treat you with indulgence'.

In the letter, Antiochus states that he is appending below a copy of the instructions that he has written to his son.[50] He was presumably referring to his last will and testament that his son adopt a benign attitude to the Jews. Now, the fact that that letter does not, in fact, appear in our source, suggests a degree of authenticity for the text. Had the writer been involved in 'creative writing', he would hardly have overlooked such an omission in his presentation.

101. But why would Antiochus have bothered to write such a letter to the Jews, naming his son as his successor?

The necessity to do so would have been quite clear to him. Alarmed at the rebellious nature of the Jews and their growing power, he would not have wanted a vacuum of leadership to be created at his death. A smooth succession makes for stability and cohesion. In the absence of a named successor, there would likely be an internal power struggle, leaving the empire vulnerable to revolt on the part of disaffected subject-states. There is thus a ring of authenticity about the letter, which, in turn, adds credence to a change of heart on the part of Antiochus. Whether that went as far as a conversion to Judaism is, however, open to question.

102. So how many battles did the Maccabees have to fight before they regained the Temple and Jewish independence?

At first, after the initial events at Modin, when the aged Mattathias assassinated the Jewish idolater, Jason, his followers confined themselves to guerilla operations. They organized themselves into area insurgent groups and weakened the Seleucid control of the country by liquidating any Jewish collaborators and imposing a disciplined loyalty among the Jewish population. As a result, the enemy supply-line connecting Jerusalem's citadel and garrison with the army bases and administrative centres around the country was almost completely severed.

This was followed by Judah the Maccabee's first major battle, thwarting an attempt by Apollonius, governor of Samaria, to break through to Jerusalem from the north. Apollonius' forces were routed and he was killed. The second major battle took place on the slopes of Bet Horon, when another Seleucid general, Seron, attempted the same objective, and met the same fate.

It was now realized that the task was too difficult to entrust to local commanders, so Ptolemy, governor of Coele-Syria and Phoenicia, took control of strategy, sending in his most experienced generals, Nicanor and Gorgias, and attempting to break through to Jerusalem from the west, via Emmaus. We have already described Judah's daring march to surprise the Seleucid army by attacking them from the south-west (see Question 95). That was the third and undoubtedly most brilliant of his battles.

The fourth victory was won against Lysias at Bet Zur, on the Idumean border; and that finally convinced Antiochus that numerical and military superiority was still not going to achieve victory against a native population fired by revolutionary zeal and led by freedom fighters willing to lay down their lives for what they perceived as a sacred national and spiritual cause.

103. Did the Seleucids immediately accept that a Jewish declaration of independence was inevitable?

Not exactly. They attempted to frustrate it diplomatically, by tempting the Jews with concessions that might allow the present political situation to remain intact. In addition, they made use of the good offices of some Roman legates who were visiting Syria at that time, persuading them to negotiate with the Jews an amicable end to the hostilities.

To that end, Lysias offered the Jews three significant concessions. These took the form of a decree to grant a free pardon to any Jewish fighter who returned to his home by a certain date, to proclaim freedom of religious practice to all Jews, and, thirdly, to replace the hated governor, Ptolemy son of Dorymenes, with Ptolemy Makron, in whom the Jews had greater confidence.

Glorying in his strength and military advantage, Judah refused to be bought off, and, spurred on by news of the death of Antiochus, he led an assault on the citadel and garrison of Jerusalem and put the enemy forces to flight.

NOTES

1. See II Maccabees 6:18–31.
2. See II Maccabees Ch. 7.
3. See II Maccabees 7:25–9.
4. Nehemiah 11:10, 12:6,9.I Chronicles 9:10.
5. See I Chronicles 24:7.
6. Ibid.
7. See Flavius Josephus, *Antiquities of the Jews* (London: Harry G. Bohn, 1845), Book XII, ch.VI. sec.1.
8. Mishnah *Middot* 1:6.
9. Talmud *Shabbat* 21b; *Bava Kamma* 82b.
10. See the *Al Ha-Nisim: Biymei Matityahu* composition, recited on Chanukah in the *Amidah* and the Grace After Meals.
11. See note 7.
12. See Genesis 49:10.
13. See below, question 156.
14. See I Maccabees 2:6–14.
15. John Bright, A History of Israel (London, SCM Press, 1964), p.407.
16. I Maccabees 1:41–2.
17. Bright, *History of Israel*, p.407.
18. Josephus, *Antiquities*, XII, V, 5.
19. See sources quoted in J. Klausner, *Historiah shel Ha-bayit Ha-sheni* (Jerusalem: Ahiasaf, 1959), II, p.178, n.24.
20. Stephen Frosh, *For and Against Psychoanalysis* (London: Routledge,1997), p.224.
21. See Klausner, *Historiah shel Ha-bayit Ha-sheni*, p.180.
22. See II Maccabees Chapter 6.

23. Ibid., Chapter 7.
24. Ibid., 7:9.
25. Ibid., 7:11.
26. See Talmud *Gittin* 57b.
27. I Samuel 2:5.
28. The classical commentators have to resort to tortuous methods of resolving this difficulty. See *Rashi* and *Radak ad loc*.
29. This thesis is argued by A. Momigliano in *Jewish History: Essays in Honour of Chimen Abramsky*, edited by Ada Rapoport-Albert and Steven J. Zipperstein (London: Peter Halban, 1988), pp.231–7.
30. Elias J. Bickerman in *The Jews: Their History, Culture and Religion*, edited by Louis Finkelstein (London: Peter Owen Limited, 1961), I, p.102.
31. I Maccabees 2:15–23.
32. See Numbers 25:1–9.
33. This name is provided by Josephus, though it does not appear in the account in I Maccabees.
34. I Maccabees 2: 25.
35. Daniel 8:4.
36. Bright, *History of Israel*, p.444.
37. See I Maccabees 2:65–9.
38. Ibid., Chapter 3.
39. Ibid., 3:29-31.
40. Ibid., 3:38.
41. Ibid., 3:33.
42. Ibid., 3:46-57.
43. Ibid., 3:40-41.
44. Ibid., 3:58.
45. Ibid., 3:56; Cf. Deuteronomy 20:5ff.
46. Ibid., 4:15.
47. A. Kahane, *Ha-Sefarim Ha-Chitzoniim* (Tel Aviv: Masada Publishing, 1960), commentary to I Maccabees 4:29.
48. II Maccabees 9:4.
49. Ibid., 9:12–17.
50. Ibid., 9:26.

II
THE RELIGIOUS
BACKGROUND

5

The Temple in our Hands

THE TEMPLE AND ITS DESIGNATIONS

104. When did the Maccabees regain control of the Temple?

It was on 25 Kislev in the year 164 BCE. And that Hebrew date was established subsequently as a day of festivity and religious significance, marking the commencement of the eight-day festival of Chanukah, in celebration of the capture of Jerusalem and the rededication of the Temple.[1]

105. The word temple is, of course, a translation. What are the original, biblical names, or terms, for that holy site?

The word *temple* probably derives from the Greek word *temenos*, Latin *templum*, with its basic sense of a demarcated place or sacred enclosure.

There are very many names for, or designations of, the Temple that appear in the Bible, though it is not possible to determine the extent of their exclusivity at the particular period they are being used. Among these are: *heikhal* ('sanctuary'), *heikhal Adonai* ('Sanctuary of the Lord'),[2] *heikhal kodshi* ('My holy Sanctuary'),[3] *ha-bayit* ('The house'),[4] *heikhal ha-bayit* ('Sanctuary of the House'),[5] *mikdashi* ('My holy place'),[6] *ha-kodesh* ('The holy place'),[7] *bet ha-gadol* ('The Great House'),[8] *bet Adonai* ('House of the Lord'),[9] *bet Adonai Tzeva'ot* ('House of the Lord of Hosts'),[10] *beitiy* ('My house'),[11] *me'on kodsho* ('His holy habitation'),[12] *bet ha'Elohim* ('House of God'),[13] *bet ha-kodesh* ('House of holiness'),[14] *bet kodsheinu vtifarteinu*, ('The source of our holiness and splendor'),[15] *bet zevul* ('The site of the [divine] habitation').[16]

106 But none of these names won acceptance as a popular designation of the Temple?

That is so. For some unknown reason – perhaps it was simply a dialectal preference in the development of spoken Hebrew during the latter half of the Second Commonwealth – the term *Bet Ha-mikdash* became the favoured designation. This term means, literally, 'home of the Sanctuary', the latter probably referring specifically to the 'Holy of Holies', the innermost sanctum where the Spirit of God was believed to be most intensely manifest. This term is the one that is most commonly found in Mishnah, Talmud and Midrash.

Another designation of the Temple, referred to in the Talmud, is *Bet Ha-bechirah*: 'Three duties were incumbent upon Israel when they entered the Promised Land – to appoint a king, to build the Temple (*Bet Ha-bechirah*) and to eradicate the Amalekites.'[17]

In spite of its infrequent usage, it is a well-known term because of its occurrence in the Passover Haggadah. It is, nevertheless, a rather curious term, meaning, literally, 'The house of choice,' probably in the sense of 'the choice, or chosen, house,' that is, the home chosen by God wherein to make His Spirit manifest. This name was probably inspired by the biblical verse, *V'attah bachartiy v'hikdashtiy et ha-bayit ha-zeh*, 'Now I have chosen and sanctified this house.'[18]

Surprisingly, Maimonides, in his Code of Law, the Mishneh Torah, employs that rare term as the heading for his section on 'Laws of the Temple' – *Hilkhot Bet Ha-bechirah* – in preference to the fairly universal term, *Bet Ha-mikdash*. Curiously, notwithstanding that section title, whenever he refers to the Temple in the body of the text, he designates it by the biblical term, *mikdash*!

This may be attributable to Maimonides having attempted to satisfy two needs. The first was to express his avowed purism, which motivated him to give priority to the original biblical term, as used by God, in the verse: 'And they shall make for Me a sanctuary (*mikdash*), and I shall dwell in their midst.'[19] On the other hand, by employing the term *Bet Ha-bechirah*, he was, at the same time, acknowledging the phraseology used in the above-quoted talmudic source.[20]

107. Are there any biblical allusions to the Temple or its holy site dating back to the period preceding the conquest of Jerusalem by King David and the building of the Temple by his son, Solomon?

Jewish tradition has it that the 'Land of Moriah' to which God directed that Abraham take his son, Isaac, and there to offer him up 'on one of the mountains',[21] was a reference to the Temple Mount in Jerusalem. Abraham's readiness to sacrifice his son on that spot (a summons that was merely a test of his faith, but never intended by God as a required human sacrifice) foreshadowed the innumerable animal sacrifices to be offered there in the future, as well as the countless sacrifices, in terms of human life, that would have to be made by Abraham's offspring in their generational struggle to retain ownership of that holiest of Jewish sites.

The above identification is based on an explicit verse in Chronicles: 'To build the house of the Lord in Jerusalem on Mount Moriah'.[22] The link between the name and the site is explained variously by commentators. The official Aramaic translator, Onkelos, renders *Moriah*, in this context, as 'the land of worship', perhaps inspired by the *Moriah*-myrrh equation, since myrrh was a primary ingredient of the sweet-smelling incense offered in the Temple.[23] The famous commentator, *Rashi*, cites authorities 'who understand "land of Moriah" in the sense of *hora'ah*, "teaching", namely, the land from which Torah, or teaching, was destined to proceed to the world'.[24] Interestingly, a reference to a central sanctuary yet to be built occurs in the Song of the Red Sea: 'The Sanctuary (*mikdash*), O Lord, which Thy hands have established' (Exodus 15:17).

The book of Deuteronomy is replete with references to 'the place which the Lord shall choose to cause His name to reside there'[25] – a central place of divine worship to which Israel will bring all its sacrifices and offerings. This is 'the land which the Lord swore unto your forefathers to give unto them and their seed, a land flowing with milk and honey.'[26]

In the light of some present-day, preposterous Palestinian revisionist attempts to deny the Jewish claim to the Temple Mount, these references, which appear in nearly every chapter of the biblical book of Deuteronomy, are incontrovertible proof that that area is bound up with the very origins of the Jewish people. They were translated from theory into a reality in the period of Kings David and Solomon, some 1,500 years before Islam came on the scene of history!

108. Can you give us a brief guided-tour of the main components of the Temple?

I'll try, though it will require a lot of imagination!

Entering via the eastern gate, one found oneself inside a large square hall, designated as the Women's Court, with each wall measuring 135 cubits (about 200 feet). Ahead were fifteen steps leading up to a higher level. Each corner of the ground floor was partitioned off to form two storerooms and two waiting rooms. The former were designated by the names 'Chamber of the Wood' and 'Chamber of the Oils'; the latter were the 'Chamber of the Lepers' and 'Chamber of the Nazarites'. There were also secondary gates leading into 'The Women's Court' from the north and the south.

Ascending the far steps, one entered, via 'Nicanor's Gate', into the middle level which housed the 'Court of the Israelites', or men's section, containing the altar and the various other ritual appurtenances.

Off three sides of this hall were ten small storerooms to house the priests' robes, the wood required for the current week's service at the altar, the salt, the bakery for the loaves, 'The Chamber of the Hewn Stones' where the Sanhedrin, or Supreme Court, sat, and a room in which the priests performed their ritual washings of the hands and feet.

As one proceeded through the centre of the 'Court of the Israelites', one entered the ritual area. To the right was situated the *Bet Ha-mitbachayim*, or 'slaughter houses' for the sacrifices; to the left, the high altar and ramp leading up to it. Just past the altar, on the left, were positioned the laver or wash bowl for the priests.

All along the south side of Solomon's Temple there stood ten magnificent *Menorahs* (candelabra), the centerpiece being the incomparable golden Menorah, crafted by Betzalel. In the second Temple, there was but one golden Menorah, which was stolen by Antiochus in the year 169 BCE. All the stolen Temple vessels were later replaced by Judah the Maccabee.

109. So have we completed our description of the Temple?

Not yet. We have so far described only two of the three levels of the Temple. From the second level there was another flight of steps leading to the most sacred area of the Temple. The area which housed the priests' laver was to the left of these steps. On reaching the top of the steps, one found oneself in the *ulam*, a long and narrow rectangular porch, with the long section stretching out to one's right and left. Crossing over the narrow porch, one could see another rectangular court stretching out, lengthwise, ahead. The front section of this was the sanctuary, with a thick veil or curtain separating it from the adjoining inner section, which was the Holy of Holies, the residence of the Divine Spirit, a place where the High Priest alone was permitted to enter but once a year, on the Day of Atonement.[27]

THE DEFILEMENT AND CLEANSING OF THE TEMPLE

110. What sight greeted the Maccabees when they entered the Temple?

The First Book of Maccabees describes the sight in this way:

> And they saw the sanctuary laid desolate, the altar profaned, the gates burned up, with shrubs growing in the courts as in a forest, and the priests' chambers pulled down. And they rent their clothes and made great lamentation. They also put ashes on their heads, fell on their faces to the ground and, blowing with the trumpets, they cried to heaven.[28]

111. Had the second Temple been a truly magnificent structure then, before the Greeks vandalized it?

Truthfully, no. It was a pale reflection of the grandeur of Solomon's Temple, which was made of the very costliest of materials and executed by the finest craftsmen of the age. The second Temple, by comparison, was a product of an impoverished Judea, and remained unadorned and of inferior materials. The one notable exception was the Menorah which, as soon as they could afford it, they made of solid gold, in conformity with biblical law (see Exodus 37:17). Indeed, when some very old men, who could still remember from their childhood the glory of the first Temple, arrived for the dedication of the rebuilt Temple, they broke down and wept at the contrasting sight. This situation prompted the prophet Haggai to reassure the down-hearted that this was only a temporary situation, and that 'even greater shall be the glory of this house than that of the former'.[29]

112. When we speak of the Greeks 'having defiled' the Temple, what exactly do we mean?

One had to be in a state of ritual purity to enter the Temple. A corpse, in Judaism, is 'the supreme generator of *tum'ah* (impurity)', and anyone coming into contact with it (and which soldier, engaging in hand-to-hand combat, did not?) could not enter the Temple without undergoing ritual purification with the ashes of the Red Heifer.[30]

In Temple times, anyone who stood under the same roof as a Jewish corpse contracted ritual impurity.

It goes without saying that pagan or gentile soldiers, or others who had dealt with the dead, would automatically convey that impurity to whatever objects or vessels they touched, so as to render them unfit for ritual use. According to Biblical law,[31] clothes, sacking, leather and wooden, metal or bone, objects can all contract impurity, and require immersion in a mikveh (ritual bath) of 'living water'. Food and certain liquids also become impure and unfit when handled by someone who is impure through contact with the dead.

Out of fear that gentiles might have slaughtered their beasts as offerings to idolatrous deities, any beast slaughtered by them was declared a source of impurity. As the Greek soldiers used the Temple as their quarters, and slaughtered their animals and prepared their meals there, the food was a natural source of contamination. Hence the reasonable assumption that the entire internal fabric of the temple, and whatever vessels remained intact, had been rendered impure.

There was also the probability that the Seleucids buried some of their dead in the earth within the Temple precincts or that fragments of human bones might be unearthed. This would render unclean any priest walking over that area, to the extent that he would be unable to perform the Temple service without purification in a mikveh (ritual bath), following a prescribed waiting period.

113. Were there any other problems of impurity confronting the Maccabeans when they reoccupied the Temple?

There were. Inevitably, the entire population of Judea would have wished to make a joyful pilgrimage to the Temple once it was in Jewish hands again, and to attend the Chanukah, or dedication service. The Greeks had destroyed the ritual baths and prohibited religious practices, including immersion. This created particular problems for the various other classes of unclean people, such as lepers, women after the conclusion of their menstrual cycle or confinement, who had to immerse in the mikveh before entering the Temple. A feverish exercise of building and repairing those facilities all over the country was required. Many would have been prevented from joining in the celebrations as a result of the inevitable delays before the ritual baths were serviceable.

114. What form did the process of cleansing the Temple take?

We have two versions of what they did. The first Book of Maccabees states that

> [Judah] chose whole-hearted priests whose delight was in the law, and they cleansed the holy place and removed the stones of abomination to an unclean place. And they took counsel concerning the profaned altar of burnt offerings as to what should be done with it. And they all inclined to the view that it should be dismantled, lest it remain a reproachful reminder of what the enemy had done to them. So they pulled it down and buried the stones on the Temple mount, in a

specially-designated place, until there might arise a prophet who could give [divine] counsel regarding the matter. And they took whole stones, according to the law, and built a new altar after the fashion of the former. And they rebuilt the sanctuary and its inner chambers and re-dedicated the courts.[32]

115. What is the meaning of that reference to a prophet who might arise in the future?

This is a most interesting notion that is taken up as a recurring concept in the later Talmudic literature. Whenever there was an halachic issue about which there was no surviving ancient tradition, and over which generations of talmudists had argued without reaching any consensus view, the Talmud brings the discussion to an end with the single word *teyku*, meaning 'the problem remains'. According to a popular view, however, this word is, in fact, an acronym for the phrase *Tishbi Yetaretz Kushiot V'ibbayot*, '[Elijah] the Tishbite will resolve all questions and problems'. Elijah is, of course, the harbinger of the Messiah, and the Talmud believes that, as a prelude to the Messiah's arrival, Elijah will resolve all problematic issues, including the establishment of the authentic Jewish and priestly pedigree of those whose status is in doubt. This reference to 'the prophet' in the Book of Maccabees appears to be the earliest reference to this concept, though in the earlier book of Ezra there is a reference to priests whose pedigree was in doubt being prevented from eating sacrificial meat, 'until there shall arise a priest [to determine the truth] on the basis of the Urim and Tumim' (see Question 294).[33]

RENEWING THE ALTAR

116. What is the meaning of the reference to them 'taking whole stones according to the law'?

In its description of the making of the desert Sanctuary – the blue-print for the permanent Temples to be built after Israel had entered the Promised Land – as well as in relation to the altar that Israel is told to erect as soon as they have crossed the Jordan,[34] the Torah states, 'You shall build the altar of the Lord your God of unhewn stones, for, if you wield your [iron] tool upon it, you profane it'.[35] The Talmud explains that iron is frequently employed violently in order to shorten human life, whereas the altar (by restoring the sinner to divine favour) prolongs life. It is inappropriate, therefore, to bring the two into proximity.[36]

117. Do we have any archaeological corroboration of the existence of altars in the way prescribed by the Torah?

We do, indeed. Although the Torah prescribes that sacrifices should only be offered 'in the place where the Lord will cause His Name to be invoked',[37] yet it is a fact that, throughout the ancient Near East, as well as in pre-Temple Israel, local sanctuaries and *bamot* (lit. 'high places') existed for sacrificial purposes.

Such altars have been unearthed at Nahariya, Megiddo, Hazor, Gezer and Arad. In the latter place, in the Negev, an Israelite sanctuary was unearthed, containing an altar of unhewn stone whose dimensions were three cubits square and five cubits in height – the precise dimensions prescribed by the Torah for the altar of the desert sanctuary![38]

118. Speaking of the altar, do not the rabbis make some connection between the altar and divorce?

Absolutely right. The actual quotation is, 'If someone divorces his wife, the very altar sheds tears'.[39]

The connection between the two should now be apparent. Kohelet promotes the permanence of marriage in the words, 'Enjoy *life* with the woman you love, all the days of your *life*'.[40] So if the main purpose of the altar is to prolong and promote 'life', and if life and marriage are, as Kohelet asserts, synonymous terms, then divorce frustrates the entire *raison d'etre* of the altar. And hence the tears it sheds for the failure of its mission.

BRINGING FIRE TO THE ALTAR

119. Do we have any supplementary information from the second Book of Maccabees regarding the purification of the Temple?

Indeed. That source adds that:

having cleansed the sanctuary they built another sacrificial altar. They then struck two flint stones together and created fire from the sparks in order to offer sacrifices after a two-year interruption. They burned incense, lit lamps and set out the shewbread.[41]

120. What was the point of striking the flint-stones to produce the spark?

It was essential that the altar fire be renewed from a pure source, and not from fire taken from any non-sacred context. As priests, the Maccabees would have been well acquainted with the biblical account of their ancestors, Nadav and Avihu, the two sons of Aaron, who took 'strange fire' to the altar, and who were struck dead for their sin.[42]

121. Was there any precedence in our religious tradition for producing fire in that way?

Not in our biblical tradition. The Midrash asserts, however, that Adam, fearful of the darkness that enveloped him when the sun set on the first Sabbath day of his creation, took two flint stones and smashed them against each other to produce fire.

Adam then blessed God as *Borei me'orei ha-eish*, 'Creator of the light of the fire'; and it is for that reason, says the Midrash, that, as part of the *Havdalah* ceremony, when Shabbat goes out, we light a candle and recite that blessing.[43]

122. Is that how the altar fire was created when Solomon built the first Temple (circa 960 BCE)?

No. According to biblical tradition, the fire of the first Temple appeared miraculously, 'having descended from heaven.'[44]

123. So when the Temple was rebuilt by Ezra and Nehemiah (circa 517 BCE) after the Jews had returned from Babylon, how was the altar fire renewed?

Here, again, we are reliant upon tradition. The Talmud simply avers that, for the second Temple, God did not repeat that miracle, to favour the Jews with any heavenly sign of grace.[45]

It is from the less authoritative second Book of Maccabees that we derive a strange tradition regarding how the fire was obtained for the renewed altar. It states there that when the Jews were about to be taken into captivity in Babylon, the priests took the holy fire from the altar and secretly concealed it within the hollow of an empty well. Now, when Nehemiah received permission from the king of Persia to rebuild the Temple, he sent descendants of the priests who had hid it to search it out.

They returned, saying that they had found no fire, but only 'thick water'. Nehemiah commanded them to bring him a specimen, and when the sacrifices had been placed on the altar, he commanded the priests to sprinkle the wood and the sacrifices with that substance.

The weather had hitherto been very cloudy; but suddenly the sun came out and ignited the substance, 'making a great blaze which astonished everyone'.[46]

124. What credence do we put by this tradition?

It certainly has a Midrashic flavour, and its rationale may well have been to inject a miraculous element into the events in order to reinforce the religious credentials of the Maccabees at a time when II Maccabees was written. By that time, the mystique of the Maccabees may well have been on the wane as a result of the religious decline of their dynasty and their militaristic and expansionist policies.

That association of the hiding of the fire with the Babylonian exile may also have suggested itself on account of the fact that the Persians, who subsequently conquered the Babylonian Empire, were fire worshipers, and therefore venerated the combustible 'thick water,' or oil. The parallels between the miracle of the Chanukah oil (see Questions 129; 139–46) and this tradition about the previously hidden 'fuel', that was 'found' and which miraculously ignited, are inescapable.

THE HISTORY AND FATE OF THE MENORAH

125. We mentioned above (see Question 111) that the impoverished, returning Judeans could not afford to restore the second Temple vessels in their costly pristine form. Do we know, then, what the replacement Menorah – the centrepiece of the Chanukah miracle – was like?

We have a Talmudic tradition that Judah the Maccabee, lacking any funds at that time, made the Menorah out of iron, overlaid with either tin or wood. Later, when more funds became available, he replaced it with a Menorah of silver. Later still, that was also replaced with a golden Menorah, as biblically prescribed![47]

The historian Josephus[48] writes, however, that, from the outset, they made the Menorah of pure gold. Writing for the citizens of Rome, he may well have been embarrassed to admit that the Jews 'made do' with inferior vessels in honour of their God.

126. Do we know what happened to that Menorah when the second Temple was destroyed by the Romans in 70 CE?

We know from Josephus[49] that it was seized by the emperor Titus and carried back triumphantly to Rome as a trophy of war. This is corroborated by the simple fact that, in celebration and commemoration of that victory, Titus had a special stone arch constructed, on one panel of which are depicted, in relief, various scenes from that event, including a representation of the Temple Menorah being transported back home by Roman soldiers, along with other Temple spoils.

127. Do we know what the subsequent fate of the Menorah was?

According to Josephus,[50] Titus deposited the Menorah, together with the other Temple treasures and booty from the city of Jerusalem, in a specially constructed Peace Temple which he built on his return to Rome. Its subsequent history is uncertain, with a popular, though probably untrue, tradition that it still resides, hidden deep in the vaults of the Vatican.

A sixth-century Byzantine historian[51] reports that when the Vandals completed their sack of Rome in 455 CE, they carried off the Jewish treasures to Carthage. He further reports that when the Byzantine General, Belisarius, returned to Constantinople, having defeated the Vandals and captured their king, he also brought back in his triumphal procession those same treasures. Later traditions refer to their having been hurriedly returned and deposited in various churches in Jerusalem out of fear that possession of them might bring in its wake the same defeat and destruction suffered by Rome and Carthage. This is contradicted, however, by medieval sources that refer directly to the Menorah as having appeared in the imperial palace at Constantinople where it was lit on state occasions, and where it was housed beneath a special 'Dome of the Seven-Branched Candelabrum'.[52]

128. Is the Menorah depicted on the Arch of Titus identical in detail to the blue-print of Betzalel's Menorah, as described in the book of Exodus?

No it is not. The Menorah of Titus, for example, has a pedestal in the shape of two octagonal casings, similar to the one displayed on the emblem of the State of Israel, which was patterned on that of Titus's arch. This conflicts, however, with Jewish sources that describe a Menorah resting on a tripodal base.[53] Clearly, the latter reflects the original design of Betzalel's, whereas the Arch depicts the last Maccabean replacement which, out of deference to the original, would not have been made identical. The pedestal would have been the obvious choice for any distinction to have been employed.[54]

NOTES

1. Many history books quote the year 165 BCE as the date for the Maccabean victory. We follow the Seleucid date given in I Maccabees 2:52 which equates to 164 BCE. The latter date is preferred, for example, by H.H. Ben-Sasson in his *A History of the Jewish People* (Harvard University Press, 1976), p.210.
2. Ezekiel 41:1. II Kings 24:13; Zechariah 6:14/15.
3. Ezekiel 43:12.
4. I Kings 6:14.
5. Ibid., 6:3.
6. Isaiah 60:13; Ezekiel 44:15.
7. Ezekiel 44:27.
8. Jeremiah 52:13.
9. II Kings 25:9; Isaiah 27:16; Jeremiah 52:13.
10. Zechariah 7:2.
11. Isaiah 56:7.
12. Zechariah 2:17.
13. I Chronicles 9:11,13, 26.
14. I Chronicles 29:1.
15. Isaiah 64:10.
16. II Chronicles 6:2.
17. See Talmud *Sanhedrin* 20b.
18. II Chronicles 7:16.
19. Exodus 25:8.
20. It remains curious that, in the subsequent two sections, dealing with further aspects of Temple ritual, Maimonides abandons the *Bet Ha-bechirah* reference and reverts to using the term *mikdash*. Hence the next sections are headed, *Hilkhot K'lei Ha-mikdash* and *Hilkhot Bi'at Ha-mikdash*.
21. See Genesis 22:2.
22. II Chronicles 3:1.
23. But see commentary of Nachmanides on Genesis 22:2.
24. See Rashi on Genesis 22:2.
25. Deuteronomy 14:23.

26. Ibid., 11:9.
27. See Jeffrey M. Cohen, *Prayer and Penitence* (New Jersey: Jason Aronson, 1994), pp.57–8, 206–9; Jeffrey M. Cohen, *1001 Questions and Answers on Rosh Hashanah and Yom Kippur* (New Jersey, Jason Aronson, 1997) pp.335–44.
28. I Maccabees 4: 37–40.
29. Haggai 2:9.
30. See Numbers Chapter 19.
31. See Leviticus 11:32; Numbers 31:22.
32. I Maccabees 4:42–8.
33. Ezra 2:63.
34. See Deuteronomy 27:5–6.
35. Exodus 20:22–3.
36. Mishnah *Middot* 3:4.
37. Deuteronomy 12:5, *et al.*
38. See Exodus 27:1.
39. Talmud *Gittin* 90b.
40. Kohelet 9:9.
41. II Maccabees 9:3–4.
42. Leviticus 10:1-2.
43. Midrash *Bereishit Rabba* 11:2; Tal. *Pesachim* 54b.
44. See II Chronicles 7:1; Talmud *Zevachim* 61b.
45. Talmud *Yoma* 21b.
46. II Maccabees 1:22.
47. Talmud *Rosh Hashanah* 24b; Avodah Zarah 43b.
48. Flavius Josephus, *Antiquities of the Jews* (London: Henry G. Bohn, 1845), 12: p.238.
49. See *Wars of the Jews* in the works of Flavius Josephus, translated by William Whiston (London: Henry G. Bohn, 1845).
50. Ibid.
51. See Encyclopaedia Judaica (Jerusalem, Keter Publication House, 1972), 11, pp.1367.
52. Ibid.
53. See Talmud *Menachot* 28b, with its reference to 'the legs of the Menorah'. See also *Rashi* on Exodus 25:31 and Rambam, *Hilkhot Bet Ha-bechirah* 3:2.
54. For a comparison between the Maccabean Temple Menorah and that represented on the Arch of Titus, see Jeffrey M. Cohen, *Blessed Are You* (New Jersey: Jason Aronson, 1993), pp.204–7. See also Maimonides, *Mishneh Torah, Hilkhot K'lei Ha-mikdash* 3:2.

III
THE SOURCES OF
CHANUKAH

6

Four Conflicting Explanations of the Basis of Chanukah

THE TALMUDIC EXPLANATION

129. What is the traditional view regarding the miracle of the Chanukah oil?

It is the view recorded in the Talmud:

> When the Greeks entered the Temple, they polluted all the Temple oils, and when the Hasmonean dynasty prevailed, they searched and found but one jar of oil with the seal of the High Priest still intact. That was sufficient, however, to burn for only one day. A miracle occurred, and they lit from it for eight days. The following year, they fixed and instituted it as a festival, with Hallel and thanksgiving.[1]

130. Popular Jewish perception, based upon this Talmudic tradition, has it that, on the very day that the Maccabees entered the liberated Temple, they searched for pure oil, and eventually found the famous jar. Did this, indeed, all happen on one day?

The process of removing the desecrated altar stones to an impure place, excavating the earth and burying them there,[2] bringing new stones and constructing the replacement altar, providing new vessels where necessary and purifying those vessels that could still be used, as well as completing the extensive rebuilding work of the sanctuary walls and partitions,[3] must have taken a considerable amount of time. It is hardly likely then, that, as popular tradition has it, they entered the Temple and immediately lit the Menorah with the sole remaining jar of pure olive oil.

There is an ancient Aramaic list, called *Megillat Ta'anit*, which chronicles specially momentous events which occurred during, or in the aftermath of, the Maccabean wars.[4] On account of the celebratory nature of those anniversaries, fasting or eulogizing was prohibited. This ancient source actually states that the Maccabean refurbishment of the Temple began on the twenty-third of the month of Marcheshvan, that is approximately one month before the dedication day of Chanukah on the twenty-fifth of Kislev.[5] Indeed, the fixing of Chanukah 'on the anniversary of the day the Gentiles polluted it',[6] suggests that this date was decided upon in advance for its appropriateness as a most auspicious anniversary. The first Book of Maccabees also makes it clear that, by the twenty-fifth of Kislev, they had already constructed an altar of burnt offerings (see Question 134).

131. So, if all the sources agree that they had plenty of time, before the official Chanukah dedication day, to obtain or prepare sufficient oil for their purposes, why, then, was there a need for a miracle ?

This is truly one of the most difficult questions to answer, and, indeed, opens up an entire scholarly debate on the origins of this festival. Suffice to say that there is no single reference, in the lengthy description of the dedication of the Temple contained in the Books of the Maccabees, to any miracle in connection with a jar of oil!

THE EXPLANATION OF THE SECOND BOOK OF MACCABEES

132. But surely the fact that they instituted an eight-day festival hints at the miraculous background that the Talmud testifies to?

In itself that is not persuasive, because there are several other explanations found in our sources to account for the eight days. Let us first examine what reason the second Book of Maccabees offers:

And they kept eight days with gladness, *in the manner of the festival of Tabernacles*, remembering how, not long before, during that festival, they had been wandering in the mountains and in caves...

Therefore, clutching 'the leaves of the thick tree', other beautiful sprigs and palm branches,[7] they gave thanks to the One who had enabled them to cleanse His habitation.

And so, by public affirmation, they ordained, for the entire Jewish people, the annual celebration of these days.[8]

So, according to this source, the eight days of Chanukah were celebrated in compensation for their inability to celebrate the eight days of Tabernacles two months earlier when the Temple was not yet in their hands. More significantly: note that there is absolutely no mention of any miracle of oil!

133. Are there any precedents for having to 'make up' later for rituals omitted by circumstances beyond one's control?

There are indeed. To give but three examples: The Torah instituted the observance of *Pesach Sheni* (The Second Passover), one calendar month later, for those who were unclean, on a journey, or prevented by some other circumstance from celebrating it at the Temple, as prescribed.[9] Secondly, the specially prescribed festival sacrifices for Shavuot, if not offered on the holy day itself, could be 'compensated for' by being brought at any time during the succeeding week. This procedure of compensation is known in the Talmud as *tashlumin*.[10] Thirdly, if one omits a daily prayer, one is expected to make a token of regret and *tashlumin* compensation by reciting two *Amidahs* at the very next daily service.[11]

THE EXPLANATION OF THE FIRST BOOK OF MACCABEES

134. So what does the first Book of the Maccabees have to say about the dedication ceremony?

It states as follows:

> They rose up early in the morning, on the twenty-fifth day of the ninth month which is the month of Kislev, in the one hundred and forty-eighth year (=165 BCE), and offered sacrifices according to the law *upon the new altar of burnt offerings which they had made*. On the very anniversary of the day the Gentiles had profaned it, they dedicated it afresh, with songs and harps, lutes and cymbals. And all the people made prostration and worshipped, and praised heaven for having bestowed victory upon them. *And they celebrated the dedication of the altar eight days*, and offered burnt offerings with joy, and thanksgiving offerings of deliverance and praise. And they decked out the forefront of the Temple with crowns of gold and with small shields ... And there was unsurpassed celebration. (Author's emphasis.)
>
> And Judah and his brethren and the whole congregation of Israel ordained that the days of dedication of the altar (*Chanukat ha-mizbei'ach*) should be observed in their season, from year to year, spread over eight days, from the twenty-fifth day of the month Kislev, with gladness and joy.[12]

Again, no mention of any miracle associated with oil! The significance of the eight-day festival according to this source was that it was an altar dedication – though with no proffered reason for its duration – whereas, according to the second Book of Maccabees, as we have seen, it was a general victory celebration whose duration was a compensatory measure for the eight days of Tabernacles, the celebration of which the Jews had had to forgo that year because of the military situation.

135. Do we have any biblical precedents for lengthy festivities of Temple dedication?

We do, indeed. Moses' installation of the priests of the Sanctuary in the desert was a seven-day event;[13] the dedication ceremony of Solomon's Temple was held for seven days,[14] as was the rededication in the days of Ezra.[15] Now, the fact that seven, not eight, days was the consistently significant number for such an event suggests that the Maccabees' choice of eight days was not, in fact, linked to the context of Temple dedication. This may lend credence to the explanation of the festival found in II Maccabees, namely that it was celebrated as compensation for their inability to celebrate the eight-day festival of Tabernacles a few months earlier.

THE EXPLANATION OF MEGILLAT TA'ANIT

136. What other explanation is offered for the eight-day duration of Chanukah?

The first century *Megillat Ta'anit* states as follows:

On the 25th [of that month] we commence the eight days of Chanukah when it is forbidden to deliver a funeral oration.

The *Scholia*, a later talmudic appendix to *Megillat Ta'anit*, adds the following:

And what prompted them to institute this festival of Chanukah for eight days? It was on account of the fact that, during the period of the Greek kingdom, the Hasmoneans entered the Temple, carrying in their hands eight iron spears which they covered with wood, and in which they lit the lamps.[16]

137. Is any credence placed on this last explanation in the later Talmudic literature?

There is an echo of this in the Talmudic reference to the various successively costlier Temple candelabra that the Maccabees designed as richer material resources became available to them (see Question 125). The first one they made was of iron overlaid with wood.[17]

138. Which source is of greater antiquity, Megillat Ta'anit or the books of the Maccabees?

The books of the Maccabees are considerably earlier than *Megillat Ta'anit*. The former are generally regarded as contemporaneous with, or shortly after, the events they describe, whereas *Megillat Ta'anit* probably received its present form around the period of the great revolt (66–70 CE.).

Regarding the books of the Maccabees, it should be noted that, although it was the Greek version of the first Book of the Maccabees to which the Church gave Canonical status – though after the Reformation the Protestants relegated it to the Apocryphal literature – it was originally written in a pure Biblical Hebrew style. The second Book of the Maccabees, on the other hand, was written in Greek.

UNRAVELLING THE EXPLANATIONS

139. We have, therefore, four conflicting explanations for the eight-day celebration: those of the First Book of the Maccabees, the Second Book of the Maccabees, Megillat Ta'anit, and the Talmudic (and later Jewish traditional) 'miraculous' explanation. Is there any way of accounting for how those respective traditions came into being?

Let us assume for the moment that the Talmudic, 'miraculous' explanation rests on an authentic tradition, and that such a miracle did, in fact, occur when the Temple Menorah was first lit. The Maccabees, as we have observed, did not actually require that miracle, because they had had plenty of time in which to prepare consecrated oil during the period of 'eight days' – referred to by *Megillat Ta'anit* – when the Menorah and the other vessels were being prepared for use (see Questions 130–131). (We may take it that the author of *Megillat Ta'anit* used the number of *eight* days simply because of its significance in the miracle of the lights, as well as because of the reference in the First Book of Maccabees – if he was familiar with that source – to the eight days of celebration of the dedication of the new altar.)

It would have been understandable, however, that the Maccabees should have wished to use, at their first ceremony of re-dedication, that sole jar of oil from the period before the Greek defilement.

140. Why would they have wanted to use just that old jar?

For two reasons. First, because the High Priest whose seal was on it would have been none other than their own father, Matityahu, who had initiated the revolt. Using his jar of oil would have been a token of nostalgia and reverence, and a most appropriate tribute to his memory and his contribution to the cause. Secondly, it would have been regarded as a symbol of spiritual continuity and a testimony to the eternity of Israel in the face of those who would put out that eternal flame.

We may assume, therefore, that the miracle occurred at that point, notwithstanding the absence of any corroborative evidence in the Books of the Maccabees. It would have been construed, therefore, by all present, as a glorious divine approbation of what Matityahu's sons had achieved in having cleansed the Temple and restored the nation to its ancestral faith.

141. But how would religious sceptics have interpreted the miracle of the oil?

They would presumably have interpreted the 'tradition' as a piece of Maccabean propaganda, calculated to vindicate the validity of their claim to being the national as well as the spiritual leaders of Israel, in the face of those who might have expected – and demanded – a ruler of the tribe of Judah and the ancestral house of David to have been restored to the throne. Sceptics would have explained the 'myth' of the miracle as a concocted piece of Maccabean propaganda, calculated to convince their critics that heavenly approbation was accorded to everything they were instituting.

142. But if the miracle really occurred, why would the contemporary authors of the Books of the Maccabees have made no mention of that wondrous occurrence?

We may but speculate that, having been involved themselves in the great military struggle against overwhelming odds, and having experienced victory over the greatest of world powers, those chroniclers would have viewed the lightning victory handed to them by God as a far more significant 'miracle' than any jar of oil which went on burning.

Furthermore, the Mishnah speaks of ten miraculous occurrences that were witnessed by all visitors to the Temple throughout the year,[18] none of which inspired any special commemorative festival. There was no reason, therefore, to establish this miracle of the oil as the rationale of the Chanukah festival.

143. Some have questioned the tradition that the seal of the High Priest was affixed to jars of oil. Do we have anything that might corroborate that tradition?

We do. Archaeology has uncovered a vast amount of pottery dating back to that early Greek period – indeed from the fifth century BCE onward – with the names of both the potter and the painter on each piece. It is now clear that attribution of source or creator was common practice; and it is not surprising, therefore, that, as regards something as important as proof of ritual suitability, the Jews would have followed suit and appended a seal of authority.

144. Could there have been another reason for the suppression of mention of the miracle of the oil by the authors of the books of the Maccabees?

There may well have been any number of rationalists who were ready to offer explanations for the augmented fuel power. Some may have speculated that its special power was to be attributed to the fact that the oil had been kept for a few years and had had time to mature, unlike most oil that was used within a short period of the olive being crushed. Others may have expressed doubt that a miracle had actually occurred, and may have entertained suspicion that the Menorah may have been secretly augmented with oil each day.

145. Have you any less speculative reason to offer?

I'll ignore that jibe! After all, speculation is the stuff of research. In any case, when dealing with such ancient sources and their conflicting traditions, the only way we can attempt to unravel their mysteries is through speculation.

I suggest that the authors of the Books of the Maccabees – eye witnesses to the events they describe – were totally involved and preoccupied with the cause of restoring their cherished Temple, the focus of their national and spiritual life. It would have been unthinkable to them, therefore, to attribute any significance to Chanukah that was not directly associated with the act of Temple rededication. And hence the name chosen for the festival, derived from the *Chanukah*, or dedication, of the desert altar,[19] the Temple of Solomon,[20] its altar[21] and the more recent project of rebuilding the walls of Jerusalem and the Temple in the days of Ezra and Nehemiah.[22]

146. But was not the miracle of the oil itself associated exclusively with the Temple?

Only in the narrow sense, for that is where it occurred. But it could have occurred anywhere. Indeed, in an earlier, biblical tradition that would have been known to every Jew, there was already a story of a miraculous jar of oil set in a domestic situation!

We refer to the famous story of the poor widow of one of the prophet Elisha's disciples who came to him to complain that her creditors were about to take her two sons as slaves. When Elisha asked what possessions remained to her, she replied that all she had was one pot of oil. The prophet told her to go and borrow from her neighbours as many empty vessels as she possibly could. He then told her to start pouring from her jar of oil. Miraculously, and foreshadowing the Chanukah miracle, the pot kept on pouring oil until all the vessels were filled up. Elishah then told her to go and sell the oil, pay off her creditors, and live, with her sons, on the proceeds of the remaining stock of oil.

Thus, a miracle based on oil augmenting either its volume or its capacity was well-attested in Jewish tradition, and would hardly have represented something so novel as to constitute the rationale for the introduction of a new festival.

147. You suggested that the authors of the books of the Maccabees, in promoting their festival of Chanukah exclusively as a celebration of the rededication of the Temple and altar, may have been influenced by biblical precedence relating to previous dedications. Can you expand on this thesis?

We suggest that their respective explanations relied on traditions relating to the previous dedications of the Temple in the periods of both Solomon (tenth century BCE) and of Ezra and Nehemiah (fifth century BCE), respectively.

Both of the books of Ezra and Nehemiah record that after permission was granted to the Jews in Babylonian captivity to return, they found the Temple in a serious state of disrepair. During the first year of their return, in the seventh month, all the newly-settled Israelites, from all over the country, gathered in Jerusalem...

Then Joshua son of Jozadak and his fellow priests, and Zerubbabel son of Shealtiel and his kinsmen, set to work and *built the altar of the God of Israel* in order to offer on it whole-offerings as prescribed in the law of Moses, the man of God. They put the altar in place first, because they lived in fear of the foreign population; and they offered on it whole-offerings to the Lord, both mornings and evenings. *They kept the pilgrim-feast of Tabernacles as ordained*, and offered whole-offerings every day in the number prescribed each day... The[se] offerings began from the first day of the seventh month, although the foundation of the Temple of the Lord had not yet been laid (Author's emphasis.).[23]

Now, it might well have been the case that the rather strange and unprecedented situation which the author of Ezra describes – of a dedication and use of the altar (in order to invoke God's aid, through sacrifices, against their hostile neighbours) a year before the Temple proper was cleansed and dedicated for general use – as well as the reference to the festival of Tabernacles, was responsible for the variant traditions in the two Books of the Maccabees.

Both authors were clearly very familiar with the book of Ezra (and the book of Nehemiah, which covers the same events), and the above passage might well have influenced them in the rationale they offered for the Chanukah of their own day. The author of the first Book of the Maccabees emphasizes the dedication of the altar as the basic rationale of the festival, since it was performed even before the general dedication. The author of the second Book of the Maccabees, on the other hand, was influenced more by the reference in the book of Ezra to the (eight day) festival of Tabernacles, which he borrowed as his rationale of the eight day festival, interpreting the latter as commemorating the more comprehensive dedication of the entire Temple.

148. Is there any other hint that the author of the second Book of the Maccabees might have been looking backward to earlier biblical traditions when he associated the Temple dedication with the festival of Tabernacles?

There is! If we consult the account of the dedication of the first Temple by King Solomon, we see that he particularly chose to celebrate his dedication on the festival of Tabernacles![24]

149. Was there any rationale for that?

We suggest that it had to do with Solomon's concept of his Temple as a universal house of prayer. He gives expression to this in his majestic petition at its dedication, which contains these lines:

> Moreover, concerning the stranger that is not of Thy people Israel, when he shall come out of a far country for Thy name's sake – for they shall hear of Thy great name and of Thy mighty hand – when he shall come and pray toward this house, hear Thou in heaven, Thy dwelling-place, and do according to all that the stranger calleth to Thee for; that all the people of the earth may know Thy name, to fear Thee, as doth Thy people Israel, and that they may know that Thy name is called upon this house which I have built.[25]

Now, given this universalistic concept of the Temple, it was natural that Solomon should have chosen the festival of Tabernacles on which to dedicate his Temple, because universalism also lies at the very core of the festival of Tabernacles.

150. Where is that universalistic aspect of Tabernacles enunciated?

Its clearest expression is found in the writings of the prophet Zechariah, in a passage that forms part of the *Haftarah* (reading from Prophetic Writings) for the first day of the festival:

And it shall come to pass, that everyone that is left of all the nations that came against Jerusalem shall go up from year to year to worship the King, the Lord of hosts, *and to keep the feast of Tabernacles*. And it shall be that whomsoever of the families of the earth does not go up to Jerusalem to worship the King, the Lord of hosts, upon them there shall be no rain.[26]

But the universalism goes further; for, according to rabbinic tradition, the seventy sacrifices that were biblically prescribed for offering during the course of the festival of Tabernacles (on the first day, thirteen sacrifices; on the second day, twelve; and so on, decreasing one sacrifice each day of the succeeding seven days),[27] corresponded to the seventy nations of the civilized world. Thus, the Temple sacrifices and prayers for rain on that festival were regarded as representing a universalistic invocation for sustenance for the entire human race, in keeping with Solomon's overall philosophy of the Temple itself.

151. So, if the authors of the two Books of the Maccabees were offering a rationale for the eight-day festival that was based on biblical precedence rather than historical reality, does that not leave us with just Megillat Ta'anit and the Talmudic explanations as credible sources?

Indeed, the non-acquaintance of Jewry with the books of the Maccabees (see Questions 53-57) might also explain why, in the course of time, the association with the festival of Tabernacles was forgotten, and the eight days of the festival were accounted for solely on the basis of the traditions underlying *Megillat Ta'anit* and the Talmud.

It should now be obvious that we are faced with a confusing picture, one which we cannot unravel with any degree of certainty. It has to be said, however, that traditionalists have always readily accepted the account of the miracle of the oil at face value. (Perhaps equally miraculous is the fact that the vast majority of the sophisticated Jewish world today celebrates this festival and accepts unquestioningly its miraculous origin. This represents a degree of acceptance that is rarely manifest in any other area of religious faith!)

152. But why does Megillat Ta'anit offer two separate explanations, one for the eight-day festival and one for the eight lights?

That late (first century CE) source, *Megillat Ta'anit*, does indeed separate the reason for the duration of *the festival* – namely, to commemorate the eight days it took to repair the altar and prepare the vessels – from the reason for the lighting of *the lights* for eight nights – namely, because of the eight staves that they converted into lamps. It would seem that the author of that work had inherited the reasons mentioned in both books of Maccabees, and he wished to find a place for them both. Thus, his explanation of the festival is clearly in line with the rationale offered by both books, which relate it to the dedication of the altar. Its separate explanation for the eight lamps, linking it to the eight staves which the Maccabees made into lamps, may also be seen to link up directly with the festival of Tabernacles – the rationale of the Second Book of Maccabees.

That association is clear from our rabbinic sources which describe the celebrations associated with the festival of Tabernacles during the period of the Second Temple, and especially the *Simchat Bet Ha-shoevah*, or Water-Drawing Celebration, the highlight of which were torch dances which took place each night in the Court of the Women at the Temple. We are now in a position to understand the source *of Megillat Ta'anit*'s tradition, relating the eight nights of lamp lighting to the festival of Tabernacles whereon lamp lighting figured so prominently.

153. But was that lamp-lighting on Tabernacles an essential part of the religious celebration, or just a popular folk practice?

It was regarded as an essential element in the Tabernacles celebrations, to the extent that the Mishnah describes the fire celebrations in full, observing that, 'he who has never witnessed the *Simchat Bet Ha-shoevah* has never witnessed real joy'.[28]

The Mishnah describes the celebration in this way:

At the close of the first festival day they went down to the Court of the Women where they made a great adjustment. There were golden candlesticks there with four golden bowls on their top, and four ladders leading up to each candlestick. Four young priests would take in their hands jars of oil holding a hundred and twenty logs and pour them into all the bowls.

They made wicks from the worn out trousers and girdles of the priests, and used them to ignite the candlesticks, and there was not a single courtyard in Jerusalem that was not bathed in the light of the *Bet Ha-shoevah*.

Men of piety and good works used to dance before the throng with burning torches in their hands, singing songs and praises.[29]

The Talmud preserves a tradition that even the Patriarch of Israel, Rabban Shimon ben Gamaliel, 'would celebrate the *Simchat Bet Ha-shoevah* by taking eight fire-torches in one hand and throwing them up into the air. He would then catch them, one by one, without one torch ever colliding with another'.[30]

154. Is there anything significant in the fact that Gamaliel used just eight torches?

It is more than coincidental that we encounter here, once again, that significant number of *eight* (torches) in relation to fire, as well as in the context of the festival of Tabernacles. We may assume that the author of *Megillat Ta'anit* – a contemporary of Rabban Shimon ben Gamaliel – was strongly influenced by the latter's eight-torch Tabernacles ritual which he chose to synthesize with the eight lights of Chanukah (under the influence of the second Book of the Maccabees). The pen of the author of *Megillat Ta'anit* simply converted Gamaliel's eight torches into eight staves of fire, which he superimposed upon the ancient Maccabees in order to provide a rationale for the eight lights of Chanukah.

155. But could there have been any other reason why the author of Megillat Ta'anit chose just that explanation, of the eight fire-staves, to account for the eight lights of Chanukah, and not any of the other traditions offered by the two books of Maccabees or the Talmudic explanation of the miracle of the oil?

We may speculate that he had a very practical purpose in mind. It is our view that the celebration of Chanukah expanded during the first century, from being purely a Temple-based to a home-based ritual, a factor which explains why the Schools of Hillel and Shammai discuss it as if it was a recent innovation, and proceed to dispute the proper way of lighting the Chanukah lights each night (see Questions 159 and 181–190).

Now, the populace of first-century Judea was, in the main, impoverished. Ordinary folk could hardly have afforded to procure for themselves a special eight-branched candelabrum. *Megillat Ta'anit*, by referring to the eight staves which the Maccabees converted into oil containers, was, in effect, offering practical guidance to the masses as to how to light their lights not only in an acceptable manner but in the authentic way, as improvised by the first Maccabees. The message was that all that people needed in order to perform the ritual of Chanukah were simple staves of wood or metal. It was a festival, they were asserting, that was within everyone's means. The raw materials were all around, and one did not need to be a 'do-it-yourself' freak to convert it into a Menorah. Eight separate supports were all that was required.

WHY THE TRADITIONAL EXPLANATION OF CHANUKAH WAS SUPPRESSED

156. But if the miracle of the oil did actually occur, why was it unknown before its disclosure in the Talmud?

It does, indeed, seem as if it was unknown; and hence there is no mention of the miracle of the Chanukah oil in the Mishnah, the core text on which the Talmudic analysis is based. However, that was not, in fact, the case; for, when the Talmud comes to discuss the way the eight lights of Chanukah should be lit (see Question 181) the dispute on the issue goes back to the traditions of Hillel and Shammai. Those two illustrious leaders lived during the turn of the Common Era, that is during the last seventy years of the Second Temple, and their dispute on Chanukah presupposes that the miracle of the oil was already the accepted explanation at that period. As they were the undoubted experts on Temple law, lore and tradition, they would have been well-placed to serve as transmitters of the traditional reason for the eight days of the festival. They would hardly have concocted such a tradition, and we may assume that its rationale was widespread within Judea.

We may but speculate as to the reason why the Mishnah itself did not devote any space to the details of this festival, according it no special tractate in the way that it does for every other festival. Commentators[31] record that the leaders of the later Pharisaic movement – whose traditions were handed down to the Mishnaic and Talmudic sages – were not at all impressed by the Maccabees. One of the main reasons was that, as a priestly dynasty, they had absolutely no right to proclaim themselves as kings, a status that biblical law reserves for the tribe of Judah. When Jacob blessed his children he vehemently proclaimed to them that, 'the ruler's staff shall not depart from Judah',[32] and it is the offspring of King David (of the tribe of Judah) who are consequently regarded in Jewish tradition as the only rightful kings.

Against this background, it is conceivable that the Talmudic sages were extremely reticent to attribute such a national miracle to the Maccabeans, a miracle that might well be construed as heavenly confirmation of their authority, and subsequent kingship of Israel (see also Questions 168–171).

157. But why would the Books of the Maccabees have suppressed any mention of that miraculous event of the lights, preferring to link the origin of Chanukah with Temple dedication ceremonies?

Again we are in the realm of speculation, although we have already suggested one reason for this (see Questions 142, 144–146). Another possibility is that it might have been a reaction to the Persian, Zoroastrian beliefs which, from the fifth century BCE, had infiltrated all the nations surrounding Judea. Fire was regarded as a symbol of truth and order in that system, and it occupied a predominant place in its worship and theology.

The Jewish Apocalyptic literature, produced in Palestine from about 200 BCE – just before the Maccabean period – to 200 CE, was strongly influenced by such ideas, as were some doctrines of the Qumran community. And fire, a recurring theme in the Persian belief system, became similarly significant in that non-mainstream, Jewish theology. Thus, the consignment of the wicked to a place of fiery eternal punishment is 'presupposed in the Qumran scrolls and ubiquitous in later apocalypses'.[33] We also encounter the notion of the God of fire, of Gabriel as the angel in charge of fire, of angels bathing in fire, emitting tongues of fire, and even made from fire. We also have references to chariots of fire, demons of fire, mountains of fire, thrones of fire, the universe as concentric rings of fire, the destruction of the world by fire, seas and lakes of fire, Abraham being tested by fire, lashes of fire and martyrdom by fire.[34]

Indeed, measures to counter Persian dualism's basic doctrine are a recurring precaution in the later Pharisaic-Talmudic system; and the fact that normative Judaism turned its back on that entire Jewish Apocalyptic literature, whose ideas were infiltrating Judea and influencing Jews at the very period of the Maccabean revolt, helps explain why any festival whose core significance was focused upon a happening associated with fire would have been an acute embarrassment to the religious leaders of Judea at that time. This might well explain why that miracle of the pot of oil, sufficient to burn for but one day and instead burning for eight, was suppressed by such writers as the religious authors of the first and second Books of the Maccabees.

THE RE-INTRODUCTION OF THE TRADITIONAL EXPLANATION

158. So, if the rationale of the miracle of the oil was suppressed, only to reappear in the period of the Mishnah and Talmud, why would the rabbis of that later period have had no qualms about promoting that reason in preference to the other two main reasons?

We may speculate that, having reinvigorated Jewish religious life, and regulated it at every turn with clear halachic guidance, and having successfully excluded such sectarian or tainted tracts as the Apocrypha (and especially the Pseudepigrapha), the sages of the Talmudic period (some two hundred years after the Books of the Maccabees were written) were not so much worried by the significance of fire in other religions. In any case, they themselves had but recently produced a chapter of Mishnah dealing with the Sabbath lights and the type of oil and wick that was and was not sanctioned for use,[35] and they were also operating with fire in a number of other halachic contexts, such as for the *havdalah* (literally, 'separation') ritual and blessings to mark the conclusion of Sabbath, the kashering by fire of metal utensils, and so on.

Perhaps those sages were also prescient. Witnessing Rome's iron grip on Judea and its manipulation of the Temple officialdom – even to the extent of selling the office of High Priest to the highest bidder – and noting the emergent Jewish resistance movement in the wake of the repressive measures of Gaius Caligula (37–41 CE) and the anti-Jewish riots in the period of Claudius (41–54 CE), the leaders of the Hillel and Shammai schools may well have been apprehensive of an imminent, full-scale Jewish revolt, with its inevitable consequences for Jerusalem and the Temple.

By the early Mishnaic period (40–70 CE), there was also a distinct lessening of interest in the Temple, as a result of its manipulation and politicization by the Romans and aided by the developing network of synagogues that was mushrooming across the country.[36] The sages may have feared that if the rationale of Chanukah continued to be promoted exclusively as a commemoration of the Temple's dedication, then, if the worst happened and Temple worship came to an end, the festival itself would be regarded as an irrelevance. The sages may well have sought to safeguard Chanukah's observance, therefore, by emphasizing the hitherto suppressed notion of the miracle of the oil that burned for eight days.

With such a unique home ritual as the kindling of lights each successive night, and the emphasizing of its miraculous background as a commemoration of a glorious revelation of divine favour to Israel in her hour of need, not only would the future observance of Chanukah be secured, but there was hope that it might also become a source of consolation for a Jewry whose turbulent history seemed to be presaging a return to an even more violent phase.

THE EMERGENCE OF CHANUKAH AS A HOME RITUAL

159. So, at what stage did the festival develop into a home, rather than an exclusively Temple, ritual?

Probably at that precise period when Hillel and Shammai first disputed exactly how the lights should be lit (see Question 181), namely during the decades preceding the destruction of the Temple, circa 40–70 CE. Had the festival been characterized by the kindling of home lights for any length of time before that, a consensus regarding the method of performing such a popular ritual would have been well established.

We may assume, therefore, that until the view of Bet Hillel won the day, there was variety in the way people chose to perform the ritual of lighting lights in their homes (see Question 190).

160. But do we have any source outside the Mishnah that might corroborate this change of emphasis in the significance and celebration of Chanukah around that period?

We do, indeed. Although the rabbis employ, exclusively, the name Chanukah, meaning 'Temple rededication', the first-century historian, Flavius Josephus, tells us that 'from that time [of the dedication by the Maccabees] to this, we celebrate this festival and call it "Lights"'.[37]

It goes without saying that that was a name that neither the authors of the Books of the Maccabees nor the sages were familiar with. We may assume, therefore, that this was either a name that the populace had begun to use in Josephus's day, on account of its main method of celebration, or one that Josephus himself had coined. Josephus wrote his works in Rome, for Roman consumption, and much of what he wrote was apologetic, in order to credit his people with greater sophistication than the Romans attributed to Jews. He may well have preferred the name Lights, to *Chanukah*, with its connotation of Temple consecration, in order not to touch any raw Roman nerve, considering that they had been responsible for the destruction of the Temple some twenty-five years before the time he was writing. It would have been impolitic to suggest that Jews were still celebrating a festival which focused on the Temple, and which might well serve as a touch-stone for 'rekindling' the flame of Jewish rebellion in an attempt to recapture the Temple from the Romans and celebrate a future 'rededication'.

The fact that Josephus felt able to promote a novel name for *Chanukah* is a further indication that the celebration was at that very time in the course of development from a purely Temple festivity to a home practice, and that its changed significance prompted many to regard the old name *Chanukah* as unsuitable to its new mode of celebration.

NOTES
1. Talmud *Shabbat* 21b.
2. See I Maccabees 4:43.

3. Ibid., 4:48.
4. On *Megillat Ta'anit*, see Ephraim E. Urbach, *The Halakhah: Its Sources and Development* (Jerusalem: Yad la-Talmud, 1986), pp.57–8.
5. See I Maccabees 4:52.
6. II Maccabees 10:5.
7. See Leviticus 23:40
8. II Maccabees 10:6–8.
9. See Numbers 9:1-14.
10. Talmud *Hagigah* 17b.
11. See Talmud *Berakhot* 26b.
12. I Maccabees 4:52–6.
13. Leviticus 8:33.
14. I Kings 8:65.
15. See Ezra 3:4.
16. *Megillat Ta'anit*, ed. M. Grossberg (Levov, 1906), p.51. On this source, *see also* Z. Lichtenstein, '*Megillet Ta'anit*' in *Hebrew Union College Annual* (Cincinnati: Union of Hebrew Congregations), VIII–IX (1931–2), pp.318–351; Ben Zion Lurie, *Megillath Ta'anith With Introductions and Notes* (Jer., Bialik Institute, 1964), and S. Zeltlin, Megillat Taanit (Philadelphia: Dropsie College for Hebrew and Cognate Learning).
17. Talmud *Menachot* 28b.
18. See *Pirkei Avot* 5:8.
19. See Numbers 7:10, 11, 84, 88.
20. See Psalm 30:1.
21. See II Chronicles 7:9.
22. See Nehemiah 12:27.
23. Ezra 3:1–6.
24. See I Kings 8:2, 65.
25. I Kings 8:41–3.
26. Zechariah 14:16–17.
27. See Numbers 29:12–34.
28. Mishnah *Succah* 5:1.
29. Ibid., 5:1–4.
30. Talmud *Succah* 53a.
31. See for example, commentary of Nachmanides (*Peirush HaRamBaN*) on Genesis 49:10.
32. Genesis 49:10.
33. James H. Carlesworth (ed.), *The Old Testament Pseudepigrapha* (New York: Doubleday, 1983), vol. 1, p.352.
34. For source of these references, see ibid., vol.2, pp.949–50.
35. See Mishnah *Shabbat* Chapter 2.
36. For the tension between Temple and Synagogue, see Jeffrey M. Cohen, *Blessed are You* (New Jersey: Jason Aronson, 1993), pp.9–13.
37. Flavius Josephus, *Antiquities of the Jews* (London: Henry G. Bohn, 1845), 12:7, (7).

7

Chanukah in Mishnah, Talmud and Liturgy

CHANUKAH IN THE MISHNAH

161. From what has just been said, you seem to be implying that there is absolutely no mention of Chanukah in the Mishnah?

No, we are not saying that. There are, in fact, seven references; but they are all indirect, and, as we have already pointed out, not one of them alludes to the great miracle that gave rise to the eight day festival!

The first reference to Chanukah is found in the Mishnah *Bikkurim* which states that 'the first fruits may continue to be brought [to the Temple] from the festival of Tabernacles *until Chanukah*',[1] though without the recitation of the biblical declaration,

162. What is the second Mishnaic reference to Chanukah?

The second reference is in Mishnah *Rosh Hashanah*, in the context of a description of the method by which messengers were sent out from Jerusalem in order to inform the Diaspora communities of the precise day that had been 'sanctified' as the first day of the new month (*Rosh Chodesh*). This information was vital to ensure that those communities observed any festival in that month on the proper Hebrew date. The Mishnah states that 'the messengers went out six times... in Kislev [to inform regarding the precise date] for the observance of Chanukah'.[2]

163. Where is the third Mishnaic reference to Chanukah?

This is found in the Mishnah *Bava Kamma*, which deals with damage caused to one's neighbour and/or his property, and the different categories and levels of required restitution.

The Mishnah relates a common occurrence in the Middle East, whereby someone was driving a camel cart over-laden with flax through a narrow street. Its load was so bulky as almost to touch both sides of the street, since the fronts of the shops lay open to the street. If the flax was so outspread that it caught the lamp inside the shop, and was set alight, with the fire spreading to the shop, then the owner of the camel cart is culpable. If, however, the shopkeeper left his lamp outside his shop, then he must bear responsibility. Rabbi Judah commented that 'if it was a Chanukah lamp (which one is enjoined to light at the entrance of one's property), then the shopkeeper is not culpable'.[3]

164. What is the fourth Mishnaic reference to Chanukah?

This is found in Mishnah *Ta'anit*, where we are told that 'We do not impose a public fast day (say, to petition for rain) on Rosh Chodesh, Chanukah or Purim'.[4]

165. What is the fifth Mishnaic reference to Chanukah?

This is found in Mishnah *Megillah*, in a chapter dealing with the sale of synagogues and their appurtenances, the central feature of the synagogue liturgy and the Reading of the Law. It also prescribes the four special readings for the month of Adar, and goes on to list the festival days when the ordinary cycle of the Reading of the Law is set aside for the festival themes: 'And for the following times they break off [from the set order]: On Rosh Chodesh, on Chanukah'...[5]

166. What is the sixth Mishnaic reference to Chanukah?

This is found in the same chapter as the foregoing reference: 'On the feast of Chanukah they read the Torah portion dealing with the installation of the Princes into office' (Numbers 7:1–89).[6]

167. And what is the last Mishnaic reference to Chanukah?

This is found in Mishnah *Moed Katan*, which deals with the laws of the intermediate days of festivals, which also have a festive dimension that may not be compromised by any unnecessary workaday activity or by performing an act that partakes of an antithetical spirit. The Mishnah states, 'On Rosh Chodesh and Chanukah...one may chant funeral lamentations and clap hands, but may not wail'.[7]

CHANUKAH IN THE TALMUD: PLAYING DOWN THE MACCABEES

168. What does the Talmud have to say about Chanukah?

Not a lot! We have already referred to the Pharisaic-Talmudic disaffection with the Maccabean dynasty on account of the latter's assumption of the mantle of monarchy (see Question 156). Not only that, but, as a priestly fraternity, the Maccabees should have been committed to the simple life, a life of service, teaching and dedication to the needs of the community, as reflected in the prophet Malachi's assertion that, 'the lips of the priest shall preserve knowledge and they shall seek Torah from his mouth' (Malachi 2:7). Theirs was not meant to be a life of luxury, diplomacy and warfare, divorced from the concerns of the simple folk.

Perhaps the strongest criticism of the Maccabees came in the wake of their affiliation to the patrician, Sadducean movement, perceived as a heresy by the populist Pharisees. This was on account of the Sadducees' rejection of the notion of an Oral Law, a doctrine that underpinned the Pharisaic tradition with its dynamic application of Judaism to the changing conditions of life. The alliance of the Maccabees with the Sadducees was probably engendered by the affinity created by their common priestly ancestry. Nevertheless, the Maccabean defection to the Sadducean movement damned them in the eyes of the Pharisees and in the eyes of the later, mainstream Talmudic tradition which developed the Pharisaic theology.

The supremos of that Talmudic (Pharisaic) tradition were the Patriarchs of Palestine, among the most illustrious of which was the author of the Mishnah, Rabbi Judah Ha-Nasi. Those Patriarchs traced their genealogy to King David, and were thus regarded as heirs of the authentic Jewish monarchy and, with it, divine authority. They, more than anyone, would have been affronted by the Maccabean usurpation of monarchy; and this may well explain why the references to Chanukah in the Mishnah are all indirect, and why the Talmud so understates the heroism and glories of the Maccabees, making the ritual of the kindling of the lights the main focus of attention.

THE MIRACLE OF THE OIL: AN ANTI-SADDUCEAN WEAPON?

169. Could there have been any other explanation of why the Talmudic sages made the miracle of the oil, rather than the exploits of the Maccabees, their main focus?

There might have been, though this explanation must remain in the realm of pure conjecture. We have referred to the fundamental difference of opinion between the Pharisees and the Sadducees on the matter of oral traditions. The Sadducees accepted the Scriptural text literally, whereas the Pharisees embraced a more flexible and adaptable interpretation, rooted, they claimed, in the oral teachings and judgements of Moses, received at Sinai and handed down the ages from teacher to disciple.

A fundamental difference between the two traditions was in their interpretation and observance of Sabbath law. The Torah states, 'Thou shalt not kindle any fire (*lo teva'aru eish*) in all your habitations on the Sabbath day' (Exodus 35:3). The Pharisaic tradition restricted this prohibition to the specific act of 'kindling' on the holy day, but asserted that enjoying the warmth of fire lit before the Sabbath, or pre-cooked food kept warm throughout the Sabbath, was not only acceptable, but was also part of the enjoyment of the holy day (*oneg Shabbat*), that was an essential element of its observance.

The Sadducees, on the other hand, took the phrase *lo teva'aru* in that verse to mean 'Thou shalt have no fire *burning* ... on the Sabbath day'. They insisted, therefore, that all lamps and stoves be extinguished at the onset of the Sabbath.

The polemical tension between the Pharisees and their rivals was often extremely acrimonious, and the Pharisees frequently introduced measures and practices that were, simply, 'to refute the ideas of the Sadducees' (*lehotzi miydei tzedukim*).

In the light of this (no pun intended!), we might explain the inordinate emphasis of Pharisaic Judaism on the kindling of lights. While the Sadducees, as a Temple-based, priestly party, had a vested interest in commemorating the rededication of the Temple and the altar by means of a festival, it would have been impossible for them to celebrate Chanukah as a festival of lights in their homes, simply because when it came to the Friday night of the festival they could not possibly have lit lights! Obviously, the whole significance of the miracle, with its uninterrupted burning for eight days, would have been severely compromised if, for one entire night, the lighting had to be suspended!

Thus, by making the miracle and kindling of the lights the central home ritual, the Pharisees were excluding their opponents from celebration of a festival which, as priests, was particularly close to their hearts. If my interpretation is correct, the festival of Chanukah would need to be re-appraised and placed at the centre of the Pharisaic-Sadducean struggle.

170. So what does the Talmud actually have to say about the Maccabees?

Well, we have already quoted the main source (see Question 129). We would merely draw attention here to the innuendo underlying that reference to them:

> When the Greeks entered the Temple, they polluted the Temple oils, and when the Hasmonean dynasty prevailed, they searched and found but one jar of oil.

In the absence of the explanations we have offered for the Pharisaic-Talmudic attitude, we would surely have regarded it as mystifying in the extreme that the name of Judah the Maccabi is nowhere mentioned! Nor is there any reference to the attempt of the Greeks to Hellenize Judea and ban the practice of Judaism – a fact that ought to have made Judah into a religious, as well as a military, hero.

The phrase, 'when the Hasmonean dynasty prevailed' is surely the under-statement of the Talmud! We have already referred to the pejorative nature of the term 'Hasmonean' (see Question 64), but to pass over their incomparable military exploits, and their victories over the professional soldiery of Greece, with the single word 'prevailed' is surely a gross injustice to them and to Jewish history.

NO MISHNAH FOR CHANUKAH

171. Can we detect an anti-Maccabean bias in any other aspects of the celebration of Chanukah?

We certainly can, especially if we compare the observances relating to Chanukah with those relating to Purim.

Let us remind ourselves that Purim commemorates a Diaspora victory, unlike Chanukah that brought relief from a threat to the very spiritual epi-centre of Judaism and the Jewish people in their Holy Land. Secondly, Purim was a mere one-day festival (except for those living in walled cities), whereas Chanukah is celebrated universally for eight days. Thirdly, Chanukah was given the status of a festival on which *Hallel* (a liturgical series of thanksgiving psalms, following the Amidah) was recited, whereas Purim was not invested with that status.

Given the greater importance of the more mainstream festival of Chanukah, we would surely have expected the sages of the Mishnah to have allocated a special tractate of that Code to the Chanukah festival, in the same way as they did to Purim. We would also have expected the sages to have included the Book of Maccabees, wherein God is invoked by name countless times, among the sacred books of the Bible, as they did for the book of Esther, though the name of God is nowhere to be found in the latter! The fact that they slighted Chanukah by such an omission, and that they went even further by insisting that the Scroll of Esther be written with all the prescriptions of a Scroll of the Law, and that it be recited both in the evening and morning of the festival – an honour accorded to no other festival book – suggests, beyond doubt, that the sages had their own agenda, and were expressing thereby their displeasure at the heroes of the Chanukah festival.

CHANUKAH IN THE LITURGY: AL HA-NISIM

172. Against all this background, one can, perhaps, understand the cool Pharisaic-Talmudic attitude to Judah the Maccabee and his monarchic dynasty. But surely the pious High Priest, Matityahu, whose zeal for God initiated and inspired the resistance movement, should have been given an honourable mention?

He is, in fact, not overlooked. When the sages came to compose the *Al Ha-Nisim*, the special liturgical insertion for the *Amidah* and Grace After Meals, which is recited throughout the festival, his name appears at the very outset:

In the days of *Mattityahu, son of Yochanan, the High Priest*, the Hasmonean, and his sons, when the iniquitous power of Greece rose up against Your people, Israel, to make them forget Your law and to force them to transgress the statutes of Your will, in Your abundant mercy You rose up for them in their time of trouble; You pleaded their cause, judged their suit and avenged their wrong. You delivered the strong into the hands of the weak, the many into the hands of the few, the impure into the hands of the pure, the wicked into the hands of the righteous and the arrogant into the hands of those who occupy themselves with Your Law. As for Yourself, You made a great and holy name in Your world, and for Your people, Israel, You effected a great deliverance and redemption as at this day. After that, Your children entered Your most holy house, cleansed Your Temple, purified Your sanctuary, kindled lights in Your holy courts, and instituted these eight days of Chanukah in order to give thanks and praise to Your great name

MASECHET SOFERIM: REDRESSING THE BALANCE

173. But is it not strange that this liturgical Al Ha-Nisim insertion also makes no reference to the miracle of the oil, merely to kindling lights 'in your holy courts'?

It is, indeed, mystifying, especially since this liturgical composition appears for the first time in the late Talmudic tractate, *Masechet Soferim* (eighth century CE), by which time Chanukah was already universally associated with the miracle of the oil.

That the author of the *Al Ha-Nisim* had his own rabbinic agenda may also be detected in the reference to God as the one who exclusively performed all the miracles, fought all the battles, and achieved glory through His exploits. Granted, it is admitted that all this happened '*in the days of* Matityahu', but it is, nevertheless, clearly ungenerous to the Maccabees of the succeeding generation, who brought to fruition Matityahu's dreams, not to grant them a mention. After all, even after the crossing of the Red Sea, the Torah states, 'And they believed in God and in Moses his servant'. Moses is given credit, even though, on that occasion, the miracle was exclusively God's! Why then, we may legitimately ask, did the sages who composed the *Al Ha-Nisim* not acknowledge Judah and his brothers, making only a passing reference to the fact that the events alluded to occurred 'in the period of' his father?

We may speculate that the author of this composition may have felt that the miracle of the oil was receiving inordinate attention as the main rationale of the festival. While wishing to redress the balance and draw attention to the more basic, and historical, aspects of the Maccabean struggle, he felt unable, however, to liberate himself entirely from the traditionally critical attitude towards the Maccabees. Hence the omission of Judah's name, and the attribution to God alone of all the glory and victory.

174. Is there any authoritative rabbinic source that adopts an even-handed approach toward the Maccabees?

The great codifier, Moses Maimonides would seem to be the exception to the rule. In the introduction to the laws of Chanukah, in his *Mishneh Torah*, he actually offers praise of the Maccabees, exonerating them from any blame in the matter of their assumption of monarchy:

> For the Hasmonean family of high priests were victorious, having slain the Greek-Syrians and rescued Israel from their hands. And they established a king from their priests, and the kingship was restored to Israel for a period of more than 200 years, until the destruction of the Second Temple.[8]

175. But how could Maimonides have ignored the unequivocal biblical prescription that 'the scepter shall not depart from Judah' (Genesis 49:10), which, as we have observed, denies kingship to members of any other tribe?

Maimonides clearly interprets that verse, uttered by Jacob on his death-bed, not as a prohibition, but rather as a prophecy. It is merely affirming that once the kingship is established in the hands of a monarch from the tribe of Judah, it shall remain the eternal right of his offspring. But that is not to say that, from time to time, leadership will not fall to members of other tribes. Thus, Saul, the first king of Israel, hailed from the tribe of Benjamin, and yet God affirmed his choice. So, according to Maimonides, kings from other tribes may also reign over Israel on a temporary basis, without establishing any permanent rights of sovereignty.

176. We mentioned that the first occurrence of the *Al Ha-Nisim* is in the late Talmudic tractate, Masechet Soferim. Is its version identical to ours?

This tractate is regarded by scholars as a compilation from at least three other sources, and the printed text that we have is characterized by considerable corruption. The text of the *Al Ha-Nisim* is a case in point, though it is easy in this case to reconstruct the original version. There is certainly no mistaking the opening phrase that, like our liturgical version which is based upon it, refers, simply, to '[In] the days of Matityahu.'

The (reconstructed) *Masechet Soferim* version reads:

> And we recite, in the *Modim* (Thanksgiving) blessing, 'And as You wrought Your manifest wonders and the salvation of Your priests in the days of Matityahu son of Yochanan, the High Priest, the Hasmonean and his sons, so may You perform miracles and wonders for us, O Lord our God and God of our fathers, that we may offer thanks to Your name forever. Blessed are You, [Whose name is] good [and to Whom it is fitting to give thanks].[9]

177. Is it not strange that, in the middle of what is meant to be a thanksgiving prayer for past miracles and victories, Masechet Soferim should have inserted a petition for future delivery, thus changing the entire focus of the prayer?

It does, indeed, appear inappropriate that the rabbis should have converted a thanksgiving into a petition. This point is taken up, from a slightly different angle, by the *Tosaphot*, which refers to those who omit that petitionary element from the composition on the basis of a Talmudic principle prohibiting the petitioning for one's needs in either the first three or the last three blessings of the *Amidah* (a series of blessings that constitute the central section of the liturgy).[10] *Tosaphot* states categorically, however, that that objection is erroneous since the prohibition only applies to personal, not communal petitions.[11]

Tosaphot proceeds to question its propriety, however, on the basis of another Talmudic principle that 'whenever anything refers to the future, the sages prescribe its recitation within a blessing for the future'.[12] The *Modim* blessing, on the other hand, is a thanksgiving blessing for past miracles, for which reason *Al Ha-Nisim* was prescribed as an insertion into that blessing. It is thus singularly inappropriate for a petition for future redemption to be included in that composition; and hence *Tosaphot* advises against its recitation, for which reason the version that ultimately entered our prayer books omits that particular petition.

THE MACCABEAN CONTRIBUTION TO LAW AND THE JUDICIARY

178. Amid all that criticism of the Maccabees on religious grounds, were the later rabbis being truly objective or was there some Maccabean contribution that was really deserving of greater credit?

It is conceivable that the later rabbis were unaware of the precise nature of the Hellenizing process in Judea some three centuries earlier. Thirty Greek cities were established within Judea as part of that process, and those cities attracted a great influx of Jewish citizenry.[13] The Books of the Maccabees make reference to a large-scale Jewish settlement, in the period leading up to the revolt, in such areas as Jaffa and Yavneh and in many localities of the Galilee and Trans-Jordan.

E. Urbach has drawn attention to the necessity for quick and accessible justice prompted by this expansion in the Jewish population, and the speed with which additional courts were set up.[14] He has also demonstrated, on the basis of *Megillat Ta'anit* and other sources, that part of the process of the Hellenization of Judea had involved the imposition of 'the law of the gentiles' upon the Jewish community. *Megillat Ta'anit*, referring to the period after the Maccabean victory, designates the twenty-fourth of the month of Av as a festive day, 'when we returned to our own laws'.[15] This also explains the references to 'The Bet Din of the Hasmoneans'[16] and 'the abolition of *Sefer Gezeirata*' (see Question 179).

It may be seen, therefore, that the Maccabees provided the impetus for the re-introduction, expansion and application of Jewish law, as well as a dramatic revision of the entire judicial system. This would, inevitably, have filtered downward, and encouraged the development of schools of law, which would have engendered an intensification of religious life, spearheaded by those religious jurists and their disciples. Adequate recognition for these major religious achievements, and the debt that rabbinic Judaism owes to the Maccabees for the religious framework they introduced, is certainly missing from our Talmudic and liturgical sources.

179. So, before the Maccabean revolt, how was the judicial system in Judea organized?

The Greek judicial system of *gerousia*, or Council of Elders, was applied in many cities throughout the empire. This even influenced the administration of justice in the highest court in Jerusalem, which was presided over by such a Council, at the head of which was the Zadokite High Priest.

Rather than rely on the memory and the legal acumen of trained judges, the Greeks had written codes of laws, often inscribed upon clay tablets, and the local *gerousia* would apply the law on that basis. This was clearly the method imposed upon Judea and swept away by the Maccabees. Hence the reference in *Megillat Ta'anit* to the fourteenth of Tammuz as a festive day, commemorating the abolition of *Sefer Gezeirata*, 'The Book of Laws'.[17] As the Sadducees were hide-bound to the written text of Scripture, and, unlike their Pharisaic counterpart, had no reservoir of developing oral tradition to assimilate and apply, their High Priests and Council members would have found *Sefer Gezeirata* far more suited to their literalist judicial approach. Its abolition by the Maccabees clearly enabled the law to become more flexible, humane and dynamic.

180. Was the transition, from the administration of gentile law under the Greeks to Jewish law under the Maccabees, smooth and instantaneous?

According to Urbach, it was certainly not. The interregnum was filled by considerable legal anarchy, leading to the imposition of zealot or vigilante law. And this situation he sees as reflected in the Mishnaic reference to several cases wherein zealots may strike a man down without due legal process. Such a peremptory punishment may be visited, says the Mishnah, upon one who loots Temple property, one who has sexual relations with a gentile woman, and one who curses by means of magical formulae.[18]

Such an anarchic means of punishment was so uncharacteristic of Jewish law that Urbach construes that Mishnah not as representing normative Jewish legal process, but rather as preserving a record of emergency measures that were introduced during that chaotic period of the Maccabean uprising and its aftermath, and before 'those who were zealous for the Law' had succeeded in establishing an authoritative, disciplined system rooted in Jewish tradition.

HOW TO LIGHT THE LAMPS: THE TALMUDIC DISPUTE

181. What does the Talmud have to say about the lighting of the Chanukah lamps?

We have already referred to the Talmudic preoccupation with the miracle of the oil (see Questions 129–145; 156–158), attested to by the historian Josephus who is the first to refer to the festival by the name 'Lights' (see Question 160). The Talmud's preoccupation is exclusively with how the ritual of lighting the Menorah should be performed, since, from the time that Chanukah became established as a domestic celebration, there existed a variety of practice depending upon whether one followed the traditions of the School of Hillel or those of the School of Shammai.

Here is what the Talmud has to say:

> The sages have taught: The [basic] mitzvah of Chanukah is that there should be one light burning in each person's home. Those who wish to perform the mitzvah with greater enthusiasm (*ha-mehadrin*) should enable each member of the household to kindle their own light each night. And for those who are ultra enthusiastic (*ha-mehadrin min ha-mehadrin*): Bet Shammai say, on the first night they should light eight, and on each subsequent night they should reduce one light. Bet Hillel say, on the first night they should light one light, and on each subsequent night they should increase one extra light.[19]

182. What reason did Bet Hillel and Bet Shammai give for their respective views?

Believe it or not, they actually do not give any reason! Or at least, no reason is preserved in their name. The best the Talmud can do is quote two later authorities from the early fourth century CE, R. Yosi bar Avin and R. Yosi bar Zevida, who offer rationales for the respective views of Hillel and Shammai nearly 300 years earlier!

183. But is that not absolutely amazing that no tradition survived within the Talmudic academies throughout those early centuries to explain the respective views of Hillel and Shammai?

Yes, it does seem surprising; though we must bear in mind our previous comments on the antipathy of the later mainstream religious authorities towards the Hasmoneans, and the fact that Chanukah was originally celebrated purely as a Temple re-dedication to celebrate a Temple festivity. Now, if, as we have suggested, its promotion as a festival of lights and its evolution into a domestic ritual emerged as a result of grassroots, lay initiative, then we can appreciate why Hillel and Shammai – who overlapped some of the closing decades of the Temple's existence – were reluctant to further undermine the authority of the Temple by over-emphasizing the new domestic ritual of lights through expositions on that theme. Such expositions would have had the effect of causing Chanukah's original significance, as a commemoration of the re-dedication of the Temple, to be completely superseded. They contented themselves, therefore, with a mere instruction to their disciples as to how they believed the lights should be lit. They did not discuss the ritual in any detail in the academy, with the result that it was left to later scholars to offer suggestions to account for their respective practices.

184. So what reason does R. Yosi bar Avin offer for Bet Hillel's practice?

He suggests that Hillel regarded the number of days of the festival that have already been (or are in the process of being) celebrated as most worthy of ritual celebration and blessing. Thus, on the first night we kindle one light, on the second night, two, and so on. For Hillel, the blessing is over experience, not expectation. Hillel preferred to celebrate what we have or have had, not what we expect to have.

185. What reason does R. Yosi bar Avin offer for Bet Shammai's practice?

He suggests that Shammai regarded the number of days of the festival still to come as most worthy of ritual celebration and blessing. Thus, on the first night he kindled all eight, corresponding with the eight days ahead; on the second night, seven, and so on. Shammai was an idealist. He focused on the entirety of the festival's experience, on how much of its all-embracing spirit remained for man to be inspired by and to bless. He had little interest in the present, that was rapidly ticking away, or the past that was already history.

186. What reason does R.Yosi bar Zevida offer for Bet Hillel's practice?

He offers a quite different interpretation of Hillel's practice, rooting it in a well-known talmudic principle of *Ma'alin bakodesh v'ein moridin*, that 'we augment sanctity; we do not reduce it'. Accordingly, Hillel's practice of increasing a light each night was influenced by the spiritual significance of light as a symbol of the Torah, on the basis of the verse, 'For the mitzvah is a lamp and the Torah is a light' (Proverbs 6:23). Hence, it is most inappropriate to decrease lights, as if to imply a corresponding diminution of Torah and spirituality.

187. What reason does R. Yosi bar Zevida offer for Bet Shammai's practice?

In his explanation we have a strong echo of the association made by the second Book of the Maccabees between Chanukah and Tabernacles that we have already fully analysed (see Questions 132, 147–150, 152). He suggests that Shammai based his practice on one of the main features of the Temple celebration of the festival of Tabernacles, namely the decrease each day in the number of sacrifices, beginning with thirteen sacrifices on the first day, twelve on the second, and so on, concluding with seven on the seventh day of that festival (see Question 150).

188. Which of the two views prevailed?

As in most matters of Jewish law, it was the philosophy of Hillel that was more in tune with the religious disposition of the masses. Shammai tended towards the dogmatic and rigorous interpretation of the law, making few concessions to human frailty and social mores. Hillel, on the other hand, was known for his profound understanding of human nature and empathy with people in their problems of everyday living. He tended therefore, wherever possible, towards a more lenient and flexible interpretation and application of principles.

Not surprisingly, the masses tended to look to the disciples of Hillel's school for their guidance and inspiration, especially after the destruction of the Temple, in the wake of the fact that the zealots, who had fomented the desperate revolt against Rome, had been devoted followers of Shammai.

189. So does the view of Shammai just disappear without trace from the ritual?

No, it does not. In an interesting, and not generally recognized way, the Shammaite view is still preserved through the manner in which we universally light the Chanukah lights.

To remind ourselves: Each night we add one extra light, increasing from the right to the left of the Menorah or *Chanukiah*, in accordance with the view of Hillel. But we kindle the lights from left to right, thereby moving from the largest number of lights on any given day, back to the first light. That notional 'decreasing' is a gesture of recognition of the view of Shammai.

190. You have mentioned earlier (see Question 159) that, until the approach of Hillel won the day, there had been considerable variety of practice in the way people lit their home lights. What is the evidence for this?

The evidence resides in a clear Talmudic report that 'there were two elders living in Zidon. One lit in the manner of Bet Shammai and the other lit in the manner of Bet Hillel. The one gave as the reason for his view the analogy with the Tabernacles offerings, while the other adduced the reason of "augmenting holiness and not reducing it"'.

We may assume that those two elders were the leading authorities in that city. Their disciples and followers would certainly have performed the ritual in accordance with their respective teacher's practice, itself rooted in the particular tradition – Hillelite or Shammaite – to which they were committed, or on the basis of whichever of the two rationales they felt was the most persuasive.

NOTES

1. Mishnah *Bikkurim* 1:6.
2. Mishnah *Rosh Hashanah* 1:3.
3. Mishnah *Bava Kamma* 6:6.
4. Mishnah *Ta'anit* 2:10
5. Mishnah *Megillah* 3:4.
6. Mishnah *Megillah* 3:6.
7. Mishnah *Moed Katan* 3:9.
8. *Rambam, Mishneh Torah, Hilkhot Megillah v'Chanukah* 3:1.
9. *Masechet Soferim*, ed. M. Higger (New York: *Hotsa'at D'bei Rabbanan*, 1937), 20 (6), ll. 34–7.
10. Talmud *Berakhot* 34a.
11. See *Tosaphot* on Tal. *Megilah* 4a. Note commencing *Pasak*.
12. Talmud *Pesachim* 117b.
13. See A. Tcherikower, *Ha-Yehudim ve-ha-Yevanim be-Tekufah ha-Helenistit* (Tel Aviv: Dever, 1930), pp.56–7.
14. See Ephraim E. Urbach, *The Halakhah: Its Sources and Development* (Jerusalem: *Yad la-Talmud* 1986), p.64.
15. See ibid., pp. 56-57.
16. Talmud *Avodah Zarah* 36b.
17. See Urbach, *The Halakhah*.
18. See Mishnah *Sanhedrin* 9:6.
19. Talmud *Shabbat* 21b.

IV
THE LAWS AND
RITUALS OF CHANUKAH

8

The Laws and Rituals of Chanukah
Women's Observance of Chanukah

191. Are there any prohibitions regarding the observance of Chanukah?

The Shulchan Arukh states as follows:

> On the twenty-fifth of the month of Kislev there begin the eight days of the festival of Chanukah, on which it is forbidden to deliver a *hesped* (funeral oration) or to observe a fast day. Work, however, is permitted, though there is a tradition for women to refrain from work while the lights are burning. Jacob ben Asher, in his authoritative code of law, the *Tur*, states that we should not permit women to be lenient in this respect.[1]

192. Why was it exclusively the women who adopted that practice of not working while the lights were burning?

The Talmud, while not addressing that specific matter, sees fit to comment on why women are obliged, in general, to observe the mitzvah of kindling the Chanukah lights (notwithstanding the fact that women are absolved from the performance of any positive ritual bound by constraints of time). The rather vague explanation of Rabbi Joshua ben Levi is that 'it is because they were also included in that miracle'.[2]

Rabbeinu Nissim of Gerona (fourteenth century) elucidates on this exception to the rule and explains that it was because the repressive measures were even more intense in regard to the daughters of Israel, for the enemy decreed that any virgin who was to be married had to submit herself first to intercourse with the local governor, Holofernes.[3] A further reason is offered in that source: that the very miracle of Chanukah was only achieved as a result of a woman, named Judith, the daughter of Yochanan the High Priest.

Judith was very beautiful, and the besieging general desired her. She went over to visit him at his camp, ostensibly to agree to his request, but first insisted on feeding him with many cheese dishes to make him thirsty. She kept plying him with wine until he became drunk and fell into a deep sleep and then cut off his head and brought it back to Jerusalem. When the enemy saw that they had lost their commander they fled in disarray.

193. Are there any parallels to this situation whereby the part played by a woman in a historical event is commemorated within the ritual celebration of a festival?

There is, indeed, an obvious parallel in the festival of Purim, which shares a similar halachic status to that of Chanukah. The Fast of Esther was instituted to commemorate Esther's heroism in entering the King's presence uninvited in order to plead for her people. As a prelude to that visit, she asked Mordechai to issue an instruction to all the Jews of her land to observe a three-day fast, and to pray for her, and their own, safe deliverance. That fast, instituted by a woman, was immortalized through the observance of the one-day, Fast of Esther.

194. Are there any other similar examples of women desisting from work as a reward for some meritorious act performed by their sex?

There is, indeed, another parallel in the tradition, quoted by the Tur, of women not working on *Rosh Chodesh* (the new moon) to recall and reward the fact that they refrained from responding to the call to donate their jewelry for the making of the Golden Calf.[4]

ABSTENTION FROM WORK DURING CHANUKAH

195. Judaism has never been without its pietists, zealous to go far beyond the basic requirements of the law. Do we know of any men who also took upon themselves that practice of not working while the lights were burning?

There is, indeed, such a tradition, referred to by the *Turei Zahav* in his commentary to the *Shulchan Arukh*. While stating his view that 'men certainly have no part in this practice', he proceeds to quote *Maharil* (R. Jacob Moellin, fourteenth–fifteenth century), one of the leading Ashkenazi halachists, to the effect that, 'It is a tradition among us that no one should do any work while the lights are burning. It was also the practice of our sages to abstain from work on the first and last days of Chanukah.'[5]

196. How widespread was the latter practice?

The practice of men abstaining from work while the lights were burning is likely to have become widespread in the late Middle Ages. The fact that the lights were not to be kindled until nightfall meant that the men had already returned home from work and had time to spend with their families. This undoubtedly accounted for the introduction of the *dreidel* or *trendel* (spinning tops) and other family games (see Chapter 13). The other practice referred to by *Maharil*, of abstaining from work on the first and last days of Chanukah, is unlikely to have been widespread; and the fact that Maharil refers to it as a 'practice of our sages' suggests that it was restricted to the sages and teachers of the schools and yeshivot of the communities under his halachic jurisdiction.

It is apposite that the compiler of the *Minhagei Maharil*, the corpus of all that illustrious leader's halachic decisions and practices, apologizes that he has been unable to incorporate all the multifarious customs practiced in the individual communities under his master's authority. His reasons are that, 'every river has its own course [namely, every place has developed its own, numerous rituals and customs], and I am unable, therefore, to enumerate them all'.[6] It should not surprise us, therefore, to learn that there were some who practiced abstention from work during the first and last days of Chanukah as a localized custom which, not surprisingly, did not win universal approbation.

WOMEN, CHEESE AND LATKES

197. Is there any other way in which the heroism of Judith has been commemorated?

The *Remah* (Rabbi Moses Isserles), in his gloss on the *Shulchan Arukh*, states that, 'some say that we should eat cheese dishes on Chanukah since the miracle was achieved by the milk foods which Judith fed to the enemy'.[7]

198. Is there any parallel situation of Jewish historical events leaving a culinary influence?

Most certainly. One only has to think of the eating of *matzah* on Pesach, to commemorate both the 'bread of affliction', eaten throughout their period of enslavement, as well as the wafers they baked at their departure from Egypt when their haste left them insufficient time to allow the dough to rise.

Another parallel is the case of Shavuot, the festival of the giving of the Torah, when dairy foods are again prescribed. This is explained either on the basis that Torah is compared to cheese,[8] or because, once the Torah was given, the Israelites realized that their utensils were no longer *kasher*, their slaughtering and preparation of meat not having hitherto been performed according to the divine law. Their cooking utensils were, similarly, now unfit for use and they could not do anything to render them kasher on that holy day. They had to restrict themselves, therefore, on that first Sinaitic Shavuot, to a temporary milk diet. And that historical situation is commemorated in the eating of dairy food on that festival.

Again, on Rosh Hashanah, there is the Talmudic tradition of *simana milta*, eating foodstuffs whose names are evocative of sweetness and blessing. Hence the dipping of the apple (and challah) into honey, and the recommendation to eat such foods as pomegranates, fenugreek, carrots, dates or the head of a sheep.[9]

On Purim there is also the custom of eating three-cornered poppy-seed cakes, called *hamantaschen* ('Haman's ears'), perhaps in mockery of Haman's readiness to listen to any rash advice given to him by 'his wife, Zeresh and all his friends',[10] to further his evil designs against the Jews.

On Tu Bishvat, the New Year for the Trees, there is also the practice of eating fifteen different types of fruit with which the land of Israel is blessed; and, last, but by no means least, there is the custom on Chanukah of eating potato *latkes*, doughnuts or any other oily dish, in order to reinforce the miracle of the Chanukah oil.

THE STATUS OF WOMEN AS REGARDS THE RITUAL OF LIGHTING

199. Is a woman's status exactly equal to that of a man as regards the mitzvah of lighting the Chanukah lights?

Yes and no! If a man is travelling away from home, his wife may light on his behalf at home, and that absolves him from lighting. It is recommended, however, that he should make a point of specifically requesting her to do so on his behalf. Nevertheless, some authorities regard it as preferable that he should still light in his place. This is because, although his wife fulfills the basic mitzvah for him (of one light per home), yet there is also the higher level of religious enthusiasm (*mehadrin*) to strive for, and referred to in the Talmud (see Question 181), wherein each person kindles his own lights. For that reason, it is recommend that, even where one's wife lights at home, the husband should light for himself or listen to the blessings being recited by someone in the place where he finds himself.

200. So if women (like Judith) played such a prominent role in the miracle of Chanukah, why do they only occupy a 'fall-back position', performing the mitzvah of lighting for the family only when their men-folk are away? Why do they not share the identical religious status as men, and have the same obligation to light?

Good question. It is a pity that I do not have an equally good answer! The *Chatam Sofer* offers the explanation that it goes back to Talmudic times, when the lights were instituted to be lit in front of one's home, outside in the street. Rabbi Sofer suggests that, in those days, it was regarded as improper for women to stand around, among the men on the street after dark, even in front of their own homes. Hence they were not accorded their otherwise rightful religious responsibility of lighting for themselves. And this tradition, of relying on their men-folk, has become entrenched to the present day, notwithstanding changes in notions of propriety.[11]

PARTYING ON CHANUKAH?

201. On Purim, a seudah (celebratory meal) is an essential halachic requirement. Is this also the case on Chanukah?

No it is not. The *Shulchan Arukh* states specifically that 'the many *seudot* that are customarily taken on this festival are, nevertheless, purely optional, for our sages did not institute partying and jollification for it'.[12] Unlike Purim, when one is free to 'let one's hair down', Chanukah's celebration is more muted, and confined, primarily, to ritual expression in the form of the lighting, the recitation of *Hallel* and the *Al ha-Nisim* composition.

202. But why was a seudah prescribed for Purim and not for Chanukah?

The reason for this is unclear. Rabbi Mordechai Jaffe suggested that it was because Purim represented a deliverance from the life or death situation facing the Jews of Persia, whereas with Chanukah the situation was not as dire. The Greeks, he alleges, did not set out to destroy the Jews. Their primary objective was merely to convert them to their own Hellenistic beliefs. Hence the relief at Purim was far greater, and the celebration far more intense and comprehensive.[13]

This theory is contested by others, however, on the view that 'the destruction of someone's faith is equivalent to, or even worse than, the taking of his life'.[14] The relief from such a threat would certainly merit the most comprehensive of celebrations.

On the other hand, the rationale might be, simply, that banquets featured so prominently in the story of Purim that it was natural that the banquet should have become elevated to a prominent means of celebrating that victory, whereas it had no place in the events leading up to the Hasmonean victory, as described in the books of the Maccabees.

203. So is there no halachic justification then for having a Chanukah party?

Judaism is never averse to celebrating, notwithstanding the fact that, nationally, we have never had much reason to do so. So it should not surprise us to find that Moses Isserles (*Remah*), the great Ashkenazi glossator to Karo's *Shulchan Arukh*, counters the latter's statement that partying and jollification were not prescribed for Chanukah. He notes that, 'Some say that there is some element of mitzvah in increasing the number of celebratory meals since the dedication of the altar [in the desert sanctuary] took place at this time'. The *Be'er Heitev* quotes several other authorities who concur that Chanukah is a time for partying and jollification, on the basis of the Midrash on *Beha'alotkha* which states that Chanukah is also the anniversary of the time when the Israelites completed the erection of the Sanctuary itself, which was celebrated with partying and jollification.[15]

A SEUDAT MITZVAH?

204. Do those authorities that recommend a Chanukah party provide any guidelines as to its conduct?

Indeed. And these are also quoted in Isserles' gloss which states that, 'it is the practice to sing hymns and verses of praise at those additional seudot, thereby elevating them into religiously prescribed meals (*seudot mitzvah*)'.

205. But how can a mere meal or party suddenly become converted into a religious ritual?

That is, indeed, a unique feature of Judaism, as reflected in the psalmist's exhortation, 'Serve God with joy'. When our joy partakes of the nature of an authentic thanksgiving to God for benefits and mercies bestowed, then our accompanying celebration is invested with a spirituality which elevates it into a religious ritual. This found tangible expression in Temple times when the meat of the Thanksgiving Offering was eaten in the Temple precincts together with the officiating priest. The banquet was, therefore, an intrinsic element of the religious thanksgiving. God was, symbolically, the guest of honour, through his priestly representative.

206. But what is it about the singing of hymns that they alone can convert an ordinary party into a religious festivity?

According to the Talmud, the singing of psalms by the Levites, while the sacrifices were being offered, represented the apogee of their divine ministrations. It was that act to which the Torah was referring in the words, 'And he shall minister in the name of the Lord his God' (Deuteronomy 18:7).[16] Hence, when songs of thanksgiving and praise to God are sung at the Chanukah party, they help set the spiritual tone and elevate that party into a *seudat mitzvah*, a religious event that the divine presence is happy to grace.

MENORAH OR CHANUKIAH?

207. Can you explain why the candelabrum is almost universally referred to as a 'Chanukiah' and not as a 'Menorah'?

This question will probably be incomprehensible to the younger generation who would probably answer, 'Because that is its name!' The older generation, however, especially those living outside of Israel, will undoubtedly have been brought up to refer to it as a Menorah – the same name given to the Shabbat candelabrum. They will know that Chanukiah is a modern coinage, not found in any of our rabbinic sources, a name that did not exist prior to the foundation of the State of Israel. It was probably popularized there in order to differentiate the (eight-branched) Chanukah candelabrum from the seven-branched Temple Menorah that is the emblem of the State of Israel.

208. So is 'Menorah' the regular term found in the rabbinic sources to describe the Chanukah candelabrum?

Surprisingly, it is not. If we read the Laws of Chanukah in the *Mishneh Torah* of Maimonides, as well as the *Shulchan Arukh* of Karo, we will not find the term Menorah anywhere. Indeed, it is as if they were studiously avoiding reference to it, preferring instead the less specific term of *ner* (pl. *ha-nerot*), 'the light(s)', the term exclusively employed in the Talmud. We may assume that the Talmud wished thereby to distinguish the eight-branched Chanukah candelabrum from the biblically prescribed, seven-branched Temple candelabrum, to which, alone, the biblical term, 'Menorah', was to be attached. It is possible that Maimonides and Karo were guided by the same consideration. Later rabbinic authorities, however, such as S. Gansfried, the author of the popular *Kitzur Shulchan Arukh*, had no qualms about employing the term 'Menorah'.

209. Are there any restrictions as regards the material from which the Chanukiah may be made?

There are no restrictions. However, since a mitzvah should always be performed in as dignified and beautiful a manner possible – a principle called *hiddur mitzvah*, 'adornment of the mitzvah' – a silver Chanukiah is the preferred choice. If one's resources cannot stretch so far, one made of any other metal is also acceptable. Unglazed earthenware, however, because it rapidly becomes discoloured, is not recommended. A new one should be provided as soon as such discoloration becomes apparent, even after one night's use.

210. Is a candelabrum or holder essential, or may one merely stick wax candles onto a surface and light them?

This hinges on a dispute between the authorities as to whether or not the oil or candleholder is also subsumed under the term *ner*. In the Temple, the candelabrum was an essential element in the ritual of the lighting, and hence the manifold laws that governed its artistic design and the skill that went into its construction.

Authorities are divided, however, as to whether or not our Chanukiah is also to be regarded as an indispensable part of the lighting process. The fact that it was the oil that was the main focus of the Chanukah miracle suggests to some that the holder or container is of little halachic consequence; and hence one may, indeed, stick candles onto a surface and light them. Other authorities, such as the *Netivot Olam*,[17] take the very opposite view, and regard the container as an essential part of the *ner*. Without a container, therefore, there is a deficiency in the provision of that *ner*. According to that way of thinking, the principle of *hiddur*, of providing the finest looking Chanukiah, would also be operative. Our observation (see Question 208), that Maimonides and Karo consistently refer to the container also by the term *ner*, would therefore be pertinent to this debate.

OIL OR CANDLES?

211. Which is preferable, an oil Chanukiah or one that uses candles?

Clearly an oil Chanukiah is the traditionally preferred method, since it is a more authentic commemoration of the miracle of Chanukah. For that reason, pure olive oil, as exclusively prescribed for the Temple Menorah, is the preferred choice also for the Chanukiah.

212. If someone took some oil belonging to another without his permission, and used it in his own Chanukiah, would he fulfill the mitzvah of lighting thereby?

No, he would not. The mitzvah is nullified under the principle of *mitzvah ha-ba'ah b'aveirah*, 'performing a religious act in a sacrilegious manner'. The intrinsic contradiction neutralizes entirely any positive benefit from the act performed.

213. If one was in a remote place, where olive oil, wax candles or any other kasher oil, were all unobtainable, could non-kasher oil be used for the Chanukiah?

The *Bet Shlomoh*[18] observes that, although we are usually particular that ritual objects should be from permitted sources – such as tefillin whose straps should be made from the hide of an animal that we are permitted to eat – yet, as regards this purely rabbinic (that is, post-biblical) institution of Chanukah lighting, it would not be necessary to insist on that prerequisite, especially given the emergency described.

WICKS AND ELECTRIC LIGHTS

214. Are wicks essential?

They are not. The reason is that, even though, in general terms, the Chanukiah commemorates the Temple situation, yet, in its specifics, the laws governing the Temple Menorah did not extend to the Chanukah lights ritual. Thus, if one had a small, perforated metal disk, floating on oil and providing an adequate and constant flame, that would satisfy the requirement of the mitzvah of the Chanukah lights.

215. If one is using oil and wicks, is it necessary to change the wicks for each successive night's lighting?

No it is not, for the reason just given. In the case of wicks there is a clear distinction between the Temple requirements and those for the Chanukiah. A new wick was provided each night for the Temple Menorah, whereas, as we have said, this was never a Chanukah requirement.

216. May one fulfill one's duty with electric bulbs?

Most authorities decide that one may not use electric bulbs, notwithstanding the fact that they may be used for *havdalah* (in an emergency) or as a *yahrzeit* (anniversary of the death of a close relative) light. This is because, for the purpose of the Chanukah lights, we require an act of *de novo* kindling, as referred to in the blessing,

'He who has commanded us to kindle (*l'hadlik*) the Chanukah light'. According to R. Zvi Pesach Frank, the activating of an electric switch is not, in fact, a primary act of 'kindling'. All it does is release and conduct a pre-existent current to its source, where it serves as a focus of illumination. The power station is the actual source of the current. The flicking of the switch is therefore only a secondary act.[19]

217. Are there any other objections to using an electric Chanukiah?

Other authorities raise the further objection that, in order for our ritual to be reminiscent of the Temple Menorah, we require that the lights be produced from fuel with an oily content, such as oil, fat or wax. For the same reason one may not light with sticks of wood, even though they might provide a good flame.

218. Could there be any practical problems when utilizing an electric Chanukiah?

Indeed. The halachah makes it a requirement that, from the outset, the Chanukiah contains enough oil to ensure that it burns uninterruptedly for at least a half hour, or that the candles are sufficiently large to guarantee that. In the case of electricity, we cannot guarantee, however, that there will be no power cut in the middle.

219. If the Chanukah lights blew out, must they be re-lit?

No, they need not be re-lit. We have already observed that not all the regulations governing the Temple lights apply to those of the Chanukiah (see Question 214). Hence, whereas in the Temple they would have had to be re-lit, because the Torah specifically states, 'that the lamp may burn continually' (Exodus 27:20), this regulation did not apply outside the Temple situation, such as in the case of the lights lit in the home on Chanukah.

THE SHAMMASH

220. What is the Shammash?

Shammash means 'attendant' or 'server', and is the name given to the extra candle that we are required to use each night, in addition to the Chanukah lights. Its purpose is to discharge all the functions of an ordinary light so that the actual Chanukah lights will not be employed for any secular purpose.

221. Why cannot the Chanukah lights be used for some other purpose?

Because they are what we call *muktzeh*, that is designated at the outset exclusively for the performance of that particular mitzvah, and forbidden to be used for any other purpose. This is in order to reinforce the principle of *pirsumei nisa*, 'publicizing [the uniqueness of] the miracle'.

The necessity to reserve the Chanukah lights for that exclusive purpose is reinforced in the *Ha-nerot hallalu* composition that we recite immediately after lighting the lights (and before singing *Ma'oz Tzur*). It states: 'Now these lights are sacred and we are not permitted to make any other use of them, except to look at them'.[20]

222. Are there any other reasons for the prohibition of utilizing the lights for any extraneous purpose?

Another reason offered[21] is that since the lights commemorate a miracle that occurred in connection with the Temple candelabrum, we preserve the same prohibition, of extraneous use that applied to that sacred Temple appurtenance.

223. So how does the Shammash discharge its purpose?

Well, first and foremost, we use that extra light in order to kindle all the Chanukah lights each night. Without it, one would probably be tempted to use the first-lit Chanukah candle in order to light all the rest. According to some authorities, this would constitute an infringement of the basic law that the Chanukah lights may only be used to look at – for their own intrinsic and commemorative benefit – not to service the kindling of any other light. The latter purpose is provided by the *Shammash*.

LIGHTING ONE CANDLE FROM ANOTHER

224. Your reference (in the previous answer) to ' some authorities' suggests that there are others who permit lighting one candle from another. Could you clarify the dispute?

This issue represents a difference of opinion between the Sephardi authority, Joseph Karo, who permits using one light to kindle another directly, and his Ashkenazi glossator, R. Moses Isserles (*Remah*) who objects to it.

Karo's view is that because the second light is being lit here for one and the same category of mitzvah, that can hardly constitute secular or external usage.[22] Isserles demurs, however, on the basis that one actually fulfils the basic mitzvah by lighting just one light each night (see Questions 181, 234–239, 245). The other lights do not, therefore, have the same religious status; and for that reason, utilizing the first light in order to light the others does, indeed, constitute a diminution of its sanctity and purpose[23]

225. Is there any circumstance in which Isserles would take a more lenient view?

There is. As the lights only have to burn for a half an hour into night in order to satisfy the requirement of the mitzvah, once that time has elapsed the lights lose their sacred status and may be used for any purpose. Thus, if one of the other lights had previously gone out, and he wished to re-kindle it after the half hour period (for an esthetic or utilitarian purpose), he could do so.

226. How else does the Shammash discharge its purpose?

In an era before electricity, when oil lights or candles provided the sole illumination for the room, the addition of Chanukah lights would serve to augment the existing illumination, enabling the occupants of the room better to see and read. With the provision of the Shammash, it is possible to attribute that additional benefit to the light that comes from that specific and non-sacred source, and feel no apprehension that one is utilizing the sacred Chanukah light for one's own benefit.

227. Are there any restrictions in the purposes for which one may use the Shammash?

None whatsoever. While not recommending the practice, if someone wished to use it, for example, to light a cigarette, it would be quite in order.

228. Since we have electric lights in our homes, may we blow out the Shammash once we have used it to kindle the lights?

Indeed, it has served its purpose, and there is no need to keep it burning as a source of illumination in the room.

TWO *SHAMMASH* CONTAINERS ON ONE CHANUKIAH?

229. I have seen in museums Chanukiahs[24] which seem to have two larger bowls, one on the right and the other on the left of the eight oil containers. Do they both serve as *Shamash*, and, if so, why are they both necessary?

They are both intended to serve as oil containers for the *Shammash*, and to reflect its dual purpose: First, to ignite the Chanukah lights, and secondly to constitute a source of secular light, by which one may read or amuse oneself in the room. *Tur* and other medieval authorities insisted on two separate lights for those differentiated tasks, and the name *Shammash* was reserved for the light with which the others were lit. The light for secular purposes was lit last, since it had no intrinsic association with the ritual, but was merely lit as a precaution to avoid misuse of the holy lights.

230. So if some authorities thought it necessary to have two Shammash lights, why did the practice not become universal?

Objections were raised against having two extra lights since it was unclear from a distance whether or not they were intrinsic, leaving the onlooker confused as to the precise night of Chanukah being celebrated.[25] Others maintained that the second, secular light was unnecessary because people invariably had a light or lights burning over their main table, which they used for general illumination.

THE POPULARITY OF WAX CANDLES

231. If the miracle of Chanukah was with oil, how do we account for the overwhelming popularity and use of wax candles?

Professor Daniel Sperber[26] attributes it to a development of the situation we have been discussing, namely the two extra lights to service the Chanukiah. He refers to authorities that felt the need to make a clear distinction between the main lights for the mitzvah, for which oil was used, and the *Shammash* light, for which they employed wax candles.

There were also communities that could not obtain oil, or for which the price of oil was prohibitive, and that used, instead, a variety of other permitted fatty fuels. But wax was generally the cheapest and most plentiful. Hence, those who could afford oil did so, while utilizing wax candles for the *Shammash*, and those who could not afford oil at all resorted to utilizing wax candles for all the lights. Hence the statement of Isserles: 'Although the choice method is to employ olive oil, if none is available he should use other pure and clear oil. In our communities, however, it is the prevailing custom to light with wax candles, for their light is as bright as that of oil.'[27] Hence the almost universal practice, in Ashkenazi communities, until recent decades, of lighting with wax candles.

THE POSITION OF THE *SHAMMASH*

232. Were any other methods used to distinguish between the sacred (mitzvah) lights and the secular *Shammash*?

There was one method that, in time, became the halachic norm and influenced the design of all Chanukiot. This was to place the *Shammash* at a different height, either higher or lower than the other mitzvah lights. The majority view favoured placing it higher than the rest, so that any activity performed in the room could be said to have been done under its exclusive illumination.

233. Were there any other methods of distinguishing the *Shammash* from the mitzvah lights?

Indeed. Another method, recommended by halachic authorities, was to place the bowl for the Shammash on the same level as that of the other lights, but to make it much longer than the rest or at a greater distance from them.[28] In the Israel Museum in Jerusalem, there is an eighteenth century Yemenite, triangular Chanukiah, made of stone, with the spout for the Shammash situated at the front, at the narrowest point. Another two Chanukiahs from Morocco make no special provision for the Shammash, but have nine uniformly spaced spouts in a row.

PERSECUTION AND THE NUMBER OF LIGHTS PER HOUSEHOLD

234. How many lights are required to be lit in each household?

We have already quoted the Talmudic source that states that the basic mitzvah is performed by a person lighting 'one light for himself and his household (included), but that the more enthusiastic will provide one light per night for each household member, while the ultra-enthusiastic will increase an extra light each night (in accordance with the Hillelite view) or decrease (in accordance with the Shammaite view)' (see Question 181).

The great Sephardi codifier, Joseph Karo, states that, 'even if there are many people in the household, they should not kindle more [than one Chanukiah]'.[29] The Ashkenazi authority, Moses Isserles, reports, on the other hand, that 'the general practice is that every member of the household lights his own'.[30]

235. How do we account for those variant practices?

R. Ezekiel Katzenellenbogen attributes this to the different conditions in which the respective communities of Spain and Franco-Germany lived.[31] In Spain, the Jews enjoyed total religious freedom in the early centuries and were therefore able to place their Chanukiahs outside their homes without fear of Gentile interference. They therefore lit just one Chanukiah so that the passers-by could tell at a glance which night of Chanukah it was. Had every member of the family lit their own in the same place, the agglomeration of lights would have obscured that indication.

In Franco-Germany, on the other hand, Jews had encountered problems from the very beginning of their settlement there. They never had the opportunity, therefore, of kindling outside and did not require to take into consideration how best to 'publicize the miracle' to the outside world. Since fear of confusing passers-by was not, for them, an issue, they therefore embraced the practice of every member of a household lighting his own Chanukiah.

236. So is it just a clear cut difference of practice between Ashkenazim and Sephardim?

Nothing in religious life is 'clear cut'! Here the matter is complicated by a statement in the code of the great Sephardi authority, Maimonides (twelfth century), to the effect that, 'it is standard practice in all our Spanish cities that each householder lights his own lights, ascending in number each night, whether there are many or only one in the household'.[32]

237. But how then could the other great Sephardi authority, Karo (sixteenth century), instruct his communities to light but one light per household if that was not their established practice?

Katzenellenbogen again elucidates. He suggests that Karo was correct in his attempt to re-assert the original practice of the Jews of Spain. It was, in fact, the communities in Maimonides' day that had stepped out of line, for pressing reasons, namely persecution at the hands of a fanatical Almohad sect. They had to abandon, therefore, their practice of lighting out of doors. In sympathy with that, Maimonides gave halachic sanction to the new practice of lighting inside the home, which, in turn, enabled each person to light his own Chanukiah without fear of confusing passers-by. By the time of Karo, the Jews of Spain had been exiled from their homeland, and hence his wish to re-establish the original Sephardi practice of lighting just one Chanukiah per family.

238. Did Karo succeed in persuading the Sephardim to revert to their original practice of having just one Chanukiah?

From a responsum of that same R. Ezekiel Katzenellenbogen,[33] it would seem that Karo's view had prevailed. Katzenellenbogen (d. 1749) describes a dispute that was brought before him, in which a Sephardi, living in Hamburg, forbade an Ashkenazi who was living in his home to kindle his own Chanukiah on the grounds that this was against Sephardi practice and therefore an infringement of the biblical prohibition of *lo titgodedu*, 'separatism'. Thus, it is clear that, a century after Karo, the Sephardim were well entrenched in their original practice.

239. As a matter of interest, how did Katzenellenbogen decide the issue?

He rejected the appeal to that principle of separatism on the grounds that, if it was at all relevant, then it was the Sephardi party that was guilty of its infringement, because he had departed from the local tradition, which was Ashkenazi. Katzenellenbogen added that, 'although the Sephardim had been the first immigrants to Hamburg, *the word of the Lord was rare in those days* (I Samuel 3:1), and, as is well-known, the Sephardim did not [summon the courage to] kindle any Chanukah lights before the establishment of the [Ashkenazi] community, after which the Sephardim began to strengthen their heart in the fear of God'.

THE CHANUKIAH: ITS SHAPE AND PLACE

240. Are there any laws governing where all the members of the (Ashkenazi) family should place their Chanukiahs?

It is essential that the number of lights on any particular night be discerned at a glance. Thus, the Chanukiahs must not be bunched together, but separated out on the table or sideboards in order to publicize that important detail.

241. Are there any restrictions regarding the shape of the Chanukiah?

Because it is necessary for the on-looker to be able to tell at a glance which particular night of the festival it is, each of the eight individual oil containers or candle holders of the Chanukiah should be in a straight line. A circular, or even a curved, Chanukiah, or one where the individual holders are at different heights, would create the illusion of merging several lights into one blaze of fire, rather than visually maintaining the separate tongues of flame. Similarly, those using wax candles are advised to ensure that they are not placed too close to each other, so that they may not melt from the heat.

242. Are there any regulations covering the minimum height at which the Chanukiah should be positioned?

There are. They should not be placed on a surface that is 'lower than three *tefachim* (handbreadths) from the ground'. The Talmudic handbreadth is just under four inches, so they should not be placed lower than about twelve inches. Placing it so low may be construed as despising the mitzvah.

243. Is there a maximum height, above which the Chanukiah may not be placed?

There is. It may not be placed 'above twenty *amot* [cubits]'. This corresponds to about thirty-six feet from the ground. Since there is a principle that the eye does not take in objects at that height, the element of 'publicizing the miracle' is lost. This has ramifications for very high Chanukiahs that are placed in public thoroughfares and for people living in high-rise buildings (see Questions 249 and 484).

244. May two people light on the same Chanukiah?

They may. However, they should take consideration of the law that two people must not position their lights close to each other, to the extent that it is no longer immediately visible to the onlooker which night of Chanukah it is. For the first few evenings, however, they may position their lights at either end of the Chanukiah, so that it is obvious that this represents two separate acts of lighting.

245. May two or more people share in the same mitzvah, with each one lighting another of the lights?

In this situation the one reciting the blessings is clearly representing the others. This is quite in order, in accordance with the basic level of the mitzvah – 'one light per household'. Once the first light has been lit, by the one reciting the blessing, the mitzvah has effectively been performed on behalf of the entire gathering. The remaining lights (in fulfillment of the highest level of religious enthusiasm) are merely for enhancement of the mitzvah, and may thus be lit by others present.

PIRSUMEI NISA – PUBLICISING THE MIRACLE

246. Is it preferable to light the Chanukiah indoors?

No it is not. We have already referred to the fact that from earliest times it was customary to light the Chanukiah in the front of one's home, in order to give maximum publicity to the miracle. Indeed, if there was a courtyard in front of the house, with a gate opening out to the street, it was the custom to affix the Chanukiah to the front gate.[34]

247. Why then was that practice abandoned?

It was abandoned on account of the antipathy and vandalism of the hostile gentiles. This was already experienced during the early centuries of the Common Era, to the extent that the Talmud, while recommending that it be placed as close to the public thoroughfare as possible, immediately adds the caveat that, 'at times of danger, let him place it on his table, and that will suffice!'[35]

248. But why should the gentiles have exhibited hostility to the Chanukiah in particular, to the extent that the Talmud made a legislative provision for that eventuality?

Rashi deals with this question, and explains it in the context of another Talmudic passage which relates that the fire-worshipping Persian Zoroastrians had a law that fire could only be formally and publicly lit in one of their own places of worship on specific festival days. Periodically one of those festival days coincided with Chanukah, when the lighting of the Chanukiah was regarded as anathema to their faith.[36]

249. So were the Jews left with just the one option of lighting them indoors?

Sadly, yes. And that remained the prevailing practice over the ages, even where there was no such threat. However, it became the custom to place the Chanukiah in the front window, looking out onto the public thoroughfare, in order to make some attempt at publicizing the miracle. This was, in any case, the only way of doing so for people whose homes were the upper stories of blocks of flats, and who had no front doors or courtyards leading out to the street.

LIGHTING IN TRAIN OR PLANE

250. If one is on a journey, is he obliged to light the Chanukiah ?

This was first discussed by the Galician authority, *Maharsham* (R. Shalom Shvadron, 1835-1911), at a time when rail travel was becoming popular. He decides that, where one will not arrive home in time to light, or if one is travelling away from home together with one's family, one is obliged to light on the journey. The rationale is that purchasing a ticket for a train compartment is tantamount to renting an enclosure for eating and sleeping. The fact that one is on the move does not, in his opinion, nullify the obligation of publicizing the miracle. The same obligation applies on an airplane journey.[37]

251. In that situation, would one have to light all the lights, as usual?

Arukh ha-Shulchan suggests[38] that if this is problematic, he may light just one light, thereby satisfying the requirement of the basic level of the mitzvah (see Question 224).

252. Does the principle of 'publicizing the miracle' have any other ramification?

It is responsible for the law that, once the Chanukiah has been lit, it should not be removed to another place, preferably even after the requisite half-hour of burning, and until the lights have burnt themselves out. The reason for this is that an on-looker, seeing one carrying the lit Chanukiah, would assume that it has been lit for the person's personal need (perhaps to illuminate another room), and not for the mitzvah. In that situation, the objective of 'publicizing the miracle' is frustrated. A further danger is that the on-looker may then proceed to make use of that Chanukiah at its final destination in a situation where it has not yet burnt for the requisite half hour.

A DEFINITION OF THE MITZVAH 'TO LIGHT'

253. At what stage is the mitzvah of lighting the Chanukiah fulfilled?

This is the subject of a discussion in the Talmud, as to whether the initial act of lighting immediately satisfies the requirement of the mitzvah (*hadlakah oseh mitzvah*) or whether this is not achieved until the moment the Chanukiah is placed in its (halachically) appropriate position (*hanachah oseh mitzvah*). The practical distinction would be that, according to the first view, if he lit them initially in a halachically inappropriate place (such as too high up, too low, or where a wind or draught would assuredly extinguish them), and then moved them to an acceptable position, he would not have fulfilled the mitzvah because at the moment of lighting, when the mitzvah was being activated, it was instantaneously nullified. According to the second view, however, the circumstances attending the lighting are irrelevant. It is the act of placing the lit Chanukiah in its appropriate position that activates the mitzvah.

254. Which of those two views was accepted as halachah?

The view that the initial act of lighting activates the mitzvah. For that reason, 'at the time the lights are lit, they have to be in their proper position and the oil containers must have enough oil for their lights to burn for the requisite time. Hence, if that were not the case at the outset, and he poured more oil in after the lights were burning, he would not have fulfiled his duty.'[39]

255. In such a situation, what should he do if that is pointed out to him?

He should re-kindle the lights, with the intention that this act alone should constitute the fulfillment of his obligation. In such a situation, he does not repeat the blessings.

TIME FOR LIGHTING

256. When is the proper time for lighting the Chanukiah?

The proper time is immediately following on from nightfall, and the lights should burn for at least a half hour into night.

257. Why was that specific time chosen?

At nightfall the streets are at their busiest, with people returning home from work, and there is the greatest opportunity, therefore, for 'publicizing the miracle'.

258. What if someone is invited out and has to leave his home before nightfall?

He may light earlier than nightfall, though there are two differing views, both quoted in the *Shulchan Arukh*,[40] regarding the precise time from which he may do so. One view is that he may do so from *p'lag ha-Minchah*, which is approximately one and a quarter hours before nightfall. Any earlier than that is pure daylight, and the lights of the Chanukiah would not be clearly visible. Passersby would also probably assume that they are merely internal lights for illuminating the home.

259. But is this not still defeating the purpose of the lighting, because at that earlier time there will be still be an insufficient number of passers-by who will see the lights, and the element of publicity for the miracle will be lost?

Good point. But those authorities are one step ahead of you! When one lights at the earlier time, they insist that one puts a sufficient amount of oil into the Chanukiah, or uses longer candles, to ensure that they are still burning for a half-hour after nightfall.

260. You said there were 'two differing views' as to the earliest period from when one may light in case of difficulty. What is the other view?

The differing views are based on variant interpretations of the Talmudic statement that 'the lights should be lit from when the sun goes down'.[41] This gave rise to a dispute as to the precise definition of 'sundown'. Simply put, the issue is whether the Talmud meant the beginning of the sundown period or its end. The first opinion, that we may light from one and a quarter hours before nightfall clearly understands the Talmudic definition as indicating from the beginning of the sundown period.

The second view, however, is that the Talmud means the end of the sundown period, in the period of transition from sundown to nightfall. This is generally defined as about one quarter of an hour before nightfall (or the appearance of three stars). According to the latter view, the window of opportunity for lighting earlier, if one needs to leave one's home, is not as generous by far.

261. What if one inadvertently lit the Chanukiah before p'lag ha-Minchah (one and a quarter hours before nightfall)?

He has not fulfilled the mitzvah as required and should therefore extinguish it and re-light it with the blessings.

MA'ARIV AND CHANUKAH LIGHTS

262. At nightfall, does one pray the *Ma'ariv* (evening) service first, or light the Chanukiah?

It depends upon one's custom in respect of reciting *Ma'ariv*. Those who are particular to recite that service at nightfall (*bizmano*) should not change their established and regular practice. They should therefore light the Chanukiah a little before nightfall, and then pray *Ma'ariv*. Those who have no strictly consistent practice, but pray *Ma'ariv* either before or after nightfall, should first pray *Ma'ariv* and then light the Chanukiah.

263. What if someone who usually prays *Ma'ariv* at nightfall forgot to light the candles beforehand. Which should he perform first after nightfall?

In this situation, he should revert to his usual practice of doing nothing at nightfall before praying *Ma'ariv*. The reason for this is two-fold. First, on account of the principle of *tadir ushe'eino tadir, tadir kodem*, that precedence is accorded to the more regularly performed ritual. *Ma'ariv* is, of course, prayed throughout the year, whereas the lighting of the Chanukiah is only an annual ritual. Secondly, the lighting is only a rabbinic institution, whereas *Ma'ariv* involves the recitation of the *Shema*, which is biblically mandated.[42]

264. Are there any restrictions governing the period between nightfall and the lighting of the Chanukiah?

The *Mishnah Berurah* states that, 'once the time for lighting has arrived, it is forbidden [to do anything else,] even to learn, and certainly to eat anything'.[43]

THE LATEST TIME FOR LIGHTING

265. Until what hour may one light the Chanukiah?

As we have observed, in Talmudic times the presence of passers-by in the street was the determinant for lighting. As there was no street lighting, people did not wander the streets much after nightfall. Hence the Talmudic definition of the *terminus ad quem* for lighting is, 'until the feet have ceased from the streets'.[44] After that, there could be no publicity for the miracle.

In our day, however, when people, and especially car occupants, do travel around for hours after nightfall, there is not the same concern to restrict the lighting to the half hour after that time. Our window of opportunity for publicizing the miracle is much greater, and so, technically, we could light the Chanukiah until much later in the night.

266. Do we have that flexibility then?

Moses Isserles addresses this question in the light of the changed circumstances since Talmudic times, coupled with the fact that, in any case, we no longer light out of doors, so that the issue of publicity should no longer be the determinant. He states: 'Some say that these days, when we light indoors, it is no longer necessary to do so before passers-by have ceased on the streets. Nevertheless, it is worthy to be concerned [to have the lights burning for a half hour after nightfall] even in our days.'[45]

267. But what if that is impossible, as in the regular situation where people do not get home from work at Chanukah time for a few hours after nightfall?

They need not fear. The *Shulchan Arukh* itself extends leeway in this situation, affirming that, 'if the prescribed time has passed, and one has not lit the Chanukiah, one may do so at any time throughout the night. However, once dawn has risen and one has still not lit, one can no longer compensate for the lost mitzvah.'[46]

268. Are there any restrictions to that concession of lighting throughout the night?

There is some doubt among the authorities as to whether a blessing may be recited by someone lighting late in the night. The principle is that, in case of doubt regarding whether a blessing may be recited, we do not recite it. *Be'er Heitev* notes an apparent discrepancy in the formulation of Joseph Karo. In his *Bet Yosef* commentary he implies that a blessing is not recited, whereas the inference from his *Shulchan Arukh* is that it is.

The view of *Maharshal* (Solomon Luria) is that only until midnight may the blessings be recited, whereas *Be'er Heitev* takes the view that they should be recited for as long as the members of the household are still awake, even if they are up all night! Once the element of publicizing to others the miracle is no longer present, and he merely lights for himself at that late hour, he does not recite the blessings.[47]

KINDLING BY ONE'S WIFE OR BY A PROXY

269. What arrangement does one make for one's family if he will not be returning home until after they are asleep or if he will not be returning at all?

We have already observed that he should formally request his wife, or another member of the family, to be his representative, and light for the family at the proper time. If he himself, will have no access to a Chanukiah, or opportunity to light one, in the place where he is, and will not be returning home, he should ask his wife or another member of the family to light on his behalf also, and to have him in mind when fulfilling the mitzvah.

270. What if one expects to return later in the evening, and has asked his wife to light for the rest of the family. May she light again for him if he is prevented from returning home that night?

She, or another member, may light a second time, exclusively on his behalf. They may only recite the first blessing (*lehadlik ner* – 'to kindle the Chanukah lights'), however, but not the *Shehecheyanu* blessing on the first night or the *She'asa nisim* on subsequent nights. Wherever possible, however, one should also light for oneself when away from home over Chanukah, even though his wife is lighting for him and for the rest of the family.

271. But in that situation, where his wife is lighting for him, and he is also lighting (away from home), does he make a blessing?

Karo states that if he is lighting where there are no other Jews (and is publicizing the miracle to the world) he may therefore recite the blessing. The *Mordechai* provides the rationale, namely that, in addition to the mitzvah of 'lighting', there is also the obligation of 'seeing' the lights burning, irrespective of whether or not someone back home is lighting for him. The purpose of the blessing he recites in this situation is to sanctify and reinforce that particular obligation.[48]

272. What if he is away from home, among Jews, and he is present when they light the Chanukiah. If his wife is lighting on his behalf back home, does he still need to light his own Chanukiah in that place?

He does not. *Remah* states, however, that 'if he wishes to be more particular for himself, he may light for himself, and recite a blessing over them. And this is our custom.'[49]

273. So is that the final word, then?

It certainly sounds like it! In reality, however, *Mishnah Berurah* adds the caveat that, in order to avoid the issue of a potentially unnecessary blessing, he must consciously dissociate himself, before he recites his own blessings, from the lighting on his behalf back home.[50]

274. So do all authorities accept that approach?

No they don't. Surprise, surprise! Some take the view that 'since the sages have absolved him from the mitzvah, through his wife having lit on his behalf, it is not for him to then go and declare, 'I do not want my wife to fulfil the mitzvah for me.' He should, therefore, light without making any blessings...Nevertheless, it is preferable for him to hear the blessings being recited by others.'[51]

275. What if a man leaves his home, together with his family, in the afternoon – say, to attend a wedding – and will not return until late that evening?

It is preferable for the family to light together on their return, however late that may be.

276. What if a man leaves his home in the afternoon, together with his entire family, and they will not return at all that night?

Then there is no obligation on him to light at his unoccupied home, and he does so at the place where the family stays.

BOARDERS, LODGERS AND STUDENTS AWAY FROM HOME

277. If someone lives permanently with a family, away from his own home, must he still light his own Chanukiah?

He is considered as a permanent member of that family, and he fulfils his basic level of obligation, therefore, through their lighting. Some authorities nevertheless prefer him to do something positive in order to acquire an equal share in the mitzvah. They therefore suggest that he contribute a nominal amount towards the purchase of the oil and wicks or the candles, and that the householder, in return, formally and verbally accepts him into partnership.

278. What if someone is only boarding on a temporary basis?

If he is staying only temporarily, or is taking some of his meals elsewhere, he is not regarded automatically as a member of the family. He should then light his own Chanukiah or contribute some money to become a partner in the ownership of the oil and wicks or candles.

279 What should an out-of-town student do?

If he lodges in a Jewish student hostel, he should light for himself in the hostel refectory. If it is a gentile college hostel, and he is uncomfortable lighting it publicly, he may do so in his own room. Since the essence of Chanukah is, however, to publicize the miracle, and we have a duty to make God's name great among the nations, it stands to reason that it is preferable to light it publicly in the college refectory.

LIGHTING ON FRIDAY NIGHT

280. If the Chanukah lights have to be lit at nightfall, what happens on Friday night when we bring in Shabbat long before nightfall?

On Friday night (*Erev Shabbat*), we have no alternative but to light the Chanukiah much earlier than usual. Indeed, since we bring in Shabbat about an hour before nightfall, we have to ensure that we light the Chanukiah *before* this time, as we cannot perform lighting once Shabbat has entered. For this reason we have to light the Chanukiah before the Shabbat candles. Furthermore, because the Chanukah lights have to burn for at least a half hour into night (see Questions 256–261), on Friday night we achieve this by using an extra amount of oil, or longer candles (such as regular Shabbat candles), which will still be burning nearly two hours later.

LEFT-OVER OIL OR CANDLES

281. May we put any of the oil, wicks or candles remaining over after Chanukah to ordinary use?

We assume that the question refers here to oil or candles that have already burnt on the last night for the requisite half-hour after nightfall, and were then extinguished.

The matter hinges on the original intention of the person filling the oil or inserting the candles. If he had no specific idea to utilize what remains after the mitzvah has been fulfilled, then we must assume that he was intending everything to be devoted to the mitzvah. In that case, the remaining oil or part of the candle is *muktzeh* (see Question 221) and may not be put to any secular use. The advice given by Karo is that 'he should make a bonfire and burn it'.[52]

282. Does this apply only to oil or candles remaining in the Chanukiah, or also to oil in the original container jar, and candles in the packet?

It applies only to oil and candles in the Chanukiah. We do not assume that an entire jar of oil or packet of candles were, ab initio, totally designated for the Chanukiah.[53]

283. But why can he not just put it aside for use on Chanukah the following year?

The reason is that our authorities feared that, during the course of the year, its origin may be forgotten and it may come to be used inadvertently.

We may consider, however, that such an apprehension was only valid in the pre-electricity period, when oil was used in the home throughout the year for lighting, and hence the container of left-over mitzvah oil, or the candles, could very easily come to be used inadvertently. In our day, however, when we only use oil for Chanukah (and would hardly put the half-burned olive oil back into our larder, together with the olive oil used for cooking!), and when Chanukah candles are of a distinctive shape and size (and would not be mixed up with Shabbat candles), it is highly unlikely that one could mistake them and come to use them for extraneous purposes.

284. So, is there any way that a poor person, or someone living in a remote place where olive oil is scarce, can avoid having to dispose of the remaining Chanukah oil?

There is. We referred above to the significance of the mental attitude at the time of preparing the Chanukiah. If, at that moment, he made a conscious mental – some prefer it to be an oral – designation that he was not consecrating to the mitzvah any of the materials that might be left over, then they may be applied to personal use.

285. Sorry to labour the point, but why, in the absence of such a specific designation, should there be any necessity to destroy the mitzvah material when this is not required? Is this the case, for example with a worn-out *sukkah* or a *lulav* after Sukkot?

Perceptive question! A disused *sukkah* or post-Sukkot lulav may indeed be merely thrown away or put to another purpose. Two reasons are given, however, for the special precautions taken in the case of the Chanukah materials to ensure that they are not treated with disrespect once their period of use has expired.

The first consideration is that the Chanukiah is symbolic of the Temple Menorah, which, together with the other sacred vessels, could never be utilized for any extraneous purpose. Such use was designated as *me'ilah*, trespass, which was a very serious matter. This is emphasized in the words of the *Ha-nerot hallalu* composition: 'These lights are sacred, and we have no permission to utilize them'.

A second reason is that *sukkah* and *lulav* are designated *tashmishei mitzvah*, 'appurtenances for a sacred ritual'. That means that they have no intrinsic sanctity, but are rather the vessels or media through which we are enabled to fulfil a mitzvah. The *sukkah* building itself is not the source of the mitzvah. The mitzvah resides in the act of sitting in it. Again, the *lulav* is but a means of demonstrating our joy on the festival and of exhibiting the species for which we require the rain we petition for on that festival. In this same category is the *shofar*. The mitzvah is 'to hear' its sound, in order to arouse our spiritual emotions. The instrument itself is but the means of procuring that sound. It has no intrinsic holiness, and therefore may be thrown away if it is rendered unusable.

286. So what sort of things do we have to dispose of more respectfully?

Objects from our religious life that are, in themselves, *intrinsically* holy. These are designated *tashmishei kedushah*, 'sacred appurtenances'. Examples of these are a synagogue Ark, *sefer torah*, *tefillin*, and *mezuzah*. All these may not be burnt, but must be stored away, buried or, in some circumstances, re-employed or re-designed and utilized for another, albeit inferior, category of sacred purpose.[54]

THE IMPORTANCE OF THE MITZVAH

287. How important is the mitzvah of lighting Chanukah lights?

The mitzvah of publicizing the miracle wrought for Israel by God was regarded as so important that the sources state that 'One must be very zealous as regards this mitzvah, to the extent that even a poor man should borrow or sell his clothes in order to purchase oil for the lighting'.[55] This was qualified by later authorities who, as with the four cups of wine on Passover, placed the obligation upon the community welfare officers of providing the poor with oil or candles. As one fulfils the basic mitzvah with just 'one light for a man and his household', the obligation to provide Chanukah lights for the poor from the communal purse extended to the provision of but one light per night.

NOTES

1. *Tur Orach Chayyim*, sec. 670.
2. Talmud *Shabbat* 23a.
3. See *Rabbeinu Nissim*'s commentary on the *Rif* (Alfasi) to Talmud *Shabbat* 23a. The tradition of the application of the *ius primae noctis* is also found in the contemporary, fourteenth century, eclectic work, entitled *Kol Bo*, whose author remains unknown. There is no historical evidence, however, of its imposition by the Greeks at that period.
4. See *Tur Orach Chayyim*, sec. 417.
5. *Minhagei Maharil* (Sabionetta, 1556), p.36a. See also H.J. Zimmels, *Ashkenazim and Sephardim* (London: Oxford University Press, 1958), p.108.
6. See *Taz* on *Shulchan Arukh* 670:1 (2).
7. *Remah* on *Shulchan Arukh* 670:2.
8. This is based on the verse 'Honey and milk are under your tongue' (Song of Songs 4:11), which Talmudic tradition interprets symbolically as referring to the Torah. The term 'Mount of *Gavnunim*' is also midrashically explained as a synonym for Sinai ('The mount of the Lord') in psalm 68:16 (see Midrash *Bemidbar Rabba* 1:8); and *Gavnunim* is connected with the word *gevinah*, 'cheese'.
9. For an explanation of the relevance of these particular foods to the festival of Rosh Hashanah, see Jeffrey M. Cohen, *1001 Questions and Answers on Rosh Hashanah and Yom Kippur* (New Jersey: Jason Aronson, 1997), pp.124–5.
10. Esther 5:14.

11. See *Chiddushei Chatam Sofer* on Talmud *Shabbat* 21a.

12. *Shulchan Arukh Orach Chayyim* 670:2.

13. This view of R. Mordechai Jaffe (*Levush*) is quoted in the commentary of *Taz* to *Shulchan Aruch Orach Chayyim* 670:2 (3).

14. This maxim, borrowed here by *Taz* in order to rebut the view of R. Mordechai Jaffe, is attributed by him to *Rashi*'s commentary on Deuteronomy 23:9. *Rashi* there expands upon his view, and offers the rationale that, 'whosoever kills another, deprives him of this world, whereas he who destroys the faith of another, ruins his life on this earth, while also depriving him of life hereafter'.

15. See *Be'er Heitev* on *Shulchan Arukh* 670:2 (3).

16. See Talmud *Arakhin* 11a–b.

17. Quoted in S.Z. Braun's *She'arim Metzuyanim B'halakhah* (Jerusalem, New York: Feldheim, 1978), vol.3, p.242.

18. Ibid., p.240.

19. For a discussion of the issue of lighting by means of elecricity, see Aharon A. Maharshak, '*Hadlakat ner chanukah bechashmal*', in *Shanah B'Shanah* (Jerusalem: Heikhal Shelomo, 5736), pp.172–7.

20. See *Ha-nerot hallalu* composition, various editions of daily prayer book, Order of Service for Chanukah.

21. See *Mishnah Berurah* 673:8 (7).

22. *Shulchan Arukh Orach Chayyim* 674:1.

23. *Remah ad loc.*

24. D. Sperber, *Minhagei Yisrael* (Jerusalem: Mosad HaRav Kook,1995), vol.5, p.53, n.35.

25. Ibid., p.51 n. 29.

26. Ibid., p. 55ff.

27. *Remah* on *Shulchan Arukh* 673:1.

28. Sperber, *Minhagei Yisrael*, pp.58–9.

29. *Shulchan Arukh Orach Chayyim* 671:2.

30. *Remah ad loc.*

31. See Zimmels, *Ashkenazim and Sephardim*, pp.205–6.

32. *Rambam, Hilkhot Chanukah* 4:3.

33. Zimmels, *Ashkenazim and Sephardim*, pp.289–90.

34. *Tosaphot* on Talmud *Shabbat* 23a.

35. Talmud *Shabbat* 21b.

36. Talmud *Gittin* 17a.

37. View of *Maharsham*, quoted in Braun, *She'arim Metzuyanim B'halakhah*, p.243.

38. See *Arukh ha-Shulchan* chap. 673, sec.5.

39. S. Ganzfried, *Kitzur Shulchan Arukh* (var. editions), *Hilkhot Chanukah*, 139:13.

40. See *Shulchan Arukh* 672:1.

41. Talmud *Shabbat* 21b.

42. *Mishnah Berurah* 672:1 (3).

43. Ibid., 672:2 (10).

44. Talmud *Shabbat* 21b; *Shulchan Arukh* 672:1.

45. *Remah* on *Shulchan Arukh* 672:2.

46. *Shulchan Arukh ad loc.*

47. For all these views, see *Be'er Heitev* on *Mishnah Berurah* 672:2 (4).

48. *Mordechai*, quoted by *Remah on Shulchan Arukh* 677:3.

49. *Remah ad loc.*

50. *Mishnah Berurah* 677:3 (15).

51. Ibid., 677:3 (16).

52. *Shulchan Arukh* 677:4.

53. See *Bi'ur Halakhah* on *Shulchan Arukh* 677:4

54. See *Shulchan Arukh* sec. 154.

55. *Shulchan Arukh* 771:1.

V
CHANUKAH THEMES AND PHILOSOPHICAL INSIGHTS

9

The Significance of Light in Judaism

288. This festival of light focuses our attention on the significance of light in Judaism. Could you say a few words on this?

Truthfully no. It is impossible to say a few words on a subject that has engaged the curiosity and wonder of man from the very beginning of time. Indeed, the heavenly luminaries, providers of light and heat – the sources of our health, energy and sustenance – were, understandably, regarded by primitive man as deities in their own right. Hence that famous Midrash, taught to all our youngsters, of Abraham's exploration of the nature of sun, moon and stars as a prelude to his profound realization that there had to be a Creator who put in place the laws of nature that also governed them.

289. But surely Judaism did not go along with that primitive, sun or moon-worshipping cult, so why did light become so significant in our tradition?

Of course Judaism regards the worship of any power, other than the Almighty God, as idolatry. Indeed, that was Judaism's unique contribution: to explode such myths and to promote in their place the absolute unity of God, His eternity, incorporeality, omniscience and omnipotence.

But the fact that there were those who worshipped nature was no reason for us to deny its grandeur as the handiwork of the Creator. It was Judaism's special contribution to explore, through nature, the nature of God; to affirm, through human relationships, the image of God in man; and to open up channels of spiritual communication through our praise of His manifold attributes and acknowledgement of our absolute reliance on His mercy and magnanimity.

Light is a powerful symbol, and according to our mystical tradition even an instrument of Creation. In the Torah, it is a metaphor for God, Himself. Thus, in the Priestly Blessing, there is an anthropomorphic description of God's 'face' as a source of light: 'May the Lord cause His face to shine upon you' (Numbers 6:25). A pillar of fire accompanied the Israelites as they travelled through the desert by night, and when Moses returned from his forty day encounter with God on Sinai, 'he did not know that the skin of his face beamed forth light' (Exodus 34:30). He had, in a sense, absorbed some of God's own essence.

Israel thought of God in terms of the element of light: 'The Lord is my light and my salvation' (Psalm 27:1). The house of Jacob is bidden to 'Walk in the light of the

Lord' (Isaiah 2:5), and for the psalmist, 'God wraps Himself with light as with garment' (Psalm 104:2).

Significantly, God's own very first recorded utterance was, *yehiy ohr*, 'Let there be light!' (Genesis 1:3); and it was that primordial light that set in motion and energized the entire creative system of the universe. As the tool of the Creator, it is easy to see, therefore, how light became transformed into a veritable spiritual element, and how fire, its source, was similarly employed in so many of our sacred rituals. Hence the significance of light in Judaism and in most other religions.

LIGHT AND TORAH ENLIGHTENMENT

290. Are there any other reasons why light should be so highly regarded?

Light was also associated, by symbolic extension, with the Torah's spiritual 'enlightenment.' In the words of the Book of Proverbs, 'For the mitzvah is the lamp and the Torah is the light' (Proverbs 6:23). And in the *Sim shalom* blessing of the *Amidah* we petition for an enhanced flow of divine light to serve as a conduit for His Torah to reach us: 'Bless us, all of us, with the light of Your countenance. For, by the light of Your countenance You have given us a Torah of life and a love of mercy.'

The soul of man is also described as 'the lamp of God' (Proverbs 20:27), and this inspired the notion of the soul as a shaft of God's illumination within us. According to the author of the book of Job, that soul-light enters into us while we are still in the womb, 'when His lamp shone above my head, and by His lamp I went through the darkness' (29:3).

It is the presence within us of that light which motivates us towards embracing God's attributes of goodness and holiness. But, as the rays of light are ethereal and can so easily be shut out, and the light of a flame extinguished, so, if the proper spiritual conditions, under which the divine light glows within us, are not nurtured, our propensity for goodness becomes dissipated. Conversely, the great spiritual insights that men of the Spirit have revealed came to them only because they created, by living lives of purity, holiness and contemplation, a reception-apparatus for an augmented degree of spirituality. This explains what the psalmist meant by the words, 'In Thy light do we see light' (36:10), and why the advent of the Messiah is conceived of by Isaiah as the 'seeing of a great light' by the entire nation (9:1).

291. Do we give any tangible expression, in our ritual, to that particular notion of the soul as a higher light?

We do. Death is regarded as the removal of that higher light of the soul. Hence the tradition of placing a candle at the head of a person immediately after death, as if to replace the light of the soul that has gone out. For the same reason, Judaism requires that a light remain burning for the duration of the seven-day *shivah* period, following the interment, and in subsequent years on the *yahrzeit*, or anniversary of the day of death.

THE LIGHT OF THE MESSIAH

292. Does this notion of the Messianic light figure in our prayers?

Judaism tends to emphasize the here, rather than the hereafter. It is concerned with the way we live out our lives, pursuing peace, purity and kindliness. The future we can safely leave to God. Hence there are very few references in our daily prayers to the Messianic era. The clearest reference, associating the Messianic era with a unique form of 'light' or enlightenment, is the verse, *Ohr chadash al tzion ta'iyr*, 'O cause a new light to shine over Zion, and may we all be worthy to enjoy its radiance speedily'. This petition occurs as the climax to the first (*Yotzer*) blessing over the *Shema*, which takes the form of a paean of praise to God for the heavenly luminaries.

Saadia Gaon (882–942), the great philosopher and purist, objected to that theological insertion of a reference to Messianic light into a blessing whose purpose did not extend beyond that of praise for the boon of physical sunlight. He therefore omitted that phrase from the (earliest) *Siddur* he popularized. But his view did not win much sympathy, due to the seamless synthesis of the physical and spiritual light in the Jewish imagination.

293. We have referred to light as a symbol for spiritual enlightenment and Torah wisdom. Does this particular characteristic find any ritual expression?

We may view it as underlying the seven branches of the Temple candelabrum. At one level, this was symbolic of the seven days of the week, with each day determined and governed by the light of the sun and moon. At another level, the seven lights connote the seven pillars of wisdom and enlightenment referred to in the book of Proverbs: 'Wisdom hath builded her house; she hath hewn out her seven pillars' (Proverbs 9:1).

294. Does the Torah provide any indication of the special spiritual significance to be attributed to light?

Indeed, it does. We have already referred at length to the Temple Menorah, the very rationale of the festival of Chanukah. Another repository of spiritual light was the *Urim v'Tumim* (literally, 'lights of perfection') worn on the High Priest's breastplate. The names of the tribes of Israel were inscribed on that breastplate in a variety of precious gems.[1] According to tradition, this formed an oracle of consultation. If the nation wished to petition God on a matter of great import, or if the High Priest was unsure as to how to proceed on a matter of judgement, they would consult the *Urim v'Tumim*, and God would give His response by means of letters from the wording on the breastplate which would light up to convey God's guidance.[2]

Yet another indication of the spiritual quality of light, and symbolic of the Temple Menorah, is the *Ner Tamid*, 'Continual Light', which is suspended over the synagogue Ark. Since the Ark is the repository of Torah wisdom and enlightenment, the light is a most appropriate symbol.

PRIMEVAL AND MYSTICAL LIGHT

295. We have already attributed some mystical dimension to light. Does the mystical literature have anything to say about the origin of that element?

Indeed, it does. And here we must repeat the caveat we gave at the outset, for we cannot encapsulate an entire and complex mystical tradition in a few lines.

The starting-point is that first divine fiat, 'let there be light'. There is a major difficulty here in understanding the nature of that primordial light, and particularly its fate once it was superseded, on the fourth day of Creation, by the sun, moon and stars.

In the mystic tradition of Isaac Luria of Safed (sixteenth century), that primordial light was conceived of as the causative element enabling the physical universe to evolve. Where nothing had previously existed, the Holy Spirit set out to create a world of finite beings and forms that were subject to physical change and characterized by imperfection and moral decline, but which, nevertheless, still bore the imprint of His own 'hand'. This could not be undertaken as an act of direct and immediate creation, for a world that was an immediate extension of God's perfect handiwork would, of necessity, be perfect. Such a perfect world was not the natural environment for the growth and moral development of imperfect man.

To overcome this problem, according to Lurianic thought, God employed ten *Sefirot*, emanations from, or extensions of, the original Divine Being, in order to bring His universe into being. As God's Spirit originally filled the entire universe, He had to perform an act of 'withdrawal' (*tzimtzum*) from its space, in order to make room for physicality to fill the vacuum. God, then, as it were, channelled His own creative light into a succession of emanations that penetrated that primeval vacuum. Each of the ten *Sefirotic* extensions of light was less bright and potent than the one that preceded it. The light of the final *Sefirah* offshoot, being so remote from its Source, was spiritually weak enough to enable it to initiate and interact with a physical universe. And it was that tenth and final emanation that was brought into being with the words, *Yehiy ohr*, 'let there be light!'

296. Do we have any description of the properties of that light?

The Talmud states that the light was so rarefied and potent that 'a person could see with it from one end of the world to the other. However, when God surveyed the generations, and particularly the degenerate acts of the generations of the Flood and the Tower of Babel [He begrudged them its use, and, instead], He stored it away for the exclusive use of the righteous in the Hereafter.'[3] And this is the sense of the verse, 'Light is sown for the righteous' (Psalm 97:11).

LIGHT AND RELIGIOUS RITUAL

297. But does light have any more practical role in our religious ritual?

It certainly does. Our religious calendar is – or was, before a fixed calendar was introduced in the fourth century CE – wholly determined by the waxing and waning of the moon. The Torah prescribes the particular day of the month in which the major festivals are to be observed, but the precise day of *Rosh Chodesh*, that is the first day of the new month, was determined exclusively by observation of the first appearance in the sky of the light of the new moon.

A special court was convened in Jerusalem, on the thirtieth of each month, to await and hear the testimony of witnesses who had seen the earliest sign of the moon's light the previous night. If the court was satisfied with their testimony, it would sanctify that thirtieth day as *Rosh Chodesh*, the beginning of the new month. If no witnesses appeared, or the testimony before them was vague or manifestly fabricated, the court would declare the following day as *Rosh Chodesh*. Thus, in the former instance, the previous month was dubbed 'a defective month', namely one of only twenty-nine days, whereas in the latter case it is 'a full month' of thirty days. Our present, fixed calendar has six months of twenty-nine days and six months of thirty days (when there are two days of *Rosh Chodesh* celebrated), providing a total lunar calendar of three hundred and fifty-four days.

Thus, light is of paramount importance in the determination of the first day of our months and, in consequence, on which day of the week any festival during that month will occur.[4]

298. Is light also a consideration in the context of our daily religious ritual?

It is. The times for the recitation of our thrice-daily prayers are determined by the daylight hours, from sunrise to sunset. This is based on the psalmist's call for us to 'express reverence of Thee with the sunlight' (Psalm 72:5). Thus, sunrise is the proper time for the recitation of the morning service, notably the *Shema* and the *Amidah*, and their recitation has to have been completed before the third and the fourth hour of the day, respectively.

For the recitation of the afternoon and evening, *Minchah* and *Ma'ariv*, services, the daylight hours are also a consideration. The proper time for recitation of *Minchah* is halachically defined as 'from nine and a half hours of the day and onwards', which, in winter (when daylight hours are from about 6 a.m. to 6 p.m.) would be from 3.30 p.m. In case of emergency this may be brought forward to 'the sixth and a half hour of the day' (that is, 12. 30 p.m.). *Minchah* should ideally be completed by one and a quarter hours before nightfall. *Ma'ariv* is similarly determined by consideration of light. Ideally, its *Shema* prayer should not be recited until three stars are visible, though this requirement was relaxed out of consideration for people for whom it was difficult to have to come back to synagogue twice, or to have to while away an hour each evening, between the afternoon and evening services, at the end of a busy day. It was therefore declared permitted to recite *Ma'ariv* immediately following *Minchah*, provided that it was within the hour and a quarter before nightfall.

We are also governed by such considerations in the computation of the times for bringing in Shabbat and festivals. The sunlight hours also determine the time when a wedding may take place, in that, for halachic reasons, it may not be solemnized during the (doubtful day or night) twilight period. Similarly, the moment of a baby's birth – either before or after dusk – may also affect the day when its *brit* (circumcision) or *Pidyon ha-Ben* (redemption of the firstborn) are performed.

299. Are there any particular blessings or rituals specifically prescribed to emphasize the sanctity of light?

There are three rituals that serve to emphasize the sanctity of the sun and the moon. The first is the *Birkat ha-Chodesh*, 'Blessing over the New Moon', recited in synagogue on the previous Shabbat, following the prayer for the government. It contains a proclamation of the day or days when *Rosh Chodesh* will occur during the coming week.

While most communities regard the new month as beginning with the recitation of the evening service, there are some communities that are particular to announce the *molad*, the precise, mathematically computed, moment of transition between one month and the next. In Talmudic times, when the Bet Din formally announced the day of *Rosh Chodesh*, they would employ the term, *mekudash*, 'It is sanctified'. Hence the term *Kiddush ha-Chodesh*, 'Sanctification of the Moon'. The more popularly employed name is, simply, *Mevorachin ha-Chodesh*, 'Blessing of the New Month'.

The second ritual is *Birkat ha-Levanah* ('Blessing of the Moon') or *Kiddush ha-Levanah* ('Sanctification of the Moon'). This is a colourful ritual, recited out of doors and in a situation where the light of the new moon is readily visible. The renewal of the moon is also an opportunity for self and national renewal, and for that reason it is recited, whenever possible, after the termination of Shabbat. According to tradition, the second Temple was destroyed, and the exile of Israel and the Divine Presence commenced, at that precise time. Thus, the renewal of the moon (and Israel's fortunes are compared in our sources to the waxing and waning of the moon) is consecrated at that very moment in order to express an optimistic hope for Israel's impending redemption from that exile.

The third, and most infrequently performed, ritual is the *Birkat ha-Chamah*, 'Blessing of the Sun', a thanksgiving prayer for its creation on the fourth day. This ceremony is held but once every 28 years, when the sun is approximately 90 degrees above the horizon in the east on the first Wednesday of Nisan, the first month. The ceremony ends with an expression of fervent hope that we may each be spared to witness the Messianic era when, according to Isaiah, 'the light of the sun shall be sevenfold, as intense as the light of seven days'. This is an evocation of that special light employed by God in order to start the creative process, a light ultimately stored away for the righteous in the Hereafter (see Questions 295–296).

300. Is light blessed in the context of any other rituals?

A blessing over the light of two (or more) candles inaugurates the Shabbat and the festivals. A special light is lit on Yom Kippur to atone for the departed souls, for as we have observed, light is symbolic of the soul (see Question 290). A candle is also used in the *havdalah* ceremony, at the conclusion of Shabbat, to indicate that use of fire may now be resumed.

Blessings over nature's lights include the benediction over the appearance of lightning, and over the light of the rainbow's illumination of the spectrum.

301. Are there any other religious contexts in which lights are used?

It is customary in some congregations to light candles in synagogue for the duration of the morning and evening services, as well as in a home where a circumcision is taking place. Karo refers to a custom in his day that, on the day he brings his child to synagogue for the first time (on a weekday), a father would also bring a wax candle to be lit there.[5]

It was the custom in medieval communities for the bridegroom's best man to carry two lit candles to the chupah. The popular explanation of this practice was that it was an auspicious augury. This is on account of the fact that the *gematria* (numerical value) of the Hebrew word for a candle (*ner*) is 250. Two candles therefore add up to 500; and that is also the *gematria* of the phrase in Genesis, *p'ru ur'vu*, 'Be fruitful and multiply!'

The fifteenth-century authority, *Tashbetz* (R. Shimon ben Tzemach Duran), also reports a rather dangerous practice of juggling with lighted candles during a chupah, in order to generate the same jollity as the Temple Succot water-drawing festivity of *Bet Ha-Shoevah*, when the great sages would do the same.[6]

The custom of carrying lights to a chupah was particularly cherished in Oriental Sefardic communities, and, through their influence, has gained in popularity in the State of Israel today, where it is generally the mothers of bride and groom who carry the candles.

BANISHING THE DEMONS WITH LIGHT

302. But surely the origin of a custom like that must have been more elemental than a mere wish to create a rather forced gematria connection?

Perceptively asked! The truth is that the origin of the custom of bringing candles to a chupah lies in the realm of pure superstition, and is intrinsically connected with the other practices of having the bride walk around her bridegroom and the breaking of a glass. An extensive and wide-ranging study of these wedding practices has been undertaken by Jacob Z. Lauterbach,[7] and we can do no more than indicate, in a few words, his conclusions.

In antiquity everyone, even the most religious, believed in the existence of malevolent demons. The Talmud itself has many references to them and advice on how to detect and counteract them. Popular belief had it that they envied human happiness, and especially coveted the beauty of young women and the sexual pleasure afforded to humans. They were thus particularly envious of bridegrooms and sought to do them physical harm in order that they might carry off their brides and gratify their passion for them.

In different places they had their own favoured methods of countering the threat of the demons. The protection of bride and groom was paramount; and hence the origin of the best man and best maid or bridesmaids, whose primary task is to stay with, and guard, their charges the entire day of the wedding.

As the groom is the first target of attack, as soon as the ceremony commences the bride walks around her groom seven times, thereby making a 'magic circle' around him, through which the demons cannot penetrate. Secondly, it was believed that demons have a preference for dark places, and eschew the light. Hence, in order to deter them, *it was the practice to bring candles to the chupah in order to intensify the illumination.*

According to the popular folklore, demons were alarmed by loud noises, especially that of breaking glass. Hence the custom of breaking a glass at the end of the chupah. The shout *mazal tov* that erupts to accompany that act also has a superstitious significance, the term *mazal* being an astrological name for each of the twelve Zodiacal signs. *Mazal tov*, in that special context, was a toast, therefore, to the young couple's 'luck' (as determined by their respective propitious Zodiacal interaction) in being able to consummate their marriage without demonic mishap. This interpretation of the practice is supported by the fourteenth century *Kol Bo*, which states that 'the glass is hurled at the northern wall of the synagogue (demons were believed to lurk in the spouts of the northern walls of houses), after which bride and groom are rushed away from the chupah to their bridal chamber'. The breaking of the glass, causing the demons to scuttle away, provided the couple with a brief window of opportunity to repair speedily to their new home and consummate their marriage. For, according to the popular belief, once she ceased to be a virgin, the demons' interest in her evaporated.

Thus, the lighting of candles at a chupah must be viewed in its wider, folklorist context, with the *gematria* 'explanation' as no more than a desperate attempt to provide a more religiously-acceptable, substitute interpretation.

NOTES
1. See Exodus 28:17–21.
2. See also, Numbers 27:21; I Samuel 28:6.
3. Talmud *Hagigah* 12a.
4. For more on the Jewish calendar, see Jeffrey M. Cohen, *1001 Questions and Answers on Rosh Hashanah and Yom Kippur* (New Jersey: Jason Aronson, 1997), pp.10–15.
5. See Bet Yosef on *Tur Orach Chayyim* 308.
6. Quoted in J.D. Eisenstein, *Otzar Dinim Uminhagim* (New York: Hebrew Publishing Co., 1938), p.274.
7. See Jacob Z. Lauterbach, 'The Ceremony of Breaking a Glass at Weddings', *Hebrew Union College Annual*, v, 2 (1925), pp.351–80.

10

The Chanukah Lights and Their Underlying Philosophy

303 Is there any philosophical significance in the fact that we go beyond the basic mitzvah of lighting just one light per night per household, to add an extra light with each succeeding night?

By lighting, not merely tonight's light, but also the lights that have burnt on previous nights, we affirm that indissoluble bond of gratitude and identity with all the 'lights', all the enlightenment and spiritual creativity, of the generations that have preceded ours. We express our appreciation, thereby, of the heritage they have handed down to us and of their heroic efforts to secure 'the miracle' of our national survival and sense of renewal.

304. From a conceptual point of view, would it not have made more sense to follow the view of Shammai and commence on the first night with all eight lights burning, to symbolize the intensity of the great miracle and redemption achieved?

One could argue that. After all, it is at the very inauguration of our major festivals that we recite the *Shehecheyanu*, which blesses God for having preserved us alive to witness the joyful and sacred occasion. We do not recite that blessing on subsequent days of the festival.

Conceptually, however, Hillel's way, which ascends gradually, adding but one light each night until the full and climactic illumination is reached on the last night, represents a far more relevant message for a festival of national deliverance. It symbolizes that every stage in our people's long and bitter struggle for survival and independence in our own land could never have been achieved without the individual contributions of countless unsung heroes. It teaches that it is not just to the famous names that we owe a debt of unbounded gratitude – men such as Theodore Herzl, Chaim Weizmann, David Ben-Gurion and Rav Kook, who blazed onto the firmament of modern Zionist history like meteorites, hastening our millennial dream along the path to fulfillment – but to countless thousands of individual 'lights', who gave of their all, by way of military, moral, material and spiritual support, and with so many surrendering their very lives in the national cause. Our achievements are their achievements. By the light of their dreams and constructive effort do we continue to enjoy the light of independence. This is symbolized in the gradual accumulations of lights, until the climactic eight are finally attained.

305. We have referred to the halachic rationales offered in the Talmud for the respective views of Hillel and Shammai regarding the number of lights to be lit on each successive night. Can their views be explained in any other way?

There might well have been an additional, psychological motivation. Hillel and Shammai lived in the turbulent period when the Roman occupation of Judea was becoming more and more unbearable. Reaction to it was split between those like Hillel (and his disciple, Rabban Yochanan ben Zaccai) who espoused a diplomatic and pacifistic approach to the enemy, and those who, like the zealot disciples of Shammai, espoused armed insurrection.

The lighting of the Chanukiah might well have symbolized, for them, the issue of how to restore the light of Jewish independence and sovereignty to the Jewish people. Hillel encouraged slow and quiet diplomacy – the slow, but gradual, increasing of the number of lights – even if it involved the laborious process of winning small, individual concessions.

Shammai, on the other hand, demanded radical action, in the form of an armed insurrection that involved the mobilization of the entire nation – the lighting of all the eight lights at the outset. Only then, in his estimation, would the nation be able to regain its sovereignty and enjoy peace.

306. Were those respective traits of Hillel and Shammai reflected in any other ways?

They were. Shammai's zeal in wishing to experience a full and immediate achievement of the national objective also motivated both his general outlook and his religious philosophy. Hence we read that he instructed his baby son to fast the entire day of Yom Kippur, and only withdrew his instruction at the earnest intervention of his close friends.[1] Again, when his daughter gave birth to a boy on the festival of Succot, he broke a space in the ceiling over the crib so that the boy might fulfill the mitzvah of Succah.[2] Not surprisingly, then, Shammai demanded the full intensity of the eight lights to be experienced from the very outset, though the festival was still in its infancy.

307. Were there any other areas in which those respective approaches of Hillel and Shammai were given expression?

Indeed. They may be discerned in their respective attitudes to converts to Judaism and to the less observant. A famous story records how a would-be convert came to Shammai, offering to convert if the master would teach him the Torah while he stood on one leg. Shammai drove him out of his presence with a rebuke. When he went to Hillel, his request was treated with respect and indulgence.[3] Thus, Hillel was prepared to kindle a single light of spirituality, however dim its initial glow, working up gradually to the highest and broadest level of illumination. Shammai, on the other hand, was prepared to entertain nothing less than a total commitment – all eight lights – from the very outset.

KARO'S FAMOUS QUESTION

308. Why do we commemorate the Chanukah miracle by kindling on eight nights? If the jar they discovered contained sufficient oil to burn for one night, then surely the miracle was that it continued to burn for a further seven nights?

This question was first aired by the sixteenth century halachist and codifier, Joseph Karo, in his magnum opus, *Bet Yoseph*,[4] and many ingenious and tortuous answers have been suggested.

Karo himself offers two solutions. The first is that the Temple authorities, realizing that it would take them eight days in order to secure fresh olives and process and refine them for use as Temple oil, actually separated the contents of the surviving jar into eighths, with the intention of having the Chanukiah burn but for a few hours each night. The miracle lay in the fact that even on the first night, though they only nourished the Chanukiah with an eighth of its normal requirement, it nevertheless continued to burn brightly throughout the succeeding twenty-four hours.

Karo's second suggestion was that the Temple authorities were resigned to the fact that they only had enough oil in the jar to burn for one day, and they therefore poured it all into the Chanukiah. At the end of that day, when they looked at the oil level, they discovered that it had hardly become depleted. Thus, even the first day was characterized as miraculous, since the oil they had found was clearly invested with unusually potent properties, enabling it to burn for eight times its normal capacity.

309. Did Karo's answers convince the authorities?

As with most rabbinic issues, there is rarely just one approach. The *Turei Zahav*, for one, is dissatisfied with Karo's answers, feeling sure that, had the situation been as Karo described, the early Talmudic sages would certainly have recorded that additional aspect of the miracle, and how the Temple authorities organized themselves in relation to the provision of the first day's allocation of oil.

His own answer is to refer to the biblical story of the prophet Elisha (II Kings ch.4), who was entreated by the widow of one of his disciples to help relieve her destitute state. Elisha asked her what she possessed, to which she replied that she had but one flask of oil in her home. He told her to borrow containers from all her friends and to pour out from her flask into those containers. Miraculously, her flask continued to pour out oil unabated until all the vessels were filled.

The *Zohar*, commenting on that episode, states that Elisha was constrained to ask her what she possessed, and to use the existing oil in her possession as the basis of the miracle to be performed, since 'God's way is never to perform a miracle *ex nihilo*.' It does not matter how minute is the base element, God will augment it. He will not repeat, however, the incomparable act of Creation to produce something out of nothing.

Thus, argues our authority, for a miracle to have occurred on the second day, there must have been some residual oil left over from the first day's burning, which served as the base element for the miracle of the second day's burning. It follows then, that not all the oil from the first day could have been exhausted; and because we are told that only sufficient oil for the first day's burning was found, of necessity a miracle must have occurred on the first day also, with the light burning for the entire day on a little less than a full day's supply of oil. (Clearly, the same miraculous procedure was followed on each succeeding day, with the basis of each day's miracle having been provided from some of the previous day's oil supply.)

310. Have we any other answer to Karo's question?

A book called *Kometz Minchah* offers a charming explanation of why we celebrate the miracle for eight days, notwithstanding the fact that there was sufficient oil for the first day. He offers a parable of a wealthy Jewish merchant who was travelling to the market town carrying with him eight bags full of gold coins in order to purchase his stock,

On the journey he was at attacked by highwaymen who seized seven of the eight bags. Miraculously, he succeeded in concealing just one bag on his person. When he arrived at the town, he enlisted the help of the community leaders, and promised them that if, through their efforts, he got his sacks back, he would donate a tenth of the money to the local charitable chest.

The community leaders immediately set about hiring some locals, and, as luck would have it, they succeeded in apprehending the robbers, and restored the seven stolen bags to the grateful merchant.

When the community leaders came to collect the 10 per cent donation that he had originally promised as reward, a dispute broke out between them. The merchant had carefully counted out a tenth of each of the seven bags that had been returned to him, whereas the leaders claimed that he was also obliged to pay a tenth of the *eighth* bag, since that bag had also played a significant part in securing the return of his money.

'After all', they claimed, 'it was only the fact that you were still, miraculously, in possession of that particular bag of money that persuaded us to go and hire the locals to apprehend the robbers. Without that, you would have got nothing back!'

It was the same, claims our author, with the sole remaining jar of oil in the possession of the Maccabees. Had it not been for the miracle of the discovery of that jar, which eluded the entire Greek ransackers of the Temple, there would have been no oil to serve as the basis of the miracle which lay, after all, in the extension of the capacity of that first day's supply. And it is for that reason that the first day merits to be placed in the same miraculous category as the subsequent seven days.

311. Surely Judaism counsels us not to rely on miracles. Once the Maccabees realized that the jar they had found possessed insufficient oil to burn for the entire period required, why did they bother to light it at all?

It is a valid question. Given their lack of expectation that any such miracle would be performed, we may well question what was to be gained by their having the Menorah burn for one day and then having to wait another seven days before the ritual could be properly reinstated?

We have no clear answer to this question. The Maccabees surely knew that, by biblical law, the Temple lights were to be 'perpetual' (Exodus 27:20), burning uninterruptedly. To have had the Menorah burning for just one day, followed by a long interruption, would actually have been not only demeaning to its ritual, but also in flagrant contradiction of that basic principle.

We may speculate, therefore, that they lit it more as a ritual celebration of victory. Light is, indeed, a symbol of joyful thanksgiving, as referred to in the Book of Esther's account of the victory of the Jews over their enemies: *And the Jews had* light *and joy, gladness and honour* (Esther 8:16). It is also a symbol of deliverance from enemies, as in the phrase, *The Lord is my light and my salvation* (Psalm 27:1). It is possible, therefore, that when they lit they had no intention to fulfil thereby the biblical prescription.

312. Is there any other underlying message to be derived from the fact that they lit it with the expectation that it would burn for but one day?

David Hartman sees the greatest significance in their willingness to light for but one initial day, in the face of many who must have counseled waiting until the conditions were ripe for the reintroduction of the full, proper and uninterrupted ritual. For Hartman,

the 'miracle' of Jewish spiritual survival throughout its history of wandering and oppression may best be described by our people's courage to live without assurance of success, and to focus on how to begin a process without knowledge of how it would end...Human initiative is undermined by the rationalization that since the completion of a task is not assured, there is no point making the required effort to begin...One ought to pour infinite yearnings even into small vessels. The strength to continue and to persevere grows by virtue of the courage to initiate a process by lighting the first flame...Those who decided to proclaim the establishment of the State of Israel in the twentieth century were Jews who had learned the message of Chanukah well.[5]

WHY THE ANTICIPATED EIGHT-DAY WAIT FOR OIL?

313. But, why did the Jews anticipate having to wait as long as eight days before they might obtain a fresh supply of pure olive oil?

Various explanations are offered, the most popular being that the olive groves which supplied the oil were located some four days journey from Jerusalem. Hence the eight days – four days there, four days back – to obtain it.

314. But do we have any proof of that?

There is no literary record that discloses the source of the olive oil at that early period. For that reason, other suggestions have been offered for the lengthy period the Maccabees expected to have to wait, such as that, as a result of the war, the entire nation was placed in the category of *temei'ei meitim*, 'those ritually contaminated through contact with a corpse'.

Now, the biblically-prescribed purification period for such impurity was seven days.[6] As they could not press and prepare the oil until they had completed their purification, they would have required a further day, the eighth, to complete that. (It goes without saying that this latter explanation takes no account of the distance that they would then have had to travel, after the completion of their purification, to obtain the oil and return to Jerusalem with it.)

315. So was there no way that, even before purification, they might handle the single jar of oil that they found with the High Priest's seal intact?

The Talmudists believed there was, and presumed that the Maccabean High Priestly family would have known how to overcome this problem by employing halachic ingenuity.

One way around the difficulty would have been to employ a wooden vice, with which to grip the jar of oil in order to pour it into the Menorah. Wooden implements (*peshutei kli eitz*) are not susceptible to ritual impurity (like the earth from which the tree's wood is obtained), and, as long as direct contact with the jar was avoided, the oil would not have become contaminated.

316. Would there have been any other way out of the problem?

Some halachists take the view that the nation's ritual impurity would not have created any problem. This is because of another law, to the effect that *tumah hutra b'tzibbur*, 'communal obligations override the prohibition of offering in a state of impurity'.[7] The Maccabees would therefore have actually been permitted to use contaminated oil in an emergency. They did not have to avail themselves of that emergency ruling, however, because they were overtaken by the miraculous occurrence of finding one solitary jar of pure oil that continued burning.

317. But would not the Menorah itself have been rendered impure?

Sorry, but again your question has been pre-empted, by the Talmud. It relates that the Maccabees actually replaced the contaminated Menorah with a wooden one that, as we have said (see Question 315) is not susceptible to impurity, and so would not itself become contaminated by having been fashioned by people who were themselves impure.[8]

318. But do we have any textual evidence to support that contention?

We do. The Book of the Maccabees states that, on regaining control of the Temple, 'they made new holy appurtenances, and *brought* the Menorah ... into the Temple'.[9]

This is clarified in the second Book of the Maccabees, where it states that, 'when they purified the Temple, they made a replacement altar...and lamps' (II Maccabees 10:3).

WHY SUCH SHORT-BURNING LIGHTS

319. Why do we only pour enough oil into the Chanukiah, or use candles of a size, to last only a half hour, when the Temple Menorah burnt the entire night?

We are essentially following here the approach of Karo's Bet Yoseph who explained that we observe eight and not seven days (there having been enough oil in their jar to last for the first day) on the basis of the assumption that, rather than exhaust all their oil the first day, the Hasmoneans poured out only an eighth of that jar's oil on the first night. The miracle occurred on that very first night, when that small amount of oil lasted the entire night – a miracle that was repeated each of the succeeding nights. And to commemorate the fact that they only used a little oil each night, we do the same. We focus on the Chanukah miracle of the Menorah, not on its normal usage.

HIDDUR MITZVAH: GRADATIONS OF BEAUTY

320. The talmudic source for the lighting of the Chanukiah refers to three qualitative levels of beauty with which the mitzvah of lighting may be endowed: The basic level, wherein one light per household is lit; a more beautiful (*mehadrin*) level, wherein each member of the household lights one light; and an incomparably beautiful (*mehadrin min ha-mehadrin*) level, wherein an increasing number (according to Hillel) or a decreasing number (*Shammai*) of lights are lit each night (see Question 181). Why is the Chanukah mitzvah endowed with these comparative levels of beauty, which are not applied to any other mitzvah?

The *Bet Ha-Levi* suggests that it was because beauty lay at the root of the act of lighting the Temple oil on that first Chanukah. He explains that, since there was enough oil to burn for one complete day, but for no longer, the Maccabees could have provided very fine wicks – an eighth of the usual thickness – which would have enabled a thin tongue of flame to be kept burning for the entire eight days, until fresh oil could be provided. That would have satisfied the requirement of the basic Temple mitzvah, as there was no law governing the minimum thickness of the wicks.

The miracle lay, therefore, in the realm of the *beautification* of the mitzvah, enabling the wicks to be maintained at their usual, impressive width, in order to provide the brightest illumination. Hence the sages applied gradations of beauty to the performance of this mitzvah alone.

321. Can we explain it in any other way?

My own view is that it may have been intended as a counter to the predominant aspect of Greek culture, which was its inordinate emphasis on the beauty of the human form and its worship of majestic and beautiful sculptures personifying the Olympian gods. Apposite in this respect is the comment of the sages on the verse, *God will enlarge Jafet* [Greece], *and he shall dwell in the tents of Shem* (Genesis 9:27), namely, that the beauty of Greece will reside within the tents of Israel.

Perhaps this was Israel's first tangible application of that prophecy. Whereas Greece made beauty her mistress, Israel made it her handmaid, pressing it into the service of God through such concepts as *hiddur mitzvah*, the beautification of the sacred act.

322. What precise sentiment is implied in hiddur mitzvah, performing the sacred act in the most beautiful way?

Concern for the aesthetics of the mitzvah betokens a desire to go far beyond the mere perfunctory response to a religious instruction, beyond the mere call of duty. It demonstrates a profound pride in and sense of commitment to what one is doing; it reflects a heightened sense of occasion and a wish to adorn everything associated with the service of one's Maker. This was expressed so directly and passionately by the Israelites in their 'Song of the Red Sea': *This is my God, and I shall glorify Him* (Exodus 15:2).

323. Why was the lighting of the Chanukiah made into a home ritual?

This is a valid query, since the miracle of the oil took place in the Temple, and in relation to the *Menorah*, the candelabrum, a ritual appurtenance related exclusively to the Temple. It would have been logical, therefore, after the destruction of the Temple, for the candle lighting to have continued exclusively as a synagogue ritual.

The simple and historical answer is that, at the time of the Chanukah miracle (165 BCE) the synagogue was not yet an established institution. The sages, in their determination to popularize an event and a festival that did not have biblical authority, and to ensure that it did not become just another Temple ritual, looked to the other main focus of spirituality outside of the Temple, namely the Jewish home.

Perhaps they were also making the point that, in the battle against assimilation – which is what the festival recalls – the most effective arsenal that we Jews can employ is the Jewish home. Its moral spirit, the vibrancy of its joyful religious celebrations and rituals, and the emotional stability that it provides, should equip the Jew to be able to counter even the most seductive enticement to assimilation.

324. Is there any deeper meaning underlying the position in the home where the lights are prescribed to be placed?

The Talmud states that

One should place the Chanukah lamp by the front door, on the outside. If one dwells in an upper storey, he should place it by the window, overlooking the street. In times of danger, however, it is sufficient to place it on the table, inside one's home.[10]

The Talmudic sages, it should not be forgotten, lived under foreign domination. In Israel it was the harsh Roman occupation. In Babylonia, the main Jewish Diaspora, it was the more benign rule of the Parthians. We may assume that the above prescription, to publicize the miracle to passers-by, originated in Israel. It was a bold and courageous gesture, therefore, effectively cocking a snook at the Romans, who assuredly would have learnt of the significance of the festival.

The celebration of a great victory over Greece, the former mistress of the world, and the annual highlighting, in that dramatic manner, of God's miraculous intervention on behalf of His people, was an implicit rallying call to Israel to aim towards a repeat of that situation, and rid the holy land of the present tyrants.

325. Is there any other significance underlying the positioning of the Chanukiah?

David Hartman gives a more symbolic explanation of the prescription to publicize the miracle by an act of external lighting, other than in time of persecution:

> In lighting the Chanukah lamp, the Jew announces to the outside world: This is my flame ... I am prepared to share my light with you and to be an active member within a shared universe of experience. If, however, you seek to extinguish my flame, then I shall remove my lamp from the windowsill and place it on my private table, to be viewed by my family alone ...
>
> We choose not to hide the flame of our spiritual tradition within the secluded confines of our people, but rather we wish to have our flame radiate light in the marketplaces of history ... Now that the Menorah has been taken off our private tables and placed in the window for all to see, we must examine whether the light itself is beautiful and inspiring.[11]

SHABBAT OR CHANUKAH LIGHTS: WHICH TAKE PRIORITY?

326. Which is the more important of the two: the Chanukah lights or the Shabbat lights?

This matter is addressed by both Maimonides, at the very end of his Laws of Chanukah,[12] and Karo (see Question 287). They both emphasize the importance of the mitzvah, to the extent that even one who is on charity should borrow or sell his clothes to fulfil it.

And yet, Maimonides points out, if one had sufficient money to buy oil for only one of those two mitzvot, he should spend it on acquiring oil for the Sabbath lights.

His reason is that the latter were introduced in order to increase the illumination in the home, and to create a serene and harmonious spirit, for 'peace and tranquillity are the most important things in life'.[13]

327. But, surely, home tranquillity, however important, cannot compete with the significance of the divine miracle which Chanukah commemorates?

It can, indeed. In the words of Maimonides, 'For the Almighty allows His own sacred name to be blotted out for the objective of restoring harmony to a strained marital relationship'.[14]

He is referring here to the wife whose husband suspects her of adultery. She is tested with the 'bitter waters' (see Numbers ch. 5), into which was placed a parchment inscribed with God's name. The waters washed away and absorbed the name inscribed, converting it into a potent and supernatural purgation for determining the innocence or otherwise of the woman.

So it is that, without light on Shabbat eve, the harmony of the home could so easily be strained, with members of the family stumbling over furniture, spilling food or dropping dishes. This could easily develop into friction between the partners. To avoid that situation is more important to God than any consideration of His own honour. It follows, therefore, that the Shabbat lights are more important to Him than the lights in commemoration even of a miracle that He wrought.

328. Can this priority of the Shabbat lights be rationalized in any other way?

We believe it can. On Chanukah, God dramatically interfered in the laws of nature, demonstrating His ability to change them at will and whim, by investing a quantity of oil with seven or eight times its natural capacity. Chanukah relates a 'tale of the unexpected'. On Shabbat, on the other hand, God consciously withdraws from the driver's seat, from presiding over nature's control system. He 'rests', and puts the world on automatic pilot, enabling it to glide along its programmed path.

Shabbat symbolizes regularity, familiarity, the security of the known, a world where little that is dramatic occurs in our daily lives – no great personal victories, no unexpected business deals, a world wherein we are at peace with ourselves and those around us. Shabbat is the antithesis of the capricious workaday world wherein man is at the mercy of unusual situations and unexpected forces. If we have sufficient money for just one light – Chanukah or Shabbat – most of us would prefer the experience of the latter. And the Halachah sympathizes with, and codifies, that decision.

329. Is there any special message underlying the recommendation that each person should light his own Chanukah light, something which is not required in the case of the Shabbat lights?

I believe there is a profound message in this. Sabbath observance presupposes and demands faith in a Creator and commitment to His exacting laws. The fraternity that is so committed is comparatively small. Chanukah, on the other hand, and the privilege of celebrating its miracle, is the legacy of the entire generation of Jews whose victory secured it.

The victory was secured by an impressive coalition and demonstration of unity on the part of Jews whose religious affiliation covered every shade of the spectrum: pietistic Chasidim, mainstream observant and less observant Jews, nationalistic Jews, modernizing, assimilating and Hellenized Jews.

The message is that, when the chips are down, none of them should be written off. The Jewish spark, nestling deep and sometimes unrecognized, within them all, can so easily be ignited, so that they may be summoned to display the greatest heroism in order to guarantee their nation's survival and the inalienable right of those of their brethren who wish to observe their faith without let or hindrance.

In the Holocaust, that message was hauntingly brought home, as Jews of every and no persuasion stood shoulder to shoulder in the line for the gas chambers. And in modern-day Israel this message is also incontrovertible. For, in all her battles for survival, young representatives of every shade of political and religious affiliation have put those differences into their proper perspective and fought under a single banner. That is the only route to survival in war and to national harmony and progress in peace. And that is the message that we need to extract and proclaim each year from the events of Chanukah.

330. Is there any other message to be derived from the Talmudic recommendation that each member of the family light his own Chanukiah?

From a homiletical point-of-view, this aspect of Chanukah, the festival of 'dedication', teaches a very practical lesson: that the only way to inspire dedication, especially in the hearts of young people, is to make them full participants in the religious experience. They will not be inspired if they are relegated to the role of spectator, or if the religion, the synagogue or community leadership does not accord them the requisite respect, concern, welcome and attention.

Everyone has a 'light' to kindle; something unique to contribute. Our national and spiritual illumination is diminished if only some are invited to do so.

WHAT CONSTITUTES A MINOR FESTIVAL

331. Chanukah and Purim are designated as Minor Festivals. In what way do they differ from the Major Festivals?

Firstly, Chanukah and Purim are not the only Minor Festivals. In this category we also include *Rosh Chodesh*, *Lag Ba'Omer*, *Chamisha Asar B'Av*, *Tu Bishvat*, and, the recently added festivals of *Yom Ha-Atzma'ut* and *Yom Yerushalayim*. They are categorized as 'minor', primarily, because they date from after the period of the Pentateuch. Unlike *Pesach*, *Shavuot* and *Succot*, there were no special sacrifices prescribed to mark their celebration in Temple times.

In this, Chanukah and Purim differ from *Rosh Chodesh* (the new moon), which is also designated a Minor Festival, notwithstanding that it is mentioned in the Pentateuch. The reason for this is that *Rosh Chodesh* originally did enjoy the status of a full festival, with a special additional sacrifice prescribed to be offered in the Temple, and a celebratory family meal taken at home.[15] The Torah did not prescribe cessation of work on *Rosh Chodesh*, as it did in the case of all the other major festivals. Hence, in the course of time, especially once the Temple was destroyed and the highlight of the occasion – the coming of witnesses to the specially-convened calendrical court at the Temple to testify to having seen the new moon the previous evening – was abandoned, the festival lost its appeal. Its significance was further eroded in the fourth century CE, when Hillel II introduced the fixed calendar, after which it became, for most, an ordinary working day. And this, for practical purposes, characterizes the difference between a minor and major festival.

332. Is there any differentiation in status within the Minor Festivals category?

There is. *Rosh Chodesh* certainly leads the rest, both for the reason we have just given, as well as on account of the fact that, halachically, a more frequently-recurring festival takes priority over the less frequently celebrated.

Chanukah follows, and leads Purim, on account of the fact that *Hallel* is recited on Chanukah, and not on Purim. Secondly, Chanukah was introduced to commemorate an event of vital importance to Jewry in the Holy Land, whereas Purim was only of consequence to the Diaspora community of Persia. Thirdly, Chanukah is an eight-day festival, whereas Purim is, for most, a one-day event; and, finally, Chanukah has a religious ritual, in which every member participates, and which permeates the home, from where it is beamed to the outside, to engage and envelop even the passers-by. The reading of the *Megillah*, on the other hand, is performed by one person, with everyone else a passive listener, and the Purim *seudah* (banquet) is a private ritual, enjoyed behind closed doors in the company of family and friends alone. At the end of the list come the other Minor Festivals referred to above.

333. Was there any wider backcloth against which the struggle between the Jews and the Greeks was enacted?

Chief Rabbi Jonathan Sacks[16] explains that struggle as part of the age-old legacy of strife between Jacob and Esau.

The Maccabean situation was not merely a struggle between Greeks and Jews, but also between traditional Jews and their Hellenized, assimilated brethren. The latter perceived Judaism as parochial, whereas to be a Greek in their eyes meant being cosmopolitan. They envied the power, wealth and self-assurance of the Greeks, and their purpose in assimilating was to broaden their horizons and transform themselves into 'citizens of the world'.

Their inability to define themselves in terms of their own heritage, and their passionate desire to don the mantle and acquire the complexion of an alien culture, is reminiscent of Jacob's naive attempt to camouflage his real identity by dressing up in Esau's clothes, in order to hoodwink his father, Isaac, into believing that it was Esau who stood before him, thereby enabling Jacob to secure his father's blessing by that subterfuge.

The Torah states, 'And he [Isaac] inhaled the scent of his [Esau's] clothes (*b'gadav*), and he blessed him [Jacob]' (Genesis 27:27). The Talmud on this verse states, 'Do not read *b'gadav* ('his clothes'), but *bogdav* ('those who would, in the future time, *deal treacherously* with him').[17] In other words, his father, Isaac, realizing subconsciously that Jacob was being disingenuous – that he was effecting the identity of an Esau – feared greatly that, in the future, Jacob's offspring might similarly emulate their ancestor, donning the mantle and trappings of their enemies, and, by attempting to exchange their faith and identity for that of an alien culture, suffer thereby a tragic fate.

The message of that internal Jewish struggle, according to Sacks, is that as long as Jacob (the one who 'grasped the heel' of Esau), continues to do just that – to be in hot pursuit of an alien culture – rather than emerging and maturing into a confident 'Israel' (one who is prepared 'to grapple with God and man'), he will never be able to meet Esau on his own terms. We only win the respect of the gentile world when we proclaim our own distinctive values and affirm our own unique identity.

334. Does Chanukah address, in any way, our contemporary situation?

It does. The message of Chanukah relates to how we Jews deal with cultural assimilation. In the days of the Maccabees the threat to our values was Hellenism. In our day it is secularism, nihilism, materialism, and the same obsession with fitness and the beautifying of the body while neglecting the soul. The Hellenistic idolatry, with its attribution of ultimate power, and the control of nature, to a panoply of capricious gods, is paralleled by the current attempt of scientific man to usurp God's position as master and controller of everything in the universe, and even, by genetic engineering, to shape man, literally, in the image of man, rather than viewing him as a unique creation, bearing within him the imprint of the Divine.

335. Is there any parallel between the way Jews reacted to Hellenism and the way they react to its modern-day counterparts?

There is. *Plus ça change* ... The same reactions may truly be discerned in our day. When there is a threat to the moral integrity of a society, when the cherished values of men of faith are derided, undermined and replaced by the quicksand of transient fads, and when the latter are so appealing to the immature and so bewitching to the gullible, there are two main responses: Those who are spiritually weak will, in the main, succumb, and jump on the bandwagon of 'modernity', with some trendy Jews in that category going even further, and becoming the arch-promoters and entrepreneurs of its philosophy. Those, on the other hand, who are more mature and perceptive, and who are fearful for what a valueless society can do to their precious offspring, will choose to retrench, to withdraw within strict, self-imposed disciplinary guidelines, and will choose to create around themselves and their families the cocoon of a society composed exclusively of like-minded souls. They will seal themselves off from the outside society and its blandishments, and will, in consequence, divorce themselves more and more from the secular reality, to live in a cosy, non-threatening, exclusively spiritually-orientated, world, ensuring that their offspring marry and bring up their children within those same confines.

In Hasmonean times it was the Essenes who reacted in that way. They fled the corrupt city life for a quasi-monastic existence in the Judean desert, with some wandering as far away as Damascus. It was impossible to infiltrate their society; and those who sought admission to their ranks had to serve several years of probation and prove themselves worthy by rigorous attention to study, purification rites, prayer, abstinence and acts of benevolence, sacrifice and piety. There was another group, referred to by Josephus as *Chasidim*, pietists, who may or may not have been Essenes. They also adopted a more rigorous religious life-style, displaying a readiness to lay down their lives for their beliefs and observances.

In modern times, we have witnessed a parallel expression of revulsion against modernity on the part of a numerically expanding religious right wing, especially in Israel, America and Britain. It was spearheaded by the unprecedented growth of Chasidic sects, the largest, most influential and high profile of which is the *Chabad* or Lubavitch movement.

The latter possess an admirable, passionate love for every Jewish soul, and a missionary zeal and degree of helpfulness second to none. They promote a Jewish self-reliance and demand of their initiates a total allegiance to the dictates of their sect, including a uniformity of dress and general life-style, commitment to religious fundamentalism and to a complex mystical system. They are also characterized by a veneration of their past leaders or *Rebbes* to a spiritual level 'just a little lower than the angels'. Indeed, their late, supreme Rebbe of Lubavitch, Rabbi Menachem Mendel Schneersohn, of blessed memory, was invested by most of his disciples with a Messianic identity.

The clannishness of most other Chasidic sects, their religious fundamentalism, and withdrawal from secular society, parallels very closely the response of the Essenes and Chasidim in the Maccabean period. And just as Jerusalem and its spiritual centre was the catalyst for such a reaction in those far-off days, so it is in the context of the ideological ferment in the present-day.

CONCEPTUAL DIFFERENCES BETWEEN CHANUKAH AND PURIM

336. Is there any conceptual distinction in the rationale underlying the respective festivals of Chanukah and Purim?

Chanukah demonstrates just how vulnerable we are to cultural assimilation, as represented by Hellenism, once we have achieved independence in our own land and are no longer unified by a common threat to our survival. Once the military commander's instructions are stilled, and replaced by those of the heavenly

Commander, from whose service there is no demobilization, the burden seems to become too heavy for many to bear. When that happens, they begin to experiment with alternative philosophies and life-styles, with a pell-mell sprint towards the freedom offered by modernity, a freedom that ultimately proves to be merely a synonym for moral licence, indiscipline and nihilism.

Chanukah demonstrates that a Jewish land must be undergirded by a Jewish religious culture. Without that, we loose that unique identity for which a land of our own is an indispensable conduit. Without that, it is difficult to justify Jewish sovereignty, a point made by the prophet Samuel when the people demanded a king, 'so that we may be like all the other nations' (I Samuel 8:20). Samuel's response was that the request was unjustifiable, because 'the Lord thy God is thy king!' (12:12)

Purim, on the other hand, represents the struggle of our people against crass anti-Semitism. Haman had no alternative religion or culture that he wished to impose on Jewry. He was merely concerned with wiping out any rival loyalties. His was also a blind and irrational hatred of the Jew, of the sort that was to bedevil Jewish history from his time onwards.

337. Which of the two – Chanukah's cultural assimilation or Purim's anti-Semitism – is the easiest to combat?

In a sense, Purim's anti-Semitism. For once the source of the antipathy was identified, overwhelmed and destroyed, the Jews of Persia were able to return to a state of security and normalcy, with their future secured.

With an insidious philosophy, such as Hellenism, however, which penetrated and captivated the minds and hearts of an entire younger generation, the defeat of its protagonists and disseminators was only the first stage in the battle to eradicate their ideas. For, it was not only the Greeks who were the conduits of Hellenism, but also the Jews that had come under its influence, and who constituted a fifth-column for its continued promotion within Judea.

What was required, in such a situation, was to replace Hellenism, root and branch, with something even more exciting, absorbing and challenging. That was the task facing the spiritual leaders of the Maccabean and subsequent periods.

338. How did they face that challenge?

By making Jewish education a state priority; by removing the mystique with which the priestly fraternity had tended to shroud the ritual and make it inordinately Temple orientated; by forcing the Temple authorities to share their spiritual hegemony with non-priestly Torah teachers, and to recognize the authority of the sages of the newly-established academies. Also, by extracting from the priestly fraternity recognition for a potentially rival institution, the synagogue (the survival of its Greek name is an indicator of the era during which it began to evolve),[18] which, together with the schools of learning, achieved a veritable spiritual revolution.

It is significant in this respect that, in the first chapter of *Pirkei Avot*, which presents a chain of named rabbinic personages who were trail-blazers and torch-bearers of the

Oral law, the first to be identified is Shimon ha-Tzaddik and his disciple, Antigonos of Socho, who were coeval with the Greek period, and who recognized that the only way to counter Hellenism was through providing dynamic Torah leadership and education for the masses.

339. Why did the sages prescribe Hallel, prayers and songs of thanksgiving for Chanukah, but not the festive banquet that is the central feature of Purim?

A Chasidic answer is that Purim commemorates the frustration of the enemy's attempt to achieve the physical destruction of the Jews. Hence we allow the physical aspect of our being to celebrate and have pleasure. On Chanukah, on the other hand, the Greeks' primary objective was not the destruction of Jewry, but the suppression of its spiritual heritage. Hence, on Chanukah, we celebrate in a primarily spiritual manner, with the recitation of psalms and prayers.

The emphasis on the spirituality of Chanukah finds expression in the words of the *haftarah* for the first Shabbat of the festival: 'Not by might, nor by power, but by My Spirit, saith the Lord of Hosts' (Zechariah 4:6).

340. Is there not a theory that the origin of Chanukah actually goes back to an ancient nature festival?

There is such a baseless contention, preserved by Hayyim Schauss in his popular work, *Guide to Jewish Holy Days*. He states:

> The Chanukah lights originated in an old nature festival, that was observed in winter by certain Jewish groups, in the season when the days began to lengthen. In time the lights were eventually tied up with Chanukah.[19]

This theory, a relic of an age when everything Israelite or Jewish was attributed by critical scholars to ancient Near-Eastern mythological notions, has been dismissed, with an appropriate economy of words, by Irving Greenberg in his engaging book, *The Jewish Way*. He states,

> The theory ignores the fact that an actual historical event – purification and rededication of the Temple – occurred and its date is attested to by contemporary accounts. Furthermore, the dedication anniversary was marked every year, and the date is far from a literary (or anthropological) convention. Moreover, 25 Kislev in the year 164 coincides with December 6, not even close to the solstice day.[20]

341. Chanukah invariably coincides with the sidrah *Mikkeitz*. (Between now and the year 2050 it fails to coincide with that sidrah on only four occasions: In 2020, 2023, 2040 and 2047.) Is there any link between the sidrah and the festival?

We can certainly construct one! The sidrah deals with Pharaoh's dream of seven lean cows devouring seven fat cows, without betraying any sign of what they had digested, and of seven lean and blasted sheaves devouring seven goodly sheaves. This could be viewed as symbolic of the small and weak Maccabean freedom-fighters who 'devoured' the mighty Greek army with the help of God, as reflected in the words of the *Al ha-Nisim* prayer: 'You delivered the mighty into the hands of the weak and the many into the hands of the few'.

Mikkeitz is also the account of Joseph rising to prominence in Egypt, acquiring a new, Egyptian name (see Genesis 41:45), being given an Egyptian wife and forgetting his Israelite roots (v.51). This has strong points of contact with the intermarriage, assimilation and Hellenizing process that forms the background to the Maccabean revolt.

Finally, *Mikkeitz* chronicles the on-going saga of the strife between Joseph and his brothers. The latter do not recognize Joseph, who has all the trappings of an Egyptian prince. He is fully assimilated to his new environment: he dresses, speaks and behaves like an Egyptian, whereas his brothers have, of course, retained their Israelite manner. This foreshadows that other aspect of the Chanukah saga: the strife between the assimilated and Hellenized Jews and their traditionalist brethren.

342. We have referred above (see Questions 156 and 171) to the fact that, unlike Purim, Chanukah was not endowed with its own biblical book, or its own Mishnah and Talmudic tractate. Is there any conceptual rationale for this?

Purim commemorates the physical struggle of the Jews of Persia against Haman. The Megillah provides a factual, almost secular, perspective on the events, and hence the name of God is missing from the chronicle. King Achashverosh gave one concession to the Jews: that they were permitted to assemble in order to defend themselves. What ensued was not therefore manifestly miraculous, though we do not rule out the hand of God. Nevertheless, the struggle bore the usual characteristics of a military skirmish between two opposing forces. And the human victory created the festival.

For that reason a Mishnah was required, with its spiritual insights, in order to convert an ordinary human encounter into a divinely ordained victory. One required a Mishnah *Megillah* in order to sanctify those events and to translate them into ritual. One needed a Mishnah and Talmud in order to elevate history into 'His story', to make the ordinary extraordinary and the secular sacred.

Chanukah was quite different. The skirmishes, the battles, the Jewish cause and the victories did not require to be elevated in that same way to the realm of the spiritual. Because, for the Talmudic sages, that was already achieved by the miraculous occurrence which climaxed the physical struggle, namely the miracle of the oil which stamped its unique complexion upon the entire spirit of the victory celebration, upon the festival and upon the ritual.

One cannot augment the uniqueness of a miracle. One cannot enhance the sanctity of a divine intervention in the laws of nature. No Mishnah can disclose any levels of spirituality not already clearly manifested by contemplation of the miraculous occurrence itself. Hence, we suggest, Chanukah did not require to be endowed with a Mishnah or talmudic tractate.

It is for every generation to recall and publicize that miracle and its implications. And that ought to be far more dramatic in its immediacy and appeal, far more profound in its educational and emotional impact, than the study of any rabbinic text.

343. But why was it that the story of Purim was prescribed to be read in synagogue, whereas the events of Chanukah were not accorded such spiritual and ritual honour?

We have already answered this historically. Philosophically, no history book, however gripping its episodes and however dramatic its literary style, can ever compete with a ritual which recalls, re-enacts, and recaptures the mystical experience of a clear manifestation of the finger of God interposing supernaturally into the history of our people. The impact of that upon the collective psyche of our nation is far more intense and far-reaching than the mere reading of some passages from a historical chronicle.

The Maccabean struggle was climaxed by a miraculous enhancement of a Temple ritual that gave a spiritual imprimatur to the entire episode. The events of Purim, on the other hand, were unrelated to any religious ritual. The only way of spiritualizing those events, therefore, was to make the reading of the Megillah an essential part of the synagogue liturgy. And it is that reading, with its reference to 'feasting and celebration' (Esther 9:17, 18) and 'the giving of portions, each man to his neighbour, and gifts to the poor' (9:22), that provides the biblical authority for the transmutation of the events of Purim into a religious ritual.

344. Could there have been any other reason why we read the story of Purim and not of Chanukah

Often it is simple practical considerations that affect liturgical evolution, rather than deep philosophical motivation. The truth is that the story of Purim was written, with contrived literary and and dramatic appeal, in a form that lent itself naturally to synagogue recitation.

We are not suggesting that it was written for synagogue use, since we may assume that it made its appearance in the Persian period, well before the rise of the synagogue as an institution. However, it was written in Hebrew, in a form that lent itself to the addition of textual punctuation and cantillation notes (*neginot*) to facilitate its being chanted in a manner similar to that of the Torah itself. Its conciseness also helped to ease it into the liturgy of Purim day.

The Books of the Maccabees, by contrast, are lengthy, rambling chronicles that would have been impossible to abridge without omitting important aspects of the account. The first book alone runs to sixteen chapters, comprising 923 verses, as contrasted with Esther's ten chapters, totaling a mere 212 verses.

Furthermore, although the first Book of the Maccabees was originally written in Hebrew, that original was lost, since the Judean religious authorities had no wish to preserve the 'external literature'. It was the Church that preserved it, in Greek, Latin and Syriac translations; and that was another reason why no place was found within the later synagogue liturgy for the account of the Maccabean struggle and victory.

345. Did not the Maccabees feel a degree of temerity when they commended their festival of Chanukah to be added to the biblical festivals hitherto observed?

The first thing to remember is that they were not, in fact, creating a precedence, since Mordechai and Esther, several centuries earlier, had already added Purim to the list of Jewry's festivals. Indeed, that festival had been merely to commemorate the deliverance of a Diaspora community, whereas the festival of Chanukah was far more comprehensive in its significance. They may well have reasoned that, while the victory itself may not have merited a special festival – there having been many other great victories in Israel's past history, in the period of the Judges and kings – yet the miraculous divine intervention on this occasion, in order to demonstrate God's special joy in the rededication of His earthly abode, did certainly merit the addition of a religious festival.

346. Could there have been any other motive behind the establishment of this festival?

Bearing in mind that the rise of localized prayer houses all over Judea corresponded with the Maccabean period,[21] and that that embryonic synagogue spelt serious competition for the High Priestly Maccabees, passionately committed to the centrality of worship at the Temple, it is not difficult to imagine that the latter saw the establishment of Chanukah, which marked a reaffirmation of God's choice of the Temple, as serving a useful additional propaganda exercise.

347. Was Chanukah willingly accepted throughout Jewry?

We suspect not. The fact that Judah the Maccabee had to send a special letter to all communities – contained in the second Book of Maccabees[22] – urging them to accept and observe his festival – suggests a certain public reticence to add something new to their tradition.

Sensitivity to the cool response of the communities may underlie the fact that Judah did not give his new festival a name, but presented it variously as, 'a festival of Tabernacles in the month of Kislev',[23] 'a festival of purification of the Temple',[24] and 'a festival of Tabernacles and fire'.[25] He was clearly attempting to soften the opposition by presenting his festival as a mere substitute for the Tabernacles festival that they had been prevented from observing at Jerusalem exactly two months earlier, when the Temple was still in enemy hands. Indeed, the first anniversary of Chanukah was celebrated, 'bearing in their hands the boughs of thick trees, [the fruit of] goodly trees and palm branches, they offered thanksgiving to the One who had enabled them to purify His habitation'.[26] (See Question 132.)

ACHIEVEMENTS OF THE MACCABEAN PERIOD

348. What lasting achievement can be attributed to the Maccabean revolt?

Primarily, it did more than kindle the lights of a Temple Menorah. It kindled numerous spiritual lights that illumined the evolution of Talmudic law and tradition for centuries to come. It is to the Maccabean period that we trace the earliest illustrious teachers and interpreters of Judaism's Oral Law, many of whom were reared in a Hellenistic environment and who, like Antigonos, even bore Greek names. Perhaps it was the challenge of the Hellenistic intellectual and philosophical tradition that energized and stimulated them to apply similar analytical methods to their own traditional lore.

349. What other achievement can be attributed to the Maccabean age?

Of all the cultures that came into contact with Hellenism, Maccabean-age Judaism exhibited the flexibility to retain its authentic identity while at the same time absorbing that which could enrich and renew Judaism. Other cultures were swept away and disintegrated in the avalanche of Greek universalism. The Jews were alone in preserving their identity. They showed themselves to be masters at throwing away the chaff while retaining the staple and nourishing wheat. Thus, for example, they borrowed from Greece the principle of *paideia*, perfection through liberal education, and set up a network of schools in every town and village of Judea. Under the Pharisees, leadership was transferred from the wealthy to the educated classes, with the Torah scholar enjoying a status hitherto reserved for kings and High Priests. Indeed, much of the bitter rivalry between the Pharisees and the priestly Sadducees hinged on that very issue of authority.

The Maccabean revolt rid young Jews of their fixation with athleticism and a life spent at the Greek *gymnasia*. It gave them a pride in their own spiritual achievement and national and cultural independence, to the extent that Jerusalem remained 'the only living centre beyond the authority of Hellenism, the one refuge of independent thought'.[27]

CHANUKAH'S CONTEMPORARY LESSONS

350. What contemporary lesson can be extracted from contemplation of the Maccabean situation?

Irving Greenberg extracts one particularly important lesson, namely, that the pious nucleus that first resisted the onslaught of Hellenism could not have done so without the active moral and military support of so many of their already-assimilating fellow Jews. The latter chose to defend their ancestral heritage rather than the alien, albeit alluring, way-of-life under whose thrall, they realized, they had so naively and readily fallen.

Greenberg's inference from this is that we must not write off assimilating Jews. 'In a showdown (as in 1967 and 1973), many more Jews will be with the cause of

Jewish survival than appears on the surface. A coalition of traditional, acculturating and assimilated Jews pulled off the Maccabean miracle.'[28]

351. Does the miracle of the burning of the oil for eight days have any symbolic message?

For Herman Wouk is certainly does:

> Our whole history is a fantastic legend of a single day's supply of oil lasting eight days; of a flaming bush that is not consumed; of a national life that, in the logic of events, should have flickered and gone out long ago, still burning on.[29]

It is not surprising that Chanukah continues to have such a special place in the hearts of our people, especially the younger generations. The oil that just kept on burning represents an on-going challenge to each succeeding generation to ensure that the Maccabean spirit is not only maintained, but augmented. It is a promise that, no matter how powerful the obstructions put in the path of our survival, and how potent the missiles directed at our breast, we will not merely survive, but will progress towards the achievement of undreamed-of national prosperity.

352. What other contemporary lesson may be derived from the miracle of Chanukah?

> David Hartman derives an important lesson from the fact that we kindle eight lights, even though they initially had enough oil for the first day, which, consequently should not have been included in the ritual commemoration of the miracle: to begin a task without guarantees that they would complete it ... [It] signifies the miracle of man's courage to begin to build within imperfect human situations ... without knowledge of how it would end...The Hanukah lamp burned for eight days because of those who were prepared to have it burn for only one day.[30]

Hartman goes on to give several examples of such modern-day miracles, the most notable of which was, of course, the most courageous decision to proclaim the State of Israel in defiance of those Jews who counselled caution and delay until Israel's military preparedness was greater and until the majority of world Jewry was ready to rally to the cause. 'World Jewry realizes that the Jewish soul must be kindled by the flame whose source is in Jerusalem ... The flame that burns in the hearts of Jews throughout the world today was initially kindled by the small flame ignited by those who heroically proclaimed: 'We are reborn!'[31]

353. Is there any further contemporary lesson to be learned?

Indeed. It derives from the earlier, and in many ways more critical, battle that preceded that armed conflict against the Greek-Syrians: the internal battle for the hearts and minds of young Jewish boys and girls.

It is clear from the accounts in the Book of Maccabees and the historian Josephus that the upper classes of Judaea had forgotten the Torah, largely abandoned their Jewish practices and embraced Hellenism enthusiastically. Even the High Priest, Menelaus, was leading a move to transform Jerusalem into a Greek city state, in order to make it eligible to stage the Olympic Games there, which would have involved acts of worship to the Greek gods.

Like the Greeks, the young Jews were becoming obsessed with their physical prowess, with keeping their bodies in peak condition, enabling them to compete in the *gymnasia*, while finding no time for worship of their own God, for study of his Torah and for nourishing their intellectual powers and their spiritual and moral sensitivity.

They were only saved and brought to their senses at the eleventh hour, as a result of having been made to stare national and spiritual oblivion in the face by an enemy that was clearly welcoming and enticing them only as a psychological and military tactic.

Many might claim that Western 'culture' – the football and drug culture, the culture of moral licence and the philosophy of the body beautiful – is a repetition of the identical Hellenistic scenario. If that is the case, then our society must know that happiness, peace and harmony, whether in the personal, national or international arena, are not to be found along that route. Judaism was saved by the moral and intellectual guidance and challenge of its Torah. Hellenism had nothing to save it from itself, so that Greece became reduced to a relic of history, as did Rome after it. It is a lesson that any godless society would do well to reflect on.

ACCLAIMING MIRACLES

354. Are there any other occasions in the Jewish year when we acclaim a miracle?

Indeed, there are. The answer is, each and every day, three times a day, in the *Modim* prayer of the *Amidah*, where we give thanks 'for Your miracles which are with us each day, and for Your wonders and favours which are with us at all times'.

We must not forget, however, that one has to be able to *recognize* a miracle. We all experience miracles in our lives, extraordinary, unexpected and sudden changes in fortune. 'A stroke of good luck', we sometimes call them. 'A miracle cure', 'a one-in-a-million chance'. Who knows whether it is really chance?

Is there not a modern-day miracle that runs parallel to, and even surpasses, the miracle of the Chanukah oil whose potential was extended from one to eight nights? Is not the extension of human life in our day an even greater miracle? Is not man's potential for an extra decade or so of active life a modern-day miracle that God has bestowed on science and medicine and, through them, on the entire human race?

Many of our miracles are not quite so dramatic, and, because they happen every minute of every day, including the miracle of birth itself, are taken so much for granted. The miracle of the divine extension of nature's potential should, on its own merit, be a source of spiritual wonderment and inspiration, and a confirmation of faith every bit as profound as that of the miracle of Chanukah itself.

THE VICTORY OVER THE GREEKS: LEGEND OR HISTORICAL FACT?

355. You'll forgive the question, but, if we were to tell the average gentile that a band of Jewish freedom fighters repulsed the military might of ancient Greece, they would probably think that we were guilty of gross fabrication and revisionism. Is it really feasible? Are our 'literary sources' reliable, or is it merely an inspirational legend?

We have no doubt as to the overall accuracy of the events described, and Chaim Raphael[32] explains how it was possible for the Jews to have achieved that extraordinary feat.

He explains that there is evidence that, following their conquest of Judea, Jewish mercenaries were employed by the Greeks in large numbers, serving in Egypt and in their homeland. In Judea an elaborate system of citadels and fortifications was established, and the mercenaries were initiated into an exacting training regimen, and were taught the most advanced military techniques and skills.

In the 150 years between the death of Alexander the Great, conqueror of Judea, and the Maccabean revolt, the Jews gained excellent first-hand experience in warfare as a result of the incessant battles between the Ptolemies and the Seleucids for control of their country. This undoubtedly explains how and where they acquired the skills to become a fifth column within their own homeland, and ultimately to win back independence.

Raphael draws the apposite parallel between the situation during the twentieth century, when many Jews in Palestine fought in, and were trained by, the Allied armies in World War II. They later drew on their military skills in Israel's War of Independence in 1948, to regain their homeland and repulse five Arab armies

THE SCROLL OF ANTIOCHUS

356. You have referred previously to the main ancient sources for the history of Chanukah. You have also said that there was no succinct account, capable of being condensed for inclusion into the synagogue Chanukah liturgy. But is there not another authentic source, the *Megillat Antiochus* (Scroll of Antiochus), which used to be included in old editions of the prayer book?

You are right about its existence and its inclusion in old editions of the prayer book, but not about its authenticity as an historical source. For that reason we have not included it in our earlier analysis of the ancient sources.

In fact, this work is referred to for the first time only in the ninth century, when it is quoted by Saadia Gaon. It purports to be a chronicle of the Hasmonean period, but it is clearly reliant on the earlier sources of I Maccabees and the Talmud. Though written in Hebrew, it is undoubtedly a Hebrew rendering of an original Aramaic work, probably of the late Talmudic period, and composed in Babylon. It has been pointed out that no native of Israel would have described Antioch as 'a coastal city', nor would a contemporary chronicle have confused, as it does, John Hyrcanus with John, son of Matityahu, or erroneously attributed a reign of twenty-three years, instead of eleven, to Antiochus, or included material that is clearly not historical.

For all that, some medieval authorities, Saadia included, held this legendary work in the highest esteem, under the mistaken impression that it was an authentic chronicle, compiled by the Maccabean brothers themselves. This explains why, from the thirteenth century, its Hebrew version was included in the Italian rite for recitation on Chanukah, from where it travelled to other places, where it was similarly included, and published in some editions of the daily prayer book, even until the beginning of the twentieth century.

MORE ON THE NAME CHANUKAH

357. We have observed that the word 'Chanukah' means 'dedication (of the Temple)'. Would one not have thought that a name more closely related to the miracle of the lights would have been chosen?

'Lights' was indeed, the name that Josephus gave to the festival (see Question 160). However, the immediacy and excitement of the miracle would have waned with the passing of the generations, whereas the significance of the regaining and rededication of the Temple remained inspirational for the following two hundred and thirty-five years of its existence.

358. Did the name Chanukah attract any other exposition?

It did. The most popular explanation is that it comprises a composite of the words, *Chanu* (literally, 'they encamped', in the sense of 'ceased fighting') and *Kah* ('on the twenty-fifth [of Kislev]'), the numerical value of the Hebrew letters *K(af)* and H(ey) being twenty-five. The popularity of this explanation is astounding when one considers its absolute implausibility!

The number twenty-five, associated with Chanukah, prompted some imaginative preachers to find a reference to this festival foreshadowed in the Torah itself. Hence, they point out that the twenty-fifth word in the Torah is *ohr*, meaning 'light'. And, as if that was not sufficiently convincing, they note that the twenty-fifth location where the Israelites encamped during their 40-year journeying in the desert was named Chashmonah (Numbers 33:29), which is, of course, the Hebrew for 'Hasmonean'!

NOTES
1. Tosefta *Yoma* 4:2.
2. Mishnah *Succah* 2:8.
3. Talmud *Shabbat* 31a.
4. *Bet Yosef* on *Tur Shulchan Arukh, Orach Chayyim* sec. 670.

5. David Hartman, *Rabbinic Responses to History as Mirrored in Hanukkah and Purim* (Jerusalem: The Shalom Hartman Institute for Advanced Judaic Studies, undated), Part I, pp.23–5).

6. See Numbers chapter 19.

7. Talmud *Yoma* 6b.

8. Talmud *Avodah Zarah* 43a.

9. I Maccabees 4:49.

10. Talmud *Shabbat* 21b.

11. Hartman, *Rabbinic Responses to History*, p.31.

12. See *Rambam, Mishneh Torah* 4:13.

13. Ibid.

14. Ibid., 4:14.

15. See I Samuel 20:18.

16. Chief Rabbi J. Sacks, 'Chanukah address to Rabbinical Council of the United Synagoue, UK', December 1998.

17. Talmud *Sanhedrin* 37a.

18. On the rise and evolution of the synagogue, See Jeffrey M. Cohen, *Blessed Are You* (New Jersey: Jason Aronson, 1993).

19. Hayyim Schauss, *Guide to Jewish Holy Days* (New York: Schocken Books, 1962), p.225.

20. I. Greenberg, *The Jewish Way* (New York: Summit Books, 1988), p. 277.

21. Cohen, *Blessed Are You*, pp.24–6.

22. See II Maccabees 1:1, 9; 10:8-9.

23. II Maccabees 1:9.

24. Ibid., 1:18.

25. Ibid.

26. Ibid., 10:9.

27. Elias J. Bickerman, 'The Historical Foundations of Postbiblical Judaism' in Louis Finkelstein (ed.), *The Jews: Their History, Culture and Religion* (London: Peter Owen Ltd., 1961), vol.I, p.110.

28. Irving Greenberg, 'Maccabean Spirit can be Rekindled,' *Jewish Chronicle*, 7 Dec. 1990, p.29.

29. Herman Wouk, *This is My God* (New York: Doubleday & Co., 1959), p.105.

30. Hartman, *Rabbinic Responses to History*, Part I, pp. 23–5.

31. Ibid., p.25.

32. See C. Raphael, *The Springs of Jewish Life* (London: Chatto & Windus, 1982), p.54.

VI
THE LIGHTING OF THE CHANUKIAH:
ITS BLESSINGS AND HYMNS

11

The Lighting of the Chanukiah: Its Blessings and Hymns

VETZIVANU – 'HE HAS COMMANDED US"

359. How, in the first blessing over the Chanukiah, may we recite the formula *vetzivanu lehadlik ner shel chanukah* ('and has commanded us to kindle the Chanukah light . . . ') when this ritual was instituted not by God, but by the sages?

This question may be asked of a whole host of rituals, such as the lighting of the Sabbath and Yom Tov lights. Granted that they are biblical institutions, but the ritual of lighting candles is certainly nowhere mentioned in the Torah.

The answer is that our concept of Oral Law means that we are bidden to accord only slightly less authority to laws that are promulgated by the sages, acting in the spirit of the Torah, than to the Torah law itself. Indeed, in certain respects, the penalty for infringing rabbinic bylaws of a Torah institution is more stringent than for infringement of the institution itself.[1]

The rabbis received a long, uninterrupted tradition, from Moses on Sinai; and they were, and remain, its custodians. All the supplementary laws and rituals that they have revealed, and which are codified in Mishnah, Talmud and later law books, must be complied with as if we, ourselves, had heard their words issuing forth from Sinai with our own ears.

The sages are the mouthpieces for God's voice to continue to be heard by man, and to speak to every generation anew, addressing its problems and guiding it through its spiritual and moral minefields. His authority is shared with them. And this explains the special blessing on seeing a sage renowned for his knowledge of the Torah: 'Blessed art Thou, O Lord our God, who has shared His wisdom with humankind.' Once we reject the authority of the rabbinic Oral Law, the next step is to reject the Written Law also.

The Torah itself adjures those who seek justice at the supreme religious court in Jerusalem to obey the decision of the sages: 'And thou shalt do according to all that they teach thee . . . thou shalt not turn aside . . . neither to the right hand or the left hand' (Deuteronomy 17:10–11). The comment of the Talmud is, 'even if they tell you that the right is left and the left is right, obey them'.[2] And it is that mantle of divine authority, that is draped around the shoulders of the sages, that enables us to recite, over purely rabbinic institutions, a blessing containing the affirmation, *asher kidshanu bemitzvotav v'etzivanu* . . . that God, 'Who has sanctified us by His commandments, has [also] commanded us . . .' to perform the said rabbinic ritual.

VARIANT FORMULAE OF THE BLESSING *LEHADLIK NER*

360. It has been said that our version of the first blessing, lehadlik ner shel chanukah, is not universal. What other versions are there?

It is true that our version is not the only one. Indeed, I recall that, as a child, we used to sing, *lehadlik ner shelachanukah*, contracting the words *shel chanukah* into one. This version is supposed to have been preferred by the illustrious R. Avraham Karelitz, the *Chazon Ish* (1878–1953).

It has been demonstrated that the one word version actually goes back to an earlier stage of the Hebrew language when the preposition *shel* was always joined together with the following word. This was common usage in the early Talmudic period, as witnessed in Hebrew and Aramaic letters from the Bar Kochba period (second century CE) and in Babylonian versions of the Mishnah, as found in the Cairo *Genizah*, a form which survived as late as the Geonic period (tenth century CE).[3]

361. But surely the later development of that prepositional form detached the word shel from the following word. Why, then, was it reintroduced in some circles into the Chanukah blessing?

It seems that this earlier form of *shelachanukah* was reintroduced under the influence of mystical and Chasidic circles that put great score by the significance of *gematria* (numerology) in our prayers. It was popularized within Ashkenazi communities by the sixteenth century Polish and Lithuanian authority, R. Solomon Luria (*Maharshal*) who attributed it to earlier illustrious authorities. It was also the regular Yemenite version.[4]

This composite form is explained as an attempt to reduce the number of words in that blessing to thirteen, which is the same number as the following, *She'asah nisim*, blessing. This significant number links those blessings to the 'Thirteen Attributes of Divine Mercy' (*Sh'losh esrei midot*), contained in Exodus 34:6–7. The total number of twenty-six words in the combined two blessings is also the gematria of the four-letter divine name.

362. Is there any other variant of the lehadlik ner blessing?

There is. Instead of our version, *lehadlik ner shel chanukah*, Joseph Karo's *Shulchan Arukh* prescribes the formula *lehadlik ner chanukah*.[5] This was also a well-established version, appearing in some manuscript versions of the passage in Talmud *Shabbat* 23a, and in the *Siddur* of Saadia Gaon. It is also the version quoted by many of the *Rishonim*, the authorities living before the publication of Karo's *Shulchan Arukh* (sixteenth century).

BAYAMIM HA-HEIM BAZMAN HA-ZEH

363. Why is it that the second of the blessings (*She'asa nisim*) concludes repetitively, with two phrases that seem to have the identical meaning?

Indeed, at first glance it does seem that *bayamim ha-heim* ('in those days') and *bazman ha-zeh* ('at this season') seem tautologous, especially as they are not linked with the conjunctive *vav*, which would give the sense of 'in those days and *also* in our present time'.

Significantly, some early sources, such as *Machzor Vitri* (twelfth century),[6] *Shibbolei ha-Leket* (thirteenth century)[7] and Maimonides (thirteenth century),[8] all have that conjunctive reading, *bayamim ha-heim u-vazman ha-zeh*.

Arukh ha-Shulchan[9] justifies the double reference in the text, as follows:

> The main miracle, the defeat of Antiochus by the Hasmoneans, did not take place 'on this day,' namely the 25th of Kislev, but during the extended period of the struggle. It was the subsequent miracle of the jar of oil that occurred 'at this time'... Thus it follows clearly that the blessing is over the two miracles [as reflected in the two expressions].

SHEHECHEYANU

364. Why is the *shehecheyanu* blessing only recited on the first night (after *lehadlik ner* and *she'asa nisim*)?

This is because *Shehecheyanu* is only recited over a new or novel situation, or a ritual that recurs infrequently or after a lengthy intermission. Examples of this are a fruit that appears for the first time in its season, a festival that has not been celebrated since the previous year (note that over Shabbat or *Rosh Chodesh* the blessing is not recited because they recur frequently) or on wearing a new garment. Hence its recitation on the first night only of the festival.

365. If someone was away, with no one at home to light on his behalf, and he was prevented by circumstances from lighting on the first night, does he recite *Shehecheyanu* on the first subsequent night that he is able to fulfil the mitzvah?

No he does not. *Shehecheyanu* is a blessing of thanksgiving that one has been 'preserved to experience *this season*', namely, the arrival of the festival, not the ability to kindle lights. (The latter he does, in any case, on a regular basis, every Shabbat.) Thus, once the festival has 'arrived', the significance of the blessing fades.

366. What if that person managed to glimpse someone else's Chanukah lights burning?

Then he has been able to visually identify with the commemoration of the miracle, which entitles him to utter a blessing. He obviously cannot recite *lehadlik ner* since he has had no opportunity 'to kindle'. He does, however, recite the second blessing, *She'asa nisim*, and, if that is the first night of the festival, the *Shehecheyanu* also.

BLESSINGS BEFORE OR AFTER KINDLING?

367. Do we kindle the lights first, and then make the blessings, or vice versa?

We always make blessings (other than Grace After Meals and lighting the Shabbat candles) *before* performing sacred rituals. This is rooted in the fact that everything really belongs to God, and man has no right to assume that he can, at will, exploit God's bounty. We therefore first acknowledge Him as the sole possessor of all existing things, and express our thanksgiving for His having shared the raw materials of His world with us, or bestowed upon us joyful festivals, before proceeding to enjoy the experience.

368. So what if one inadvertently lit the candles and then realized that he had omitted the blessings?

Because one fulfils the basic mitzvah by lighting just one light each night (see Questions 234–239), if one realized his omission on one of the later nights, before he had lit all the lights, he should stop at that point, recite the blessings, and light the remaining light(s). If, however, he had already lit all the lights, then he omits the first blessing (*lehadlik*), over the act of 'kindling', and merely recites the following blessing. On the first night, if he remembered after the kindling, he recites just the *She'asa nisim and Shehecheyanu*.

THE POSITIONING AND LIGHTING OF THE LIGHTS

369. How are the lights positioned and lit within the Chanukiah?

The first night's light is placed into the right-hand side of the Chanukiah, and, on each succeeding night, a new light is added to the left of the total number of lights kindled the previous night, thereby building up each night from the right to the left of the Chanukiah.

When it comes to the lighting, however, we light the left-hand (that is the new) light first, and then continue lighting to the right, so that the last light we kindle is the first night's light at the right-hand side of the Chanukiah.

370. Is there any special significance in lighting the new light, on the left first?

By lighting the new night's light first, he is not only drawing attention to the on-going augmentation of the miracle, but is also recalling the Temple procedure which was that whenever one made a turn, it was preferably towards the direction of the right.[10]

Mishnah Berurah provides another rationale, taking account of the fact that by lighting that first additional light each night, the basic mitzvah is already fulfilled. Thus, by ensuring that we start each night with the new light on the left, we also fulfil the prescription of *ein ma'avirin al ha-mitzvot*, not to bypass mitzvot[11] (see also Question 189).

HA-NEROT HALLALU

371. How old is the *Ha-nerot hallalu* composition?

It is found for the first time in one of the minor tractates of the Talmud, *Masechet Sofrim*, which dates back to the eighth century. Jacob ben Asher (1270–1340), author of the *Tur*, quotes it in full, and then states, 'and Rabbi Meir of Rothenburg and my revered father, the *Rosh*, were accustomed to recite it'.[12] The implication is that, although it was clearly recited in Israel in the period of *Masechet Sofrim*, yet its recitation had not subsequently become more universal. Those distinguished scholars of the thirteenth and fourteenth century, referred to by *Tur*, were clearly attempting to reintroduce its recitation.

372. At what stage do we recite it?

Mishnah Berurah[13] recommends that it be recited immediately after the first of the lights has been lit, because once that light is burning the basic level of the mitzvah has been fulfilled (see Questions 234 and 370). He quotes the *Pri Megadim*, however, who takes the view that to recite it after he has lit all the lights is also acceptable.[14]

373. What is the purpose of this composition?

This question requires to be asked, since, at first sight, it may appear to be an unnecessary insertion, interrupting the ritual to provide an explanation of its purpose ('We kindle these lights on account of the miracles, the deliverance and the wonders that You performed . . .'). Other than the requirement to explain the significance of *Pesach*, *Matzah* and *Maror* on Seder night,[15] we are never required to provide an explanatory recitation of why we are fulfilling any particular mitzvah! (The mystics of sixteenth century Safed did, however, favour introductory formulae whose purpose was to generate religious concentration on the mitzvah as well as to indicate its higher spiritual purpose and effect.)

The primary objective of this composition is to constitute a solemn warning to the members of the household to stay at a distance from these particular lights since they may not be used for any purpose whatsoever, not even to study Torah by their light: 'Throughout the eight nights of Chanukah, these lights are sacred; and we are not permitted to make any other use of them, excepts to look at them.'

Because it came naturally, in an age before electricity, for people to crouch under the light of a lamp in order better to see the particular task they were performing, a special warning against this had to be issued, in the form of the *Ha-nerot hallalu*.

374. If it is an introductory warning, would it not have been more logical to recite it at the very outset, before the blessings are recited and the candles lit?

It is our universal practice for the entire family to sing aloud, and with gusto, the most popular *Ma'oz tzur*, known almost by heart because of its tune, by even the very young children. It was composed by an Ashkenazi poet of the thirteenth century by the name of Mordechai ben Isaac,[16] and, according to A.Z. Idelsohn, its popular tune became traditional from the sixteenth century.[16]

But we have to go back, however, to the period before *Ma'oz tzur* was invested with that popularity, and when its words were not, therefore, so well-known. People would then have required to hold their text to the light in order to recite it. The instinctive tendency would have been to employ the Chanukah lights to illumine the page. Now, bearing in mind that the attempts to popularize the recitation of *Ha-nerot hallalu* were made (on the evidence of *Tur*) not long after the composition and dissemination of *Ma'oz tzur*, we may conjecture that these situations are inter-linked. In other words, the popularity of *Ma'oz tzur* called for a cautionary prelude, advising people not to make any use of the lights in order to view their texts of this recently-introduced hymn. *Ha-nerot Hallalu* was not prescribed for recitation before the blessings are recited, in case an interruption and delay in the lighting might subsequently occur in the home.

375. We referred previously to the significance of the number of words in the two blessings over the lights (see Question 361). Is there anything significant about the number of words in *Ha-nerot hallalu*?

The *Mishnah Berurah* points out that there are thirty-six words in this composition, corresponding to the *total* number of Chanukah lights kindled during the eight nights. The *Sha'ar ha-Tziyyun* observes that we should not include the word *heim*, therefore, in the phrase *ha-nerot hallalu kodesh heim*, since the addition of that word gives a total of 37, which destroys the numerical significance.[18]

MA'OZ TZUR

376. What is the subject matter of this hymn?

It is an overview of the cycle of oppression and deliverance experienced by Israel down the ages, commencing with a plea for the Temple to be rebuilt and for the enemies of our people to be finally silenced (Stanza 1). It goes on to express the hardship and bitterness of the Egyptian bondage, followed by the drowning of

Pharaoh and his host in the Red Sea (Stanza 2). Nationhood in the Promised Land was followed once again by exile in Babylon, justified as a punishment for the nation's idolatry. However, within seventy years, the Babylonian empire was swept away and Israel's woes ceased (Stanza 3). Haman's hatred for Mordechai, the former's ignominious fall from grace and his and his sons' execution, is referred to (Stanza 4), followed by a reference to the Greeks' wholesale assault on the Temple, defilement of the sacred oil in the days of the Hasmoneans, and the miracle of Chanukah and institution of the festival that followed (Stanza 5). The initial letters of each stanza make up an acrostic of the author's name, *Mordechai*.

MA'OZ TZUR'S CONTROVERSIAL FINAL STANZA

377. In some prayer books is there not a final, sixth stanza?

There is, indeed. Seligman Baer (1825–97), in his *Seder Avodat Yisrael*, observes that,

in some recent prayer books there is an additional stanza, commencing with the words, *Chasof zero'a kodshekha*. This does not appear, however, in any old prayer book. It is not by the same poet, but an addition, conceivably derived from the laws of Chanukah found in the *Abbreviated Writings of the Shela* (Isaiah Horowitz, 1565–1630).[19]

This view is contested by modern scholars on internal and stylistic evidence, as well as on the basis that 'its acrostic [*chazak*] seems to show that it is part of the original composition'.[20]

That acrostic, meaning 'Be strong!' is formed from the initial letters of the opening three words, and it is a sentiment that invariably follows at the end of a poem bearing a name acrostic, and is intrinsic to it.

378. But if it was intrinsic, why was it omitted from most printed prayer books?

A glance at the translation of the stanza might help explain:

> O bare Your holy arm, and hasten the time of salvation.
> Wreak vengeance upon the wicked nation,
> On behalf of Your faithful servants.
> For deliverance has too long been delayed,
> And the evil days are endless.
> O thrust the enemy into the shadow of death,
> And bring to our aid the seven Shepherds.

We may assume that, as was often the case, sentiments in the liturgy that were regarded as offensive by the Christian censor, were removed, and, with the advent of printing, were never reproduced. The Jews also exercised their own internal censorship in order to avoid violent repercussions. It is not surprising, therefore, that, given an anti-Christian allusion that appears in this stanza, it was not reproduced, and survived only in some rare manuscripts.

THE ENIGMATIC FINAL LINE OF THE POEM

379. Where does that offending sentiment occur?

It is contained in the final line of the poem: *D'cheih admon b'tzeil tzalmon*. The above quoted modern rendering, by my late, revered teacher, Rabbi Eli Cashdan, 'O thrust the enemy (*Admon = Edom =* Rome) *into the shadow of death*',[21] is derived from the emphatic duplication of the nouns *tzeil* and *tzalmon*, in the sense of 'shadow of the shadow', or 'the darkest possible shadow', namely, the darkness of the tomb.

However, *tzalmon* could also be a reference to the Cross, from the word *tzelem*, 'an image', 'an idol', because the crucifixion was widely represented on icons and 'images'. (Note also the popular Yiddish pronunciation of the word for the Cross, as *tzeilem*). Hence, a censor with a sharp nose for a veiled allusion, ruled the entire stanza out of order.

I am more inclined, however, to detect here an oblique reference to Islam, on the basis of the almost identical sound of the words *tzalmon* and *izlam*), and to view the poet as looking forward to the fall of Edom (Rome /Christianity) at the hands of the more benign rule of the Muslims.

There is a long tradition of such sentiments being alluded to in poetry. As early as the seventh century, we find Yochanan Ha-Kohen bar Yehoshua, in his *Izzun shema' medubbar*, calling for the fall of Edom (Byzantium) at the hands of the invading Arabs: 'Subdue Mount Seir and Edom . . . Strike them with the forces of *pere*''.[22] The latter is, of course, a reference to Ishmael, the primogenitor of the Arabs, who is referred to by the term *pere'* in Genesis 16:12.

380. But why, just at this period, should Jews have expressed such bitterness in a Chanukah poem that ought to have exuded joy and gratitude for redemption?

The Crusades left a legacy of great hatred and bitterness with the decimated Jewish communities of Central Europe; and the thirteenth century, during which *Ma'oz tzur* was composed, witnessed an unprecedented explosion of anti-Semitism and an increasingly hostile attitude towards the Jews as official Church policy, culminating in the Fourth Lateran Council (1215) which ordained that the Jews wear a 'badge of infamy' on their outer clothing, to distinguish them from Christians. During this century the Church conducted public disputations with a view to exposing Judaism as a pernicious and flawed religion; Christian art began widely to stereotype Jews; ritual murder (blood libel) charges were frequently brought, and European monarchs formally imposed the status of serf upon the Jews of their countries as punishment for the sin of deicide.[23]

It would have been unnatural therefore, for European Jewry not to have looked, albeit naively, to the other great religion (of which they had had little or no experience!) as the only realistic alternative to Christianity, offering a measure of future hope and relief to Israel. And hence, we suggest, the appeal to *tzalmon*, Islam, in the final stanza of *Ma'oz tzur*. The phrase is therefore to be rendered: 'Thrust the Edomites into the shadow of the Muslims', or paraphrased as, 'Let the Muslims overwhelm the Edomites'. In our day, we would strongly support the continued omission of this stanza!

381. Were Jews uncomfortable about expressing such sentiments?

The Jews of nineteenth century Germany, who were acculturating to the mores of the wider society, established a Reform tradition that set out to rid the liturgy of sentiments and concepts that were not in keeping with the modern, enlightened outlook. They were embarrassed by the many references to the ancient sacrificial order and such notions as the restoration of Israel to its own land, and they consequently excised them from their prayer books. The final stanza of *Ma'oz tzur* was, inevitably, unacceptable to them, and they either omitted or rewrote it. Indeed, numerous Reform variants of the entire poem, not only the final stanza, have appeared, all with the objective of softening its call for the subjugation of Christendom.

The current Reform prayer book, *Forms of Prayer for Jewish Worship*, contains only four of the six stanzas, and omits not only the final stanza but also the fourth,[24] which recounts the downfall of Haman, ending with the words, 'But the enemy's name You blotted out. His numerous sons and his household You hanged on the gallows.' Perhaps the notion of Israel gloating over the downfall of her enemies was not one the Reform tradition wished to promote. It is possible, however, that, subsequent to the reality of the modern State of Israel's daily acts of necessary retaliation for terrorist atrocities, Reform tradition might be a little less reticent to acknowledge Israel's need to counter force with force.

382. Presumably Orthodox Rabbinic authorities were implacably against such changes in the liturgy as those introduced by the Reformers in respect of *Ma'oz tzur*?

One might have thought so. However, a translation of the version of that last stanza as found in the *Bet Ya'akov* prayer book of the illustrious Rabbi Jacob Emden (1697–1776) and a comparison with the original version (see Question 378) is enlightening:

O bare Your holy arm, and hasten the time of salvation.
Do it, we pray You, for Your name's sake, that we may have salvation.
For our salvation has too long been delayed, and the evil days are endless.
Blot out transgression and unrighteousness,
And bring to our aid the seven Shepherds.[25]

Ignoring the repetitiveness of the word 'salvation', Emden's version was clearly a similar attempt to disguise the poem's strong nationalistic sentiments and its plea for the downfall of Jewry's contemporary persecutors. Emden was a passionate inquisitor against any sentiment that could be construed as *Chillul Ha-Shem*, calculated to bring the name of Jewry into disrepute, and it is probably against that backcloth that we may explain his dilution of the sentiments inherent in the *Ma'oz tzur* composition.

MA'OZ TZUR'S CONTROVERSIAL MELODY

383. What can you tell us about the almost universal melody to which *Ma'oz tzur* is sung?

To be honest, not a great deal, given my woeful lack of knowledge on the subject of music. However, to save you the effort of looking up an encyclopedia, I shall report what the received wisdom is on the subject.

Apparently, the melody dates back to the early fifteenth century and has its origin in a group of early Protestant chorales and a German soldiers' song. I must admit to having felt a slight shudder go down my spine when I read that, for, although that was a good few hundred years before the Holocaust, yet the fifteenth and sixteenth centuries witnessed a growing hatred of Jews on the part of German townsfolk, exacerbated by their increasingly large debts to Jewish money-lenders. That situation culminated in state edicts cancelling any debts owed to Jews, coupled with their expulsion from many cities, beginning with Nuremberg in 1498 and Regensburg in 1519.

One can almost hear those German soldiers, singing their *Ma'oz tzur* melody while breaking down the doors of Jewish homes and beating their occupants senseless. It seems a trifle ironic, that, in an age when Israeli songs can win the Euro-Vision Song Contest, we should remain reliant upon, and continue to hallow, a melody from an anti-Semitic source by according it such popularity.

NOTES
 1. See Mishnah *Sanhedrin* 11:3.
 2. *Sifrei* on Deuteronomy 17:11; Talmud *Shabbat* 23a.
 3. See M. Rafeld, '*Ha-nuscha'ot hashonot shel birkat ner chanukah*', in D. Sperber, *Minhagei Yisrael* (Jerusalem: Mosad HaRav Kook, 1995), p.79 n.5.
 4. Ibid., p.81.
 5. *Shulchan Arukh Orach Chayyim* 676:1.
 6. *Machzor Vitri*, sec. 236, p.199.
 7. *Shibbolei ha-Leket*, p.72.
 8. *Rambam, Hilkhot Megilah* 1:3.
 9. *Arukh ha-Shulchan* 676:3.
10. Talmud *Yoma* 58b.
11. See *Mishnah Berurah* 676:5(11).

12. *Tur Orach Chayyim* sec. 676.
13. See *Mishnah Berurah* 676:4(8).
14. Ibid.
15. See Jeffrey M. Cohen, *1001 Questions and Answers on Pesach* (New Jersey: Jason Aronson, 1996), pp.142–3.
16. See I.M. Elbogen, *Ha-tefillah Beyisrael* (Tel Aviv: Dvir, 1988), p.418, n.6.
17. See A. Idelsohn, *Jewish Liturgy and its Development* (New York: Holt, Rinehart and Winston, Inc., 1932), p.162.
18. See *Sha'ar ha-Tziyyun to Mishnah Berurah* 676:4(13).
19. Seligman Baer, *Seder Avodat Yisrael* (Jerusalem: Schocken, 1937; reproduction of original Roedelheim edition,1868), p.440.
20. See, for example, *Encyclopaedia Judaica* (Jerusalem: Keter Publishing House Ltd, 1971), vol.11, p.910.
21. Rendering of E. Cashdan, *The Authorised Daily Prayer Book of the United Hebrew Congregations of the Commonwealth* (London: Singer's Prayer Book Publication Committee, 1992), p.710.
22. See Leon J. Weinberger, *Jewish Hymnography: A Literary History* (London: The Littman Library of Jewish Civilisation, 1998), p.39.
23. See H.H. Ben-Sasson, *A History of the Jewish People* (Cambridge, MA: Harvard University Press, 1976), pp.477–89.
24. See *Forms of Prayer for Jewish Worship* (London: The Reform Synagogues of Great Britain, 1977), pp.268–9.
25. See Jacob Emden, *Siddur Bet Ya'akov* (Lemberg D. Balakan, 1904 edition), p.369.

VII
CHANUKAH IN
THE SYNAGOGUE
AND THE HOME

12

Chanukah in the Synagogue

AL HA-NISIM

384. Are there any special prayers or compositions prescribed for recitation on Chanukah?

As one might have expected for a festival, albeit a minor one, the sages prescribed the recitation of *Hallel* together with a special portion of the Torah to be read in the morning services each day of the festival, as well as a thanksgiving composition for inclusion into the thrice-daily *Amidah* prayer and into the Grace After Meals throughout Chanukah.

The specially composed thanksgiving prayer, for insertion into the *Modim* blessing of the *Amidah*, is popularly referred to as *Al Ha-nisim*, after the introductory statement which praises God, in general, 'for the miracles (*Al ha-nisim*), the redemption, the mighty deeds, and for the victories in battle which You performed for our fathers in those days and at this season'. (This same introductory formula is employed for the special insertion for Purim, also recited at this point.) There then follows the specific composition prescribed for Chanukah, commencing *Biymei Matityahu ben Yochanan kohein gadol*, 'In the days of Matityahu, son of Yochanan, the High Priest' (see Questions 172–173).

385. Why is *Al Ha-nisim* introduced into the *Modim* blessing of the *Amidah*?

Because, contextually, that is the most appropriate blessing, being a thanksgiving blessing for all the protection God has afforded Israel over the millennia. The opening phrase, *Al Ha-nisim* ('for the miracles') also constitutes a textual link with the phrase *v'al nisekha shebkhol yom immanu*, '[We thank You for] *Your miracles* which are daily with us', in the *Modim* blessing of the *Amidah*.

386. Is there not a problem of syntax in the introductory *Al ha-nisim* phrase, which seems to hang in mid-air, without any subject?

Well spotted! If we translate *Al Ha-nisim*, it reads, simply, 'For the miracles, the redemption, the mighty deeds and the victories', without any subject, such as 'We thank You for'. Most translations have to provide that, in order to give some sense.

This explains why *Mishnah Berurah*, quoting *Pri Chadash*, states, without elucidation, 'It is written in some works that we should recite *V'al ha-nisim*, with a conjunctive vav, both in the *Amidah* and in the Grace After Meals'.¹ By adding the vav, the phrase is now rendered, '*And* for the miracles'. This makes our list of divine interventions a mere continuation of the list given in the host blessings of the *Amidah* and Grace After Meals. The words *Modim* and *Nodeh* ('We thank You'), in the *Amidah* and Grace blessings, respectively, now govern our *Al ha-nisim* references also, and hence the difficulty we encountered is removed.

387. What if one inadvertently omitted to recite *Al ha-nisim* in the *Amidah*?

If he remembers the omission before he has recited the name of God (*Barukh attah Hashem [hatov shimkha . . .]*, in the concluding blessing of *Modim*, he inserts *Al ha-nisim* at that point. If that point has been passed, he concludes the *Amidah* and does not recite it.

388. Why is *Al Ha-nisim* inserted into the second blessing of the Grace After Meals?

Because that is also a thanksgiving blessing, commencing with the word *Nodeh* ('We thank You'), which is almost identical to the opening word *Modim* of the *Amidah* blessing into which *Al ha-nisim* is inserted. Furthermore, this *Nodeh* blessing thanks God for the heritage of 'a desirable, goodly and spacious land', and the miracle of Chanukah was performed in the context of the battle for Jewish sovereignty over that land of Israel.

389. What if one inadvertently omitted *Al Ha-nisim* from the Grace After Meals?

Again, the same law applies as for the omission of *Al Ha-nisim* in the *Amidah*. Thus, if he remembers his omission before he has recited the name of God in the concluding formula, *Barukh attah Hashem [ha-tov shimkha ul'kha na'eh l'hodot]*, then he *inserts Al Ha-nisim* at that point. If that point has passed, however, he does not interrupt, but continues with the Grace After Meals. However, he does have a further opportunity to recite it during the course of the list of *Harachaman* blessings towards the end of Grace.

Most prayer books will indicate the point at which to insert the belated *Al Ha-nisim*. It follows on immediately after the phrase *b'einey Elokim v'adam*, at the point where we normally insert mention of any special holy day (Shabbat, Rosh Chodesh, or festival) that we are celebrating.

390. But, according to my prayer book, the belated version does not use the usual *Al Ha-nisim* introduction?

Nor in mine! In fact, we again employ that common liturgical device of contextually linking the opening words of an inserted composition to a key phrase in the host composition. Thus, because the Chanukah piece is to be inserted into the

Harachaman section of Grace, the usual *Al Ha-nisim* was replaced by a new introductory formula, commencing with the identical word, *Harachaman* ('*May the All-Merciful One* perform miracles and wonders for us, as He performed for our forefathers in those and at this time').

391. What if he has passed that point in Grace before he realizes his omission?

Then he has missed the opportunity of praising God in this way, and he does nothing further.

HALLEL

392. Why was *Hallel* prescribed for Chanukah and not for *Purim*?

Logically, it should have been prescribed for both festivals. We do not need to query its prescription for Chanukah, as the great deliverance of the Jews certainly merited a thanksgiving service in the form of recitation of joyful psalms.

Two reasons are given, however, for its omission on Purim. The first is that the deliverance of the Jews of Persia was not, in fact, complete, because they remained there in exile as subjects of King Achashverosh. A second explanation is that the reading of the *Megillat Esther* constitutes, of itself, a veritable and dramatic thanksgiving composition.

393. Why do we recite the full version of *Hallel* on the rabbinically prescribed festival of Chanukah, whereas we only recite an abbreviated version on, say, the biblical holy day of *Rosh Chodesh*?

The reason is that, because the miracle of the Temple oil was continuous for the entire eight days, each and every day was construed as a separate and unique demonstration of unparalleled divine revelation, meriting the fullest of thanksgiving.

394. If one is praying the morning service at home, before going to work, are there any restrictions governing the time for the recitation of *Hallel*?

In the first instance, *Hallel* should not be recited before sunrise. This is derived from the verse, in the opening psalm of *Hallel*, 'From the *rising of the sun* and until it goes down praised is the name of God' (Psalm 113:3).[2] However, a concession is given to those that have to leave their home early in the morning in winter to get to their place of work. They were permitted to recite *Hallel* at dawn, though not before.

395. Since when was Judaism so flexible as to relax the halachah for materialist considerations?

Some may regard it as surprising, but Judaism is flexible, and is most concerned that people should have work and not loose their jobs and livelihood. 'Six days shalt thou labour' is regarded by some authorities as a positive command, in the same category as the continuation of that fourth commandment, 'and the seventh is a day of rest to the Lord thy God'. Countless laws are relaxed in the rabbinic codes, *mishum chisaron kis*, for the avoidance of financial loss.[3]

The concession to recite *Hallel* before sunrise is based on that concept of the pursuit of work as a mitzvah in itself.

396. *Hallel* contains some verses that are recited responsively by *Chazan* and congregation, and in which the *Chazan* summons the congregation to respond with praise of God? How important is it, then, for people to attend synagogue on Chanukah and on the other occasions when *Hallel* is recited?

I think you've already answered your own question! Although *Hallel* may be said at home, yet its proper and desired context is the synagogue. Hence, if one arrived late in synagogue, at a point where the congregation was almost at *Hallel*, he should not commence the recitation of his own prayers, but should wait to recite *Hallel* together with the congregation, and only then should he commence his own prayers.

397. Is there more than one version of the *Hallel* blessing, *Barukh ... likro' et ha-Hallel*?

The original, Talmudic version is *Barukh ... ligmor et ha-Hallel* ('Blessed ... who has commanded us *to complete* the *Hallel*'),[4] and this is the version preferred by the Sephardim. Ashkenazi authorities, on the other hand, were concerned by the implication of the word *ligmor*, 'to complete', since it could easily happen that a person was distracted or interrupted, and did not 'complete' every word of the Hallel. Furthermore, there are several festival days when only Half-Hallel is recited. In order to avoid a contradiction between the implication of the blessing and what is actually being recited, and in the interest of consistency, Ashkenazi authorities reduced the obligation of the blessing to *likro'*, that of, merely, 'reading' the *Hallel*.

CHANUKAH TORAH READINGS

398. What readings are prescribed for Chanukah?

Each day of Chanukah (except Shabbat), we call up three people to the reading of the section of the Torah describing the sacrifices offered by each of the twelve princes of Israel on the day that the altar of the desert sanctuary was dedicated (Numbers 7:1–89).

There is a dispute as to the point at which we commence on the first day, with Karo's *Shulchan Arukh* prescribing that we commence five verses earlier, to include the Priestly Blessing (6:22–7), as a tribute to the Priestly family at the centre of the Chanukah victory. Ashkenazi tradition, as codified by Moses Isserles,[5] was more purist in that respect, and did not countenance any allusion to a basically extraneous subject.

399. Why was that particular biblical portion dealing with the princes chosen as the Torah reading on Chanukah?

Because there is a tradition that all the work on the desert sanctuary was finally completed on 25 Kislev, the day on which the miracle of Chanukah was later to occur. Now, although the princes did not offer their contributions until the first day of the month of Nisan (some three months later), nevertheless, since those contributions were for the dedication of the Sanctuary, the two events become interconnected. And this is underscored by that choice of reading for Chanukah, the festival of Temple re-dedication.

400. How are the daily readings divided up between the three who are called up each day?

The idea was to read on the first day of Chanukah the verses which describe the offering brought on the first day of dedication by the first prince (*Nachshon ben Aminadav*); on the second day of Chanukah, the verses which describe the offering brought by the second prince (*Netan'el ben Tzu'ar*), and so on. The only problem is that only six verses are accorded to the description of each prince's offering, and we have to call up three people and read a minimum of three verses for each! Even dividing the six verses into two call-ups of three verses is not going to solve the problem.

The only solution, therefore, was to tack on to each day's reading the verses that describe the following day's princely offering. In order to weight the call-ups on the side of the appropriate day of Chanukah, we break up the reading of the relevant day of Chanukah into two, reciting the first three verses for the *Kohein* and the second three for the *Levi*. We then call up the third person (*shlishi*), and read for him the entire account (six verses) of the following day's princely contribution.

401. Is that the universal solution to the problem?

Universal? It's Judaism we're talking about! No, that is the Ashkenazi solution to the problem. Joseph Karo, reflective of the Sephardi tradition, states that the third person is not called up to the next day's reading (which, after all, is not relevant to the day of Chanukah being observed), but, instead, the portion for the present day, already read, is repeated in its entirety as the third person's reading.

402. But that section of the Torah describes twelve princes' contributions. Do we only cover the reading of eight of the twelve princes during Chanukah?

No. The liturgical approach is rather to complete the reading of an entire episode, even if only part of it is relevant. Thus, on the eighth day, we commence with the eighth prince (v. 54) and we complete the entire reading of the rest of the princes, concluding with the first paragraph of the following sidrah (Numbers 8:4).

403. But why slide over into the following sidrah? We never bridge two sidrot on any other weekday of the year?

The reason we do this on Chanukah is because the first four verses of the next sidrah (*Beha'alotkha*) deal with the commandment to Aaron and his offspring to keep the Sanctuary Menorah continually alight. This is, of course, a most relevant reading for Chanukah, and an opportunity that our sages felt should not be missed.

404. What do we read on the intermediate Shabbat of Chanukah?

We do not forgo the reading of the ordinary week's sidrah for a minor festival such as Chanukah. For this reason, we take out two scrolls, and we read the ordinary week's sidrah from the first. After that we recite half-*Kaddish*, and then read the six verses of the portion for the particular day of Chanukah from the second scroll.

405. What Haftarah is read on Shabbat Chanukah?

Tradition chose a reading (*Roni v'simchi*) from the prophet Zechariah 2:14–4:7. This was on account of the reference it contained to the Temple Menorah.

The prophet relates that an angel confronted him suddenly and asked him what vision he was experiencing. Zechariah answered, 'I see a candlestick all of gold, with a bowl upon the top of it, and seven lamps thereon' (4:2). The prophet then elucidates the meaning of that vision of light: 'This is the word of the Lord unto Zerubbabel, saying: "Not by might, nor by power, but by My spirit, saith the Lord of hosts"'.

Zerubbabel was the governor of Judea in the period following the return from exile in Babylon in 538 BCE. He had encountered many problems in attempting to re-invigorate the national spirit as a result of the adverse conditions facing the returnees. This prophecy of the Menorah was meant to hearten and inspire him to proceed vigorously with his mission to restore the Temple in the face of great internal and external opposition, and to reassure him of the light of God's presence blessing all his endeavours.

The parallel with the adverse conditions that faced the Hasmoneans in their similar struggle, and the place of the Menorah at the heart of that struggle, makes this a most relevant choice of Haftarah for Chanukah.

406. Are there not occasions when there are two Sabbaths during Chanukah? What Haftarah is read, then, on the second Sabbath?

When the first day of Chanukah occurs on a Shabbat, the last day of Chanukah will obviously also coincide on Shabbat. When that happens, we read as Haftarah on the last day a passage from I Kings 7: 40–50 describing the many Temple vessels and appurtenances commissioned by King Solomon for his Temple. These were fashioned by Hiram, a famous brass worker, son of a father who hailed from Tyre and an Israelite mother. This is also a most relevant theme for the festival of Chanukah, commemorating the restoration and rededication of the second Temple and its vessels and appurtenances.

407. But does not *Rosh Chodesh Tevet* also coincide with Chanukah? How is the Torah reading organized on that occasion?

If the two days of *Rosh Chodesh Tevet* occur on weekdays of Chanukah, we take out two scrolls. To the first scroll we call up three people for the usual *Rosh Chodesh* portion. (However, because we usually break up that reading into four portions, on Chanukah we link together the first and second portions, reading for the *Kohein* from Numbers 28: 1–6.). We then take the second scroll for the fourth call-up, and read the specific day's portion from the Chanukah reading.

408. Why does *Rosh Chodesh* take priority of place here, to read it before the Chanukah section?

Because of the principle, *Tadir ush'eino tadir, tadir kodem*, 'When one occasion recurs regularly and another less regularly, the regular one is accorded primacy'. *Rosh Chodesh* naturally occurs more frequently than Chanukah, and hence we read its portion first.

409. Why do we use two separate scrolls? Why not just roll the Torah to the Chanukah reading after concluding the *Rosh Chodesh* passage?

The main reason is in order not to interrupt the service with a vacuum, and burden the congregation with having to wait silently while the scroll is rolled to its place. It is also a glory for God's house that it be endowed with several scrolls, all of which are used during the course of the year.

410. What if *Rosh Chodesh Tevet* happens to coincide with Shabbat?

On that occasion, which occurs most regularly, we take out three scrolls. We call up the first six people to the reading of the regular week's sidrah from the first scroll. We then take out the second scroll, and call up the seventh aliyah to the reading of the *Rosh Chodesh* portion, commencing *Uv'yom ha-shabbat* (Numbers 28:9–15). We then recite half-*Kaddish*, take out the third scroll, and read from it the portion of the particular day of Chanukah. For Haftarah, as we have said (see Question 406), we read the passage from I Kings, dealing with the preparation of the vessels of Solomon's Temple.

411. But, surely, if that Shabbat is also *Rosh Chodesh Tevet*, we should apply the principle of *Tadir* (see Question 408), and, since *Rosh Chodesh* occurs more frequently than Chanukah, we should read the Haftarah for *Shabbat Rosh Chodesh*?

The precedence principle of *Tadir* is only applied where there are two readings, both of which are to be recited, and we wish to establish which to read first. Here, however, it is a matter of choosing between the two. In that situation the principle of *Tadir* is not adduced.

The reason we choose the Chanukah Haftarah, above that of *Rosh Chodesh*, is on account of the most important principle of *Pirsumei nisa'*, 'publicizing the miracle' of Chanukah.

412. Are there any other changes in the daily liturgy for the festival of Chanukah?

Yes. We do not recite *Tachanun* during Chanukah. This is the intercession prayer, bemoaning Israel's abject condition, the loss of her Temple and sovereignty, and calling upon God to protect His defenceless nation. The sentiments are given dramatic resonance by being recited, in part, leaning one's head on one's arm in a pose of desperate resignation. Understandably, it was regarded as wholly inappropriate for recitation on this joyful and optimistic festival.

For the same reason, we omit, on Monday and Thursday mornings, before the opening of the Ark, the *El erekh apayim* lines, which similarly echo Israel's state of sin and the resultant desperate condition she is suffering. In similar vein, we omit *Lamnatze'ach* (Psalm 20), which commences with the sentiment, 'May the Lord answer you in time of trouble'.

And, finally, on the Shabbat afternoon of Chanukah, we omit recitation of the *Tzidkatkha tzedek* paragraphs. Tradition has it that Moses, Joseph and David departed this life on Shabbat at the time of Minchah, and that the three *Tzidkatkha* verses constitutes a memorial to each of the three, respectively. The very word, *tzidkatkha* has an association with *Tzidduk ha-din*, 'the justification of the divine decree', which is the main part of the burial service. Understandably, it was regarded as inappropriate to be reminded of death, especially that of such spiritually illustrious personalities in our tradition, on the joyous festival of Chanukah.

413. Why is there no special *Musaf Amidah* prescribed for Chanukah, such as there is for *Rosh Chodesh* and the major festivals?

Simply because *Rosh Chodesh* and the major festivals are biblically prescribed, and were accompanied by special additional offerings offered in the Sanctuary and Temple. The synagogue *Musaf* (Additional) Service was introduced to commemorate those additionally prescribed sacrifices. Chanukah, however, was post-biblical, and not therefore endowed with any additional Temple rituals. It did not, therefore, justify a *Musaf Amidah* that deals primarily with the special sacrifices biblically prescribed for that particular festival.

LIGHTING THE CHANUKIAH IN SYNAGOGUE

414. What is the purpose of lighting the Chanukiah in synagogue when there is an obligation upon each person to light his own at home?

Again, it is simply in order to fulfil the duty of publicizing the miracle at all possible times. It is also possible that someone may be called away to an emergency immediately after synagogue and arrive home too late to light his Chanukiah, or may completely forget to do so. The *Levush Mordechai* adds a third reason, namely that it is performed on behalf of travellers staying overnight in town.[6]

The thirteenth-century Italian authority, Zedekiah ben Avraham Anav, author of *Shibbolei ha-Leket*, is most critical of this practice, stating,

Although it is also our custom (to light in synagogue), I do not understand its origin or basis. My teacher, R. Judah, refrained from kindling in synagogue, in order not to have to recite [unnecessary] blessings, and I am inclined toward that view. After all, if everyone is lighting their own lights at home, why should we require a synagogue lighting? If there are guests being accommodated at synagogue, it is they who need to light, and if there are no guests, then why light?[7]

415. Are there any differences between the ritual of lighting in the synagogue and that in the home?

Only that, in synagogue, many have the custom for the one lighting the lights and the congregation to recite responsively, after *Ha-nerot hallalu* and before *Ma'oz tzur*, the verses of *Mizmor shir chanukat habayit*, 'A song for the dedication of the House' (Psalm 30).

The synagogue is regarded as a *mikdash me'at*, a Temple-in-miniature; and hence the relevance of that psalm for the synagogue context on Chanukah.

416. When is the Chanukiah lit in synagogue?

It is lit between *Minchah* and *Ma'ariv*, in order to publicize the miracle for the duration of the Evening Service.

On Friday afternoon, most synagogues commence the Minchah service after Sabbath has already entered. Obviously, one could not then light the Chanukah lights in synagogue. To overcome the problem, synagogues set the time for Minchah earlier on Shabbat Chanukah – say, a quarter hour before the time of the commencement of Shabbat – to enable them to recite the service and then light the Chanukiah before the onset of Shabbat.

417. At what point in the service do we light the Chanukiah at the termination of Shabbat?

It is lit just before the recitation of *V'yiten lekha*, giving the congregation just a short period in which to contemplate the miracle of the lights.

418. But does not the lighting of the Chanukiah before *Havdalah* contravene the precedence principle of *Tadir* (see Questions 403 and 411)?

Theoretically it does. However it is outweighed by two other considerations: the overriding principle of *pirsumei nisa'* ('publicizing the Chanukah miracle') and, secondly, the principle of delaying the departure of the Sabbath as much as possible.[8]

419. On arrival home, what do we attend to first, *havdalah* or the lighting of the Chanukiah?

This is the subject of much debate among the authorities. Unlike the procedure in synagogue, where the lighting of the Chanukiah precedes *Havdalah*, at home we first make *Havdalah*, to see out the Shabbat, before inaugurating the lighting of the new night's lights. However, this accords neither with the view of Karo, in his *Shulchan Arukh*, nor with that of his great Ashkenazi commentator, Moses Isserles. The latter observes that, 'It goes without saying that at home one lights [the Chanukiah] first and then makes *Havdalah*, since he has already heard the *Havdalah* recited in synagogue'.[9]

Mishnah Berurah finds Isserles' view confusing, on the grounds that we do not have the intention to fulfil our duty of *Havdalah* through the synagogue recitation. He states that

> *Taz* and many latter-day authorities take issue, therefore, with the basic law of Karo and Isserles, and insist that *Havdalah* should precede the lighting, because of its greater frequency (*Tadir*).[10]

Mishnah Berurah concludes:

> Therefore, as regards synagogue practice, one should not change the custom that Israel has espoused, of lighting before *Havdalah*. At home, however, whichever custom he adopts has its champions![11]

NOTES
1. See *Mishnah Berurah* 682:1 (1).
2. See *Teshuvot Maharsham* 1:1.
3. See, for example, *Shulchan Arukh* 248:4 (end).
4. See Talmud *Erakhin* 10b.
5. See *Remah* on *Shulchan Arukh Orach Chayyim* 684:1.

6. See *Levush Mordechai* sec. 671:8.

7. *Shibbolei ha-Leket* (Venice, 1546), p.185.

8. See *Mishnah Berurah* 681:2 (2).

9. See *Shulchan Arukh* 681:2 and *Remah ad loc.*

10. *Mishnah Berurah* 681:2 (3).

11. Ibid.

13

Chanukah in the Home

CHANUKAH *GELT*

420. From where did the custom of giving children money, called 'Chanukah *gelt*', arise?

One of the most exciting aspects of the festival for children is the expectation and realization of receiving Chanukah *gelt* from parents and relatives. Some have the custom to give it each night of the festival, after the lighting of the candles.

We cannot be sure precisely when the practice arose, though it is plausible that it was nothing more than a counterbalance to the Christian practice of giving Christmas presents. Jewish children may well have envied the good fortune of their Christian peers around the same period of the year. Perish the thought that our little *kinder* should be deprived!

I speculate that it may also have been inspired by the Talmudic passage dealing with Chanukah, which states that 'it is forbidden to change money by the lights of the Chanukiah'.[1] As there are a host of other activities that could have been used as an exemplification of the prohibition of making use of the lights, it might be inferred that coins were counted and handed out to the family after the lighting of the Chanukah lights.

This may, in turn, have inspired the playing of games for money, which became a prevalent practice in the Middle Ages, and probably accounts for the origin of the *dreidl*, *trendl* or, to use its Modern Hebrew name, *sevivon*, though it is more plausible that Jews borrowed these practices from their Christian neighbours. It is known, for example, that long before the playing of *dreidl* was popularized, Christians played the identical game at Christmas time!

THE *DREIDL*, *TRENDL* OR *SEVIVON*

421. What is the *dreidl*?

It means 'little top', and is essentially a small, four-sided spinning top, with one of the Hebrew letters, *nun*, *gimmel*, *hey* and *shin* marked on each of the four sides. These are the initial letters of the four Yiddish words, *nichts* ('nothing'), *ganz* ('take all'), *halb* ('take half') and *shtell* ('put in'), which constitute the instructions that have to be followed by the players when the *dreidl* comes to rest with one of those letters face up. It is a game that was originally played for money, with the rules against gambling being relaxed for Chanukah in many circles, even without rabbinic sanction.

422. But I don't recall hearing our young children use those Yiddish instructions when they play dreidl?

No, you won't have. During the early part of the last century, with the influx of Jews to Western countries, coupled with the widespread abandonment of Yiddish as their *lingua franca*, a new significance was given to the four letters on the *dreidl*, which henceforth were construed as the initial letters of the verse, *Nes Gadol Hayah Sham*, 'A great miracle occurred there'.

With the rise of the State of Israel, many Israelis were uncomfortable with the implication of the last word (*sham*). They objected that, as the miracle occurred in Israel, surely the phrase should read, 'A great miracle occurred *here*!' The only problem was the letter shin. As there was no Hebrew word for 'here' commencing with a *shin*, they had no choice but to replace the latter with the letter pey, standing for *poh* ('here'). So much for tradition!

423. What is the difference between the names *dreidl*, *trendl* and *sevivon*?

They are simply the variant words derived from the main provenance from which the custom derived. The word *trendl* is pure German. The Yiddish (Judeo-German) term is *dreidl*. Other terms, originating in Eastern Europe, were *fergel* or *varfel*,[2] though these names have not survived into the modern period. The Modern Hebrew term for 'spinning top', *sevivon*, has become almost universal, except in more Right Wing, Yiddish-speaking, Orthodox communities. The popular children's Chanukah songs from Israel, as taught in all our nurseries and Hebrew Classes, have ensured the universal adoption of the term *sevivon* in the modern period. (As I am over 60, and reared on the name *dreidl*, I trust my readers will not be offended if, for nostalgic reasons, I continue to use that term here!)

424. From where did Jews derive the practice of playing *dreidl* for money?

Although the ancient Greeks and Romans utilized dice and spinning tops for gambling, its introduction into the Chanukah context was clearly a borrowing from the gambling device used in mediaeval Germany. Although gambling was not a Jewish preoccupation, and, indeed, was vehemently condemned by rabbinic authorities, on Chanukah people relaxed their opposition and made a concession to the joyful occasion, allowing their families a little flutter. The Hebrew letters on the *dreidl* helped to give the game a 'Jewish' complexion, and thus banish any suggestion of 'aping the customs of the gentiles'.

425. So how is *dreidl* played?

The game can be played with any number of participants. Before play commences, an equal number of coins (some use nuts, raisins, match sticks, sweets, or counters which can be cashed in later) is distributed to each player. (This is the preferred way, so that players can be eliminated when bankrupt, thus preventing the game continuing interminably.)

The *dreidl* is spun by each player in turn to determine who commences first; he or she being the first to throw a *gimmel*. Each player then feeds the kitty with one coin (or its alternative). The first player spins the *dreidl*. If it lands with top surface bearing the letter *nun*, then no action is taken; the player neither takes from, nor feeds, the kitty. If a *gimmel* is thrown, the player takes the entire kitty, though leaving in one coin as contribution to the next round. At that point (and whenever anyone spins a *gimmel*), all the other players must contribute another coin to the middle, whether or not it is their turn to spin. If a *hey* is spun, then half the contents of the kitty is won, though giving the advantage to the kitty. Thus, if there are three coins in the middle, the winner takes one; if there are five, he only takes two, and so on. If a *shin* is spun, one must 'put one in' to the kitty, and play passes to the person on his left, and so on, around and around and around – literally like a spinning wheel, until one overall winner emerges, or until everyone collapses from boredom! That is, apart from the kids, who can play it for hours on end.

In Galicia they practised a variety of the game, whereby each player bet in advance on which letter the *dreidl* would land.

426. Is *dreidl* restricted to the Ashkenazi, Central and Eastern-European tradition?

Originally this was the case, with the Sephardim doing little more than the kindling of the lights and the provision of special feasts for the children. Since the in-gathering of Jewry to the State of Israel, and the mutual borrowing and adaptation of traditions, *dreidl* has also become popular among Sephardim and other denominations.

JEWS AND GAMBLING

427. You referred (in Question 424) to gambling being opposed by rabbinic authorities. What do our sources actually have to say on the subject?

Compared with other ancient civilizations, Jews adopted gambling rather late in their development, for it is unknown until the age of Herod (first century BCE).[3] Jews at that time seem to have been so seduced by it, clearly as a result of the Roman occupation, that the Mishnah[4] saw fit to introduce the strongest measures in order to outlaw the practice, declaring the *mesachek bekuviah* (dice-player) unacceptable as a witness in a court of law. This was subsequently limited to one who became a professional gambler, and who, by pursuing no other gainful occupation, was undermining the progress of society. The later limitation may have been a concession forced upon the sages in the light of its widespread popularity as a leisure-time practice.

428. But why did those early sages oppose it so vigorously?

Undoubtedly because they feared the social consequences of a people, living not far above the bread-line, and with far more time on their hands than present-day folk, indulging in a pastime that, with the throw of a dice, could totally impoverish them.

They also believed that it countermanded the biblical law against theft. The reason given was that, at the beginning of a round, when players put their coins into the kitty, they were not truly giving the coins as a gift to the one who wins the round. Their clear hope and intention was that they, themselves, would win the round and gain back the coin they had put in, together with those of all the other players. The result was that the one who won that kitty was technically 'taking away' money from the other contributors against their real will. And, from the halachic perspective, that is theft!

429. So what sort of gambling did the ancients indulge in?

In addition to dice playing, the Mishnah refers to pigeon racing (*mafrichei yonim*). This involved betting on the pigeon that would reach a marked destination first, or betting on pigeons, trained to recognize from afar the shrill beckoning calls of their owners, to see which one could be recalled first.[5]

In the mediaeval period, Jews in France and Germany indulged in a greater variety of gambling, such as 'back or Edge', played with a knife which was thrown into the air. Players bet on which side of the knife would fall uppermost. From the fifteenth century, however, gambling became more widespread and sophisticated, with the introduction of playing cards, and it was not uncommon to find rabbinic authorities, in their sermons and writings, bitterly condemning the practice. In some communities, especially in Italy, communal enactments, or *takkanot*, were promulgated, prohibiting, under pain of fine or even excommunication, the assembling together in any premises for the purpose of gambling.[6] Nevertheless, the 'Chanukah *shpiel*' (card game) became *de rigueur* in many communities, and the religious authorities wisely turned a blind eye to it.

430. Did the practice of gambling on Chanukah have any defenders?

The great defender of Israel before the heavenly throne, Reb Levi Yitzchok of Berdichev, is credited with having defended the practice by claiming that, by staying up late in the night, playing cards on Chanukah, our young men were merely conditioning themselves to be able to stay up later during the rest of the year, in order to study Torah!

431. Is *dreidl* invested with any other significance?

Ever on the trail of mystical manifestations, one Chasidic Poirot discovered that the numerical value (*gematria*) of the four letters (*N G H S*) added up to 385, the same value as – wait for it – *mashi'ach* (the Messiah). Now, what this is meant to imply, I am not too sure. Perhaps it comes to reassure us that, in the Messianic era, *dreidl* is destined to become a universal pastime!

432. Could there have been any other purpose underlying the playing of *dreidl* on Chanukah?

It might have arisen out of a desire to provide a comparably pleasurable pastime to that offered by Purim, with its *seudah*-feast, fancy dress, dramatic plays, and greggers to drown out the very sound of Haman's name.

If Purim was in the mind of those who introduced the *dreidl*, we may speculate that it was inspired by the very name 'Purim', reminiscent of the lots drawn by Haman to determine which day of the year to destroy the Jews. Just as he chose a game of chance, and the day he chose was turned into a day of victory celebration for the Jews, so on Chanukah we play a game of chance, indicative of the unexpected victory that God handed the Maccabees.

433. Do any sources make such an association between the dreidl and Purim?

Indeed. The *B'nei Yisaschar* states that, on Chanukah there was a heavenly arousal, in the form of a miraculously wrought salvation; and hence we spin the *dreidl*, which is grasped from above. On Purim, however, the deliverance appeared in the form of a more natural victory, with heavenly support working from below, at the human level. Hence, on Purim, we spin the *gregger*, which is held from below.[7]

434. Has any other origin been suggested for the *dreidl*?

There is an unsubstantiated tradition, quoted in the *Otzar Kol Minhagei Yeshurun*, connecting it to that period when the Greeks forbade the study of Torah. Jewish children and their teachers obviously disregarded the edict, but the children kept by them a spinning top, so that, if any enemy soldiers appeared, they could pretend that they had gathered there simply to play.

435. So when is the proper time for *dreidl* to be played?

It is played while the Chanukiah is burning. As women have the custom not to do any work during that period, in tribute to the part played by Judith in killing the Syrian commander, Holofernes, it was always considered appropriate for the mother of the home to participate in the game.

And yet, the players also expected their Chanukah *latkes* to appear on the table at the same time! Well, if anyone can perform a modern-day Chanukah miracle, it is mum!

LATKES AND CHEESE BLINTZES

436. Now, what exactly are *latkes*?

Well, *latkes* are, simply, grated potato pancakes, fried in oil. This is, of course, to reinforce the motif of the miracle of the Chanukah oil.

They are quite lip-smackingly delicious, and are generally eaten until indigestion is assured. One of the modern-day Chanukah miracles – I am reliably assured by a pious doctor friend – is that people with higher levels of cholesterol do not need to be apprehensive. For, however many *latkes* one consumes on Chanukah, it has absolutely no effect! He quotes the Talmudic maxim, 'Whoever is engaged in the performance of a mitzvah is never harmed'. And what greater mitzvah could there be than eating *latkes* on Chanukah?

437. And from where did the custom of eating cheese-*blintzes* arise?

Well, this custom was certainly older than that of eating *latkes*. It probably derives from the story of Judith and Holofernes (see Question 192). The beautiful Judith is supposed to have taken with her various cheeses when she went to visit the tent of the Syrian commander. When, as a result, he became terribly thirsty, she poured him glass after glass of wine, until he was so drunk that he sank into a deep sleep, enabling her to cut off his head. In commemoration of her act, Jews ate cheese foods, and especially cheese-filled *latkes*, called *blintzes*, on Chanukah. The potato *latke* was probably a development of that practice.

GEMATRIA ENTERTAINMENT

438. We have referred to *dreidl* playing (for money or its substitute) and *latke* eating while the lights are burning. Were there any other pastimes reserved specifically for Chanukah?

Our sources refer to the popularity of table amusements, such as those employing *gematria*, arithmetical word equivalence. Thus, 'endless entertainment could be obtained by the discovery that certain words had the same arithmetical equivalence as other words, which might then be connected with them for moral or humorous purposes'.[8]

Another harmless game was *Samech* and *Pey*, the letters that are used, without any clear consistency, to demarcate the end of open (*petuchot*) or closed (*setumot*) paragraphs of the chumash.[9] This involves each player choosing either of the two letters as his own, and then, in turn, opening the chumash at random in an attempt to turn up his chosen letter the greater number of times.

ACROSTICS AND RIDDLES

439. Were there any other pastimes created especially for Chanukah?

Although its history long predates the medieval period and its association with Chanukah, a source of popular amusement on that festival was the creation of mnemonics, acrostics and riddles, centring on aspects of the festival or playing on the letters of the word *Chanukah*. One interpretation was that its letters represent An acronym for, *Chet Nerot V'halachah KeHillel*, 'Eight lights, and the halachic approach of Hillel' (namely, that of kindling an increasing number of lights each night, as opposed to the view of Shammai, that we should decrease each night).

The importance of providing harmless and challenging recreational activities was recognized by such distinguished scholars as the great Bible commentator, grammarian, poet and philosopher, Abraham Ibn Ezra (1089–1164), who composed some very profound and ingenious examples of this genre.

To give but one example: We have referred to the fact that Chanukah generally coincides with the sidrah *Mikkeitz*. In that sidrah we have the phrase, *shivru lanu me'at okhel*, 'buy for us a little food' (Genesis 43:2); and it was observed that that phrase contains within it a cryptic reference to the total number of lights kindled during Chanukah! This is not straightforward, other than to rabbinic minds accustomed to working along such obscure lines!

The solution is as follows: *Shivru* may also mean 'break into two' (from the root *shavar*). Hence *shivru lanu* may be construed as an instruction to 'break the [numerical value of] the word *lanu* – which is eighty-six – into two', giving a total of forty-three. The next phrase, *me'at okhel*, is construed as an instruction to add to that total 'the little one (*me'at*) of the word *okhel*', which is the letter *aleph*, whose numerical value is *one*. This gives a grand total of forty-four, which is the total number of lights (including the eight *shammash* lights) required for the entire festival! *QED!*

CHANUKAH PLAYS AND MASQUERADES

440. So have we exhausted all the types of Chanukah celebration?

No we have not. There is one more important aspect of Chanukah that we have not yet referred to, namely the staging of charades, and particularly the special Chanukah plays. This practice is several centuries old, having probably originated in the eighteenth century German ghettos, and is still perpetuated to this day in many Jewish schools and Hebrew classes. It is likely that the custom was actually borrowed from the Purim theatricals.

One of my own earliest recollections, in the cheder I attended in Manchester, England, in the 1940s, was of participating in a Hebrew Chanukah play, written by the principal who had arrived a few years earlier as a refugee from Germany. This pleasurable and educational experience ensured a sound basis of Modern Hebrew vocabulary (a year or so before the State of Israel was declared) which stood me in good stead for my later Hebrew language studies.

There are also references, in the seventeenth century, to Oriental communities staging masquerades on Chanukah, with men dressing up as women and parading through the streets.[10]

CHILDREN'S CHANUKAH SONGS

441. We referred previously (see Question 423) to popular children's Chanukah songs referring to the *dreidl*. Can you please cite one of the most popular of this genre?

With pleasure. The song, entitled *Likhvod ha-Chanukah* ('In honour of Chanukah'), is a must in every nursery and Junior school. It was written by Modern Hebrew Literature's most famous poet, Hayyim Nachman Bialik (1873–1934). I reproduce it here in transliteration and with my own free verse translation:

Avi hidlik neirot liy,	Father lit the lights for me,
V'shammash lo avukah.	With the Shammash there for all to see.
Yod'im attem likhvod miy?	Do you know in whose honour it is done?
Likhvod ha-Chanukah.	It's for Chanukah – oh what fun!

Moriy natan sevivon liy,	Teacher gave me a sevivon,
Ben 'oferet yetzukah.	Of brightly polished lead.
Yod'im attem likhvod miy?	We spin it in honour of Chanukah,
Likhvod ha-Chanukah.	Before we go to bed.

Immiy natnah levivah liy,	Mummy gave me a doughnut,
levivah chamah metukah.	A doughnut warm and sweet.
Yod'im attem likhvod miy?	When do we save them for?
Likhvod ha-Chanukah.	For Chanukah they're good to eat!

CHANUKAH AND CHRISTMAS

442. Are there any points of contact between Chanukah and the Christian festival of Christmas that is celebrated around the same time?

As Christian festivals are mostly rooted in the mother religion's ritual (Note that John Chrysostom, in his Pentecost sermon delivered in the year 386 CE, refers to Christianity's three great festivals of 'Epiphany, Pascha (Passover) and Pentecost'),[11] it would not be surprising to find such borrowings in the case of Chanukah. One would hardly have expected Christianity to employ a tree – a harvest symbol – as a ritual object in the middle of winter. On the assumption that Christmas was inspired by Chanukah, however, we have a simple explanation, bearing in mind that the Second Book of Maccabees refers to Chanukah as having been celebrated, as a substitute Tabernacles festival, with 'the boughs of thick trees and palm trees' (see Question 132).

The Christmas trees are also endowed with lights, as one would have expected if the roots of the festival lie in Judaism's 'festival of lights'. Indeed, in 381 CE, Gregory of Nazianzus, preaching in Constantinople, refers to the Epiphany as 'the festival of lights', a reference to the baptism of the one who, in Christian eyes, was 'the true light'.[12] Furthermore, the identical dates, Christmas on 25 December and Chanukah on 25 Kislev, the month that always coincides with December, seem hardly coincidental.

443. Has there been any reverse borrowing?

Inevitably. We have already referred to the giving of chanukah gifts. The sending of greetings cards was certainly influenced by Christmas custom. It has to be said that the Lubavitch practice of setting up a giant Chanukiah in the main thoroughfares of towns – something that is not required by or referred to in Jewish law, which restricts the Chanukiah to Jewish residences – is viewed by some as an aping of the Christian practice of setting up giant Christmas trees in town centres and public places.

444. Did the events of Chanukah have any more profound significance for Christianity?

According to Herman Wouk they decidedly did:

> The two festivals have one real point of contact. Had Antiochus succeeded in obliterating Jewry a century and a half before the birth of Jesus, there would have been no Christmas. The feast of the Nativity rests on the victory of Chanukah.[13]

NOTES

1. Talmud *Shabbat* 22a.
2. M. Grunewald, *'Ha-sevivon u-sevivato'*, in Y. Levinsky (ed.), *Sefer Ha-Moadim* (Tel Aviv: Dvir, 1957), vol. 5, p.225.
3. See Israel Abrahams, *Jewish Life in the Middle Ages* (Phildelphia: The Jewish Publication Society of America, 1958), p.390ff.
4. Mishnah *Sanhedrin* 3:3.
5. Ibid.
6. See Abrahams, *Jewish Life in the Middle Ages*.
7. See *B'nei Yisaschar*, section *Chodesh Kislev/Tevet*.
8. Abrahams, *Jewish Life in the Middle Ages*, p.382
9. On the *petuchot and setumot*, see Jeffrey M. Cohen, *Blessed Are You* (New Jersey: Jason Aronson, 1993), pp.180–1.
10. See Hayyim Schauss, *The Jewish Festivals* (New York: Schoken Books, 1962), p.236.
11. See entry 'Christmas' in *Encyclopaedia Britannica* (William Benton, 1970 ed.) vol. 5, p.705.
12. Ibid.
13. Herman Wouk, *This is my God* (New York: Doubleday & Co. Inc., 1958), p.106.

14

A Selection of Bereavement Regulations

TZIDDUK HA-DIN: THE BURIAL SERVICE

445. Why, on most festivals, is the usual *Tzidduk ha-Din*, pre-interment composition, replaced by the recitation of *Michtam le-David* (Psalm 16)?

The pre-interment service is called *Tzidduk ha-Din*, the justification of the divine edict. Its core theme is encapsulated in the verse, 'The Lord has given, the Lord has taken away. Blessed is the name of the Lord.' It draws attention also to the fact that His ways are inscrutable, that whatever fate is meted out to man is absolutely just, and it is accordingly improper for us to criticize them in any way; and it includes a prayer for mercy for the bereaved and life for 'the remnant of thy flock'.

It was felt that this composition was too poignant and possibly psychologically troubling to be recited on a festive day. The reference to the futility of life and man's inability to make any permanent impact upon it ('If a man live a year or a thousand years, what profiteth it him? He shall be as though he had not been.') could turn the already sad thoughts of the mourners, as well as the others attending the funeral, to morbid preoccupation. The reference to death as always being deserved might also upset the mourners and prompt feelings of religious rejection, especially in a situation where, for example, a person died prematurely. And the reference to God 'turning away His anger and not stirring up all His wrath' may also prove inexplicable to those brooding over the reality of their loss. Hence on festive occasions, characterized by the non-recitation of *Tachanun*, the *Tzidduk ha-Din* is replaced with psalm 16.

446. Why was *Michtam le-David* (Psalm 16) chosen as a replacement for the recitation of *Tzidduk ha-Din*?

This psalm, while referring to the inevitability of death, is primarily an optimistic affirmation of life and life eternal. It also expresses, on behalf of the bereaved, the many other blessings of life that they continue to enjoy, and for which they ought to remain grateful ('The Lord is the portion of my inheritance...Fate has dealt pleasantly with me...goodly things are my inheritance...My heart rejoices...My family will dwell secure...Thou hast made known to me the path of life...'). Hence the choice of this psalm as containing sentiments that are appropriate to festive days of the religious calendar.

447. So, is it the universal custom to substitute Psalm 16 on Chanukah?

It is certainly the universal Ashkenazi practice, though the *Taz* mentions that for a sage an exception may be made and the *Tzidduk ha-Din* recited. This is probably because the preoccupation of his life and the depth of his faith have totally removed death's sting from him, making the prospect of reunion with the Almighty a cause for a joyful expectation that the awesome sentiments of the *Tzidduk ha-Din* can in no way neutralize.

Sephardi authorities, on the other hand, were never troubled by the effects of reciting *Tzidduk ha-Din* on festive days, and they do not have the practice of substituting psalm 16.

448. Are there any other changes in the burial service during Chanukah?

Another variation in the burial service concerns the recitation of the lengthy *Kaddish* prescribed for children at the interment of parents. This is known as *Kaddish ha-Gadol*, ('The Great *Kaddish*'), and makes specific reference to the resurrection of the dead, their return to Jerusalem and the rebuilding of the Temple and the restoration of its service. It is also referred to as *Kaddish L'itchadata* ('The *Kaddish* of the Renewal') on account of the reference therein to 'the world which will be renewed' (*di hu atid l'itchadata*).

This *Kaddish* was regarded as a conclusion to the *Tzidduk ha-Din*, for which reason, on festive occasions such as Chanukah it is also omitted, and replaced with the ordinary 'Mourner's *Kaddish*'.

FUNERAL ORATIONS ON CHANUKAH

449. We referred previously (see Question 136) to the prohibition of delivering a *hesped* (funeral oration) on Chanukah. But if one attends a funeral (or stone-setting) these days, will one not hear the rabbi deliver such an oration?

It depends. There are Orthodox communities which will not permit it, while others take a more lenient view. The *Shulchan Arukh* itself opens the door to a measure of leniency in permitting a *hesped* to be delivered in honour of a sage, prior to his interment.

A rationale for taking a more lenient view in general is that our modern-day orations do not correspond, in intention or execution, to the ancient and medieval tear-jerking variety. Our presentations partake rather of the nature of an appreciation of the life of the departed. Their purpose is not to arouse deep emotions and lamentation on the part of the bereaved, but, on the contrary, to calm their spirits and still their anguish. Such low-key presentations do not measurably dilute the joyful spirit of the festival for those attending the funeral any more than does the inevitable sadness engendered by the death itself.

The present writer has attended funerals taking place at cemeteries administered by communities whose authorities prohibit orations on such occasions, and has witnessed the anguish caused to the mourners at the prospect of their loved one being interred without so much as a word of tribute. If anything, the upset caused by such an insult to the memory of their departed is a greater diminution of the joyful spirit of the festival than that engendered by the introduction of a *hesped*.

TZIDDUK HA-DIN ON THE EVE OF CHANUKAH

450. Normally, the afternoon leading into a festival already partakes of the festive spirit. At such a time, therefore, we omit, in the Minchah service, the recitation of *Tachanun*, with its reference to King David's sorry plight: *Tzar liy me'od* ('I am in great distress'). Do we omit *Tzidduk ha-Din* and the special *Kaddish ha-Gadol*, therefore, when an interment takes place after noon, prior to Chanukah?

Logically, we should omit it. However, it was a matter of dispute between Ashkenazim and Sephardim as to whether, even on *Chol Ha-moed*, the *Tzidduk ha-Din* may be recited. Karo insists that it should, whereas Isserles reports that the consensus in Ashkenazi communities was not to recite it.[1] The *Mishnah Berurah* maintains, however, that on the afternoon prior to Chanukah it is to be recited,[2] presumably because Chanukah does not partake of the same *simchat yom tov*, joyful spirit, as a major festival or even its intermediate days. By the same token, the special *Kaddish ha-Gadol* (see Question 448) should also be included.

THE PUBLIC, POST-INTERMENT '*SHURAH*-GREETING' OF THE MOURNERS

451. At the end of the service of interment throughout the year it is customary for the mourner to walk between two rows (*shurah*) of comforters, and to be greeted by them with the words *Ha-Makom yenacheim*... 'May the Almighty comfort you among all other mourners in Zion and Jerusalem'. Is this ritual performed during the days of Chanukah?

The question is presumably motivated by the fact that we do not offer formal comfort on the main festival days of our calendar. Nevertheless, according to the Talmud and the major codes, there is no objection to doing so, and in previous ages it was indeed performed. Since people go about their daily work on Chanukah, Rosh Chodesh and Purim, those minor festivals were deemed ordinary days as regards the making of the *shurah* lines and the offering of public consolation.

KINDLING THE CHANUKAH LIGHTS BY A MOURNER IN THE PERIOD BETWEEN BEREAVEMENT AND BURIAL

452. Normally, an *onen* (a mourner prior to burial) is absolved from the performance of all positive religious duties. Is that also the case regarding the lighting of the Chanukah lights?

Here the authorities seem to take a midway position, advising that the *onen* should preferably have the lights kindled, and the blessings recited for him, by his wife or another person. This is because *pirsumei nisa*, 'the publicizing of the great miracle', is such an overriding principle at this period.

453. Does the *onen* respond with *Amen* to the other person's recitation of the blessings?

The problem is that to respond with *Amen* to the blessing that another makes on one's behalf is tantamount, in halachah, to reciting the blessings oneself. *Mishnah Berurah* states that the authorities are in fact divided on this point.[3]

454. What should the *onen* do if there is no one available to light the candles for him?

He should light them himself, but without reciting any blessing.

OBSERVANCE OF *SHIVAH*

455. Does Chanukah cancel out the requirement of sitting *shivah*, as is the case with other festivals?

No, it does not. *Shivah* is observed in the usual manner. It is only a biblical festival, for which there is an overriding obligation of 'Thou shalt rejoice on thy festivals' (Deuteronomy 16:14), that neutralizes any formal and public demonstration of mourning, as represented by the *shivah*. As Chanukah is not a biblical festival, and does not partake, therefore, of that degree of festivity, the norms of *shivah* and mourning proceed as usual.

456. If the first night of Chanukah occurs during the period of *shivah*, may the mourner recite the *Shehecheyanu* blessing?

The question is based on the fact that the *Shehecheyanu* blessing is intended to underscore and reinforce the joy of the occasion, and may thus be construed as inappropriate for someone in mourning. The ruling is that the mourner does recite that blessing, however, on the first night of Chanukah, 'just as he is obliged to recite that blessing on all other occasions for which it is prescribed'.[4] The spiritual joy which that blessing engenders is of a higher quality. Its roots are in national pride and gratitude to God, and are not perceived as being inimical to a state of personal mourning.

457. Do we perform a public lighting of the Chanukah lights in a *shivah* house?

Although there is the overriding principle of *pirsumei nisa* ('publicizing the miracle'), for which reason one might have regarded it as most appropriate to have a public lighting before the service, yet it is not our custom to do so. The joyful voices of a crowd singing the *Ma'oz Tzur* creates a light-hearted spirit that is inappropriate to the atmosphere of the memorial service being observed.

THE *SE'UDAT HAVRA'AH* (MOURNER'S MEAL)

458. On returning from the interment, mourners do not eat of their own food, but have it prepared for them by others. This meal consists of hard-boiled eggs and rolls. It has also become customary to add some salt herring. On some occasions this meal is dispensed with. What is the situation regarding its provision after a Chanukah interment?

It is, indeed, dispensed with on late Friday afternoons, or on the eve of a festival, after the ninth hour of the day. The reason is so that the mourner will retain an appetite for the obligatory Sabbath or festival meal. On Chanukah, however, where there are no such obligatory evening meals, the special mourner's meal is provided.[5]

HALLEL IN THE HOUSE OF MOURNING

459. Where a morning service is being held on Chanukah in a *shivah* house, is the joyful *Hallel* composition included in the prayers?

The recitation of *Hallel* on Chanukah is talmudically mandated. Authorities are divided, however, as to whether it should be recited publicly in the house of mourning. Some take the view that the mourner recites it with the rest, in order not to separate himself from the community. Others require him to withdraw to an anteroom while the other worshipers fulfill their duty of reciting it; while there are some authorities who assert that *Hallel* should not be recited by anyone in a house of mourning, and that those who attend should recite it for themselves when they return home. The custom of one's community should be followed.

ATTENDING A CHANUKAH PARTY

460. May a mourner, during his or her year of mourning for parents, and thirty days for other relatives, attend a Chanukah party?

No, they may not. The Talmud lays down the clear guideline that Chanukah is to be commemorated exclusively 'by the recitation of *Hallel* and (*Al Ha-nisim*) thanksgiving'. Indeed, the *Tur* quotes the unequivocal ruling of the illustrious Ashkenasi halachist, Rabbi Meir Mi-Rothenburg, that 'the customary increase in Chanukah celebratory meals is an optional matter, for the sages did not prescribe [as in the case of Purim] 'banquets and celebrations', but only *Hallel* and the thanksgiving composition'.[6]

A MOURNER AS *CHAZAN* ON CHANUKAH

461. May a (post-*shivah*) mourner lead the services in synagogue on Chanukah?

The majority view is that a mourner may lead the afternoon and evening services on Chanukah, and the morning service until *Hallel*. There are some communities, however, such as the Chasidim, who do not permit a mourner to lead any service. Their view is that, try as he inevitably would, it would prove impossible for the mourner totally to conceal the sadness in his heart. This would be detectable in the intonation of his voice, and it would tend, therefore, to detract from the joy of the festive period.

YAHRZEIT ON CHANUKAH

462. If a near relative died on one of the days of Chanukah, is it safe to assume that every year the *yahrzeit* will occur on that particular day of the festival?

No, it is not. The precise Hebrew date should be noted and observed. The reason for this is that the sequence of days is broken by the incidence of *Rosh Chodesh* (the new moon of) *Tevet*, which occurs in the middle of Chanukah. In some years there are two days of Rosh Chodesh, and in others only one. Thus, in the year 2006, the 2nd of Tevet is the eighth day of Chanukah, whereas in 2007 it is the seventh day!

NOTES

1. See *Shulchan Arukh Yoreh De'ah* 401:6.
2. See *Mishnah Berurah* 429:7; *Shakh* on *Shulchan Arukh,Yoreh De'ah* 401:3.
3. See *Mishnah Berurah* 671:12.
4. *Gesher ha-Chayyim*, chapter 23:3 (8).
5. Ibid., Chapter 20:2 (11).
6. *Tur* section 670.

VIII
CHANUKAH CUSTOMS
FROM AROUND
THE WORLD

15

Chanukah Customs from Around the World

THE WAY CHANUKAH IS CELEBRATED

463. Are the customs of Chanukah, as practised by different Jewish communities, as varied as they are in the case of the other festivals?

They are not. In fact one encounters a surprising uniformity in the way Chanukah is celebrated all over the world. This may be accounted for as a result of the synagogue liturgy being little different from that of any other day of the year, with the exception of the addition of *Hallel* and *Al Ha-nisim*. While there is a special Torah reading each day, yet, unlike, say, *Rosh Chodesh*, it is not endowed with a *Musaph* (Additional) *Amidah* and was never, at any time, celebrated with any cessation from work. For this reason, there was little scope or time available for the introduction of any liturgical poetry or other customs and ritual innovations. The celebration was generally confined to the home, with the lighting of candles, the evening meal and the family games and diversions.

In Western countries, as we have observed, the general Christmas and New Year festive period influenced some of the ways Chanukah was celebrated in families, and served to ensure that Jewish children did not feel that they were missing out. In Muslim countries, on the other hand, there was no such influence or consideration, and Chanukah tended to be celebrated, therefore, as a rather low-key event.

464. Is the giving of Chanukah gifts to family and friends an example of that Christian influence?

It might well have been, as we have already suggested. However, many would prefer to view it as a borrowing from the festival of Purim, which enjoys a similar religious status and a kindred spirit. On Purim there is a biblical instruction to celebrate by sending *mishloach manot*, 'gifts of goodies' to one's friends,[1] and this may well have been taken over into Chanukah.

465. Could the giving of 'Chanukah *gelt*' similarly be traced back to native Jewish practice?

We have already indicated a Talmudic source which might be interpreted as providing a precedence for the giving of Chanukah money to one's children (see

Question 420). We should add that children were not the only beneficiaries. In the *shtetl*, it was also customary to send such *gelt* to one's Hebrew teachers as well as to the poor.

The origin of the custom could also be attributed to the Maccabees themselves! On regaining their country's independence, they immediately threw out all the currency that the hated Antiochus had minted, and which had displayed the head of that murderous and idolatrous tyrant, and replaced it with Jewish coinage. The children would naturally have been given the new coins by parents, grandparents and family who would have been in a particularly generous and happy mood at such a time.

466. Speaking of the *shtetl*, was the Chanukah spirit much in evidence there?

From chroniclers of Jewish life in the East European *shtetl*, and particularly from writers such as Sholom Aleikhem, Agnon and Mendele Mokher Seforim, we learn that Chanukah was a heady period of the year when everyone was expected to join in with the festive spirit and to liberate themselves from the drudgery that characterized much of their day-to-day routine.

Chanukah was a time for parents and teachers to overlook the young people's pranks, to relax their firm opposition to gambling so that such games as chess, draughts, cards and a variety of Bingo might all be played, with the additional challenge and thrill of some modest financial gain. The teenage children would inevitably have been allowed to join in on this one occasion in the year; and, with their pockets unusually jingling with Chanukah *gelt*, the temptation to double their money – for children who knew nothing of spending-money or birthday gifts – must have been overwhelming. The lucky ones would frequently treat themselves to a sleigh ride around the town. Such materialistic indulgence!

The shops would all put up their shutters well before nightfall, so that the proprietors could attend the evening service at synagogue on their way home to light the candles, after which families would entertain, or be entertained by, other family members, neighbours or friends. This was a time when hostess's reputations for their potato pudding and *latkes* could be made or unmade! Unlike Purim, it was not a time for inebriation, though a few more drinks than normal were undoubtedly downed.

The local Hebrew schools would stage an annual Chanukah event, the centrepiece of which was the Chanukah play. The programme would also include a concert by the local chazanim, a performance by the town band and a succession of stand-up comics who would tell jokes at the expense of Antiochus and perform sketches which set out to parody him and cast him as a buffoon. As this performance was repeated on several evenings of the festival, it was seen by most of the townsfolk. Scouts for the Yiddish theatre, which developed in the nineteenth century, would watch out keenly on Chanukah (and Purim) for any emerging talent. Even on Chanukah, the rabbis would not countenance young boys and girls acting together, and would certainly not permit the singing voices of 12-year- old girls to be heard. A concession to the demands of the Chanukah script was frequently made, however, to allow the boys to dress up as women.

THE CHANUKAH PLAY AND THE ENTERTAINMENT INDUSTRY

467. Were there any spin-offs from those Chanukah plays?

I suppose that 'spin-off' has to be a most appropriate word for a Chanukah performance! It is, in fact, an under-statement, for it is probably true to say that the Chanukah and Purim plays of the *shtetl* were a major contributory factor to the Jewish fascination with theatre. This, in turn, inspired our unique contribution to the modern entertainment industry.

In New York, for example, the first performance of a Yiddish play took place on 18 August 1882. Before the end of the century, three of the actors had already opened their own theatres, and Jews were providing the acting, singing, song-writing and literary talent that laid the groundwork for the stage and cinema industry of the twentieth century.

A NORTH-AFRICAN CELEBRATION

468. Were there any similar women's celebrations reserved for Chanukah?

There were. In some North-African communities, young girls were welcomed to the synagogue on the seventh day of Chanukah. They would ascend the steps, and pass, in single file, before the opened Ark where they would proceed to kiss the scrolls of the Torah. The *Haham* (spiritual leader) of the community would then raise his hands over the girls and bless them with the traditional priestly blessing. He would also arrange a *siyyum*, or conclusion of the study of a Talmudic tractate, to coincide with that occasion, and the banquet that always accompanied a *siyyum* was held specifically in honor of the young women.

SEPHARDIC CUSTOMS OF THE OLD YISHUV OF PALESTINE

469. Did the Sephardim of the old Yishuv practice any unique Chanukah customs?

We have literary reminiscences of the way Chanukah was celebrated among the Sephardi community of Jerusalem in the late-nineteenth and early-twentieth centuries.[2] There was a particularly popular custom, calculated to make Chanukah doubly appealing for the youngsters. This was 'The pupils' Feast', celebrated in school on the final day of the festival. During the first seven days of the festival, the teachers and their pupils, for whom Chanukah was a school holiday, would visit all the homes in the Yishuv, and collect gifts of rice, flour, garlic, onions, beans, oil and coal – all the raw materials for a grand culinary banquet – and money with which to purchase the meat and chickens. That was also the occasion to elicit funds to buy clothing for the poor children of the community, and to ensure that they were adequately and warmly dressed for the cold winters of hilly Jerusalem.

The teachers and their pupils would enter each house during the course of the festival evenings and sing a few songs and recite some *grammen*, or humorous rhyming lines, for the entertainment of the family, after which suitable remuneration would be proffered.

During the course of the seventh day, an entire army of volunteers helped to cook all the food, and on the last morning they would bring it in large cauldrons into the school-house of the Old City, next to the Synagogue of R. Yochanan ben Zaccai, where, in the presence of the *Rishon le-Tzion*, the Sephardi Chief Rabbi of the city, and other distinguished sages and personalities, a special Chanukah service, presentation and party was held. Rice, beans, pastilles and delicacies were also distributed at the door of that synagogue to poor widows. For the children, that was *the* banquet of the year, and the excitement at receiving their 'going home gifts' of food, money and, for the poor, new clothes, knew no bounds.

In some Sephardi communities they would also light fireworks and burn effigies of Antiochus.

470. Do we know of any other unique Chanukah customs emanating from the old Yishuv in Palestine?

In Hebron, the ancient city where the Patriarchs are buried, the Sephardi women had the practice of celebrating the last day of Chanukah as an occasion for a women's only dairy banquet. License was granted by their husbands for them to eat and drink to their hearts' content. They sang and danced until the early hours, and their entertainment also involved some good-natured mockery of the male sex. In addition to the celebration, however, it was also expected that any feuds between women would be patched up before the night was over. Similar parties were also celebrated within the Jewish community of Greece.

A TURKISH CUSTOM

471. Are there any unique customs emanating from the Jewry of the old Turkish empire?

We have a tradition that in Ismir, famous as the birthplace of the pseudo-Messiah, Shabbethai Zevi, it was the custom to weave the wicks of the Chanukiah from the fibre in which the *etrog* had been packed. The preparation of those wicks was done by the women, for tradition had it that a woman, the prophetess Deborah, would weave the wicks for the Menorah of the Sanctuary.

The Turkish Jews would also save the remains of the Chanukah candles, which they would melt down to make a candle to be used for the searching of the *chametz* on the eve of Passover. This was in keeping with the tradition that one should not discard a material that has once been used for the performance of a mitzvah, but should rather employ it in the performance of another mitzvah.

On the last day of Chanukah, the Sephardi community in Turkey celebrated the festivity of *Merenda*, a picnic, shared by the entire family and friends. The individual invitees brought with them a specific course or delicacy. *Bimuelos* or *Loukomades* are the popular Sephardi equivalent of the Ashkenazi latkes. They come in various forms, some as puffy fritters, some as muffins, and others like flat pancakes baked on a griddle. They are dipped in warm syrup and generously sprinkled with cinnamon.[3]

YEMENITE AND KURDISTANI CHARMS

472. Were there any beliefs regarding the oil left in the Chanukiah?

There was a belief, in such countries as Yemen and Kurdistan (and probably in other countries in the region), that the remains of the Chanukah oil possessed, or attracted, miraculous properties. In the Yemen it was used as a medication, and was also believed to afford protection against the Evil Eye. Pregnant Jewish women in Kurdistan would rub it on their bodies, and believed that it was efficacious as a charm for ensuring a safe delivery. It was also used as a medication to cure infant illnesses. The Pesach *Afikoman* was believed to be similarly efficacious.

Another Kurdistani custom was for the children to burn a doll made of wood and rags at the end of the Chanukah week. The doll would be endowed with a beard and pipe, and carried a large candle in its hand. As with the English celebration of Guy Fawkes Night, the Kurdish children would march the doll around the streets, extracting donations from passers-by. At the conclusion of Chanukah, they would tear off the beard – a method of male humiliation going back to biblical times – and then set fire to it. While it burnt they would cry, mockingly, '*Antiochus! Antiochus!*'

ORIGIN OF THE CHANUKAH BONFIRES

473. Could the practice of lighting bonfires, or setting fire to effigies at the conclusion of Chanukah, have any roots in traditional sources?

It may well have developed out of a ritual prescription. Early authorities, such as *Avudarham* and *Shibbolei ha-Leket*, quote the eighth century Babylonian Gaon, Ahai of Shabcha, author of the *She'iltot*, as requiring that, because the oil placed in the Chanukiah each night was mentally designated as exclusively for the purpose of fulfilling the mitzvah (*huktza lemitzvah*), any oil remaining after the wick had burnt out on the last night of Chanukah could not be used for any other purpose. 'One should therefore make a bonfire and burn it away.'[4] It is possible that the various post-Chanukah bonfires, burning of effigies or fireworks, were extensions of, and inspired by, that practice of burning off the remaining oil.

A PERSIAN CUSTOM

474. Do we know of any unique Persian Chanukah customs?

We hear of an exotic variation of the previous custom, whereby the children would go around the houses to secure a seasonal gift, holding fire pans of burning coals. On receipt of a gift, they would toss onto their pan a particular herb that made a sizzling and explosive sound. They would then bless the householder with the words: 'So may the eyes of all your enemies explode'

SYRIAN CUSTOMS

475. Did any other community inject a superstitious element into the Chanukah ritual?

Syrian Jews recall that the teachers of the Hebrew school in Damascus used to send the infant pupils five-branched Chanukiahs shaped to look like the human hand. This was the popular shape of the talisman popularly employed in Oriental communities to ward off the pernicious effects of the Evil Eye. Hence its name, *hamsa*, from the Hebrew *chamesh*, 'five', a reference to the five fingers of the hand that deflects the evil. Such a talisman was regularly found in synagogues, schools and other places where people congregated in numbers, and was even incorporated into synagogue ritual appurtenances.[5] Its popularity has been restored in Modern Israel, thanks to the paramount influence of the Sephardi community and its propensity to superstitious belief in the Evil Eye.

It was also a Syrian practice for the children to be given Chanukah candles made from the drippings of the wax candles that had been used to light the synagogues over Yom Kippur.

CHANUKAH IN BOMBAY

476. Do we have any reminiscences of how Chanukah was celebrated among the ex-patriot Iraqi Jewish community of Bombay?

I am grateful to my friend and congregant, Mr Eddie Ezra, for sharing his personal recollections as a child in Bombay. In 1970 that community numbered over 10,000 Jews, which a steady immigration to Israel has now reduced by half. Mr Ezra states as follows:

If Rip van Winkle, or Yankle Vandenberg, had woken up in the Jewish club in Bombay on Chanukah, he would be forgiven for thinking that it was in fact a Purim festivity that had disturbed his 100-year sleep. This is because most of the children under the age of twelve would have been in fancy dress, parading up and down and creating quite a din. This local tradition would take place on the last night of Chanukah, soon after the eighth candle had been lit. As on Purim, prizes were awarded for the most creative costumes. This would be followed by playlets on the theme of Chanukah.

'Our family would only light one Chanukiah, and it was the exclusive prerogative of my father, the head of the household, to light it. Instead of using the *Shammash* to light the candles, we would use matches or a candle separate from the *Shammash* [see Question 229], and I or one of my sisters would then light the *Shammash*. This seems to have been a widely accepted practice, especially among Sephardim of Iraqi origin.

Another custom of the Iraqi Jews was to distribute to all the congregants coloured prayer and song sheets with gold Hebrew writing. A popular Chanukah song was *Yah hatzeil yonah m'chakah*, ('Lord, save the waiting dove'), the dove being the symbol of Israel that is 'awaiting' redemption.

The traditional Chanukah food in our community was not doughnuts, but a sweetmeat called *halaawa*, made from semolina, flour, water, oil, sugar and almonds. I am not biased, but my mum's version was undoubtedly the best! Throughout the festival it was customary to eat dairy foods, to recall the miracle wrought by God through Judith.'[6]

CHANUKAH IN COCHIN

477. Did the Jews of Cochin have any distinctive Chanukah observances?

They did, indeed, have some very distinctive Chanukah customs, unknown outside their own community. On the Shabbat before Chanukah, prior to the Torah being read, they would read aloud the *Megillat Antiochus* (see Question 356), in the same way as it is customary in many other traditions to read the 'Five Megillot' in synagogue on the biblically-prescribed festivals.

On the first day of the festival they observed a communal *Yahrzeit* in memory of the revered mystic of Cochin, Rabbi Nehemiah Motha, who had died on the first day of Chanukah in the year 1615. They would also visit his grave, recite prayers and make vows.

Following the kindling of the lights at home, the families would walk to synagogue, singing the hymn, *Al eim ha-derekh* ('Along the highway'), following a route that had already been decorated and festooned with candles and banana stalks on both sides of the road. At synagogue they would participate in a communal lighting, after which they would assemble each night at a different home to spend the evening in song and dance. This would include a traditional Chanukah dance for women. During the evening, fireworks would be set off and an effigy of Bagris, Antiochus's second-in-command, would be set alight by the children.[7]

CHANUKAH AND THE BENE ISRAEL OF INDIA

478. Did the Bene Israel of India observe Chanukah?

Historically, they did not. Toward the end of the nineteenth century, however, when travellers and Orientalists began to visit the community, bringing with them reports of the rituals and practices of their fellow Jews the world over, they became attracted to the celebration of Chanukah.

H.S. Kehimkar, an authority on the Bene Israel, takes the view that the community's religious observances approximate closely to that of the Kingdom of Northern Israel after its separation (following the death of King Solomon) from the Kingdom of Judah. The community was cut off from mainstream Judaism and its historical evolution and development down the ages, and was consequently left in ignorance of Chanukah, as well as of Purim and the four historical fast days of national mourning for the loss of the Jerusalem Temples.

Kehimkar believes that they pulled up their roots, in the province of Galilee, and moved to India, some time between the fourth and the third centuries BCE, and certainly before the events of the Maccabean period. Their own tradition, however, is that they actually left as a consequence of the persecutions inflicted on the Jews of Palestine by Antiochus Epiphanes, and that their ship was wrecked just off the coast of Bombay. Isolated from Jewish life, they remained in ignorance of the Maccabean struggle, its victory and the introduction of the festival of Chanukah.

Since their adoption of the festival, they made Chanukiahs, which they attached to a wall in their living room, in the form of a brass frame, holding eight glasses in a row, with a ninth glass pendant above the row of eight.[8]

A QUESTIONABLE LIBYAN CUSTOM

479. Do we have any Chanukah traditions emanating from Libya?

In 1951, some 37,000 Jews emigrated to Israel from Libya, leaving a present-day remnant of some fifty souls. They report an ancient Libyan custom related to the Reading of the Torah on each day of Chanukah. This was to honour the *Shammash* (sexton) of the community with the first *aliyah* ('call-up') on each day of the festival, as a mark of appreciation for all his efforts on behalf of the community.

This is a questionable practice, however, since Jewish law allows no exception to the rule that it is a *kohein*, a member of the priestly fraternity, who has that exclusive prerogative. The only time that may be set aside is if there are no priests in synagogue. The mystery remains!

As to why this honour was reserved just for the festival of Chanukah, we may conjecture that it arose through some association with the word *shammash*, which is both the Hebrew title of that communal servant and, of course, the 'servant light' of the Chanukiah.

A HUNGARIAN CHANUKAH CUSTOM

480. Do we know of any unique Chanukah custom practiced in East-European communities?

It was the custom in some Hungarian communities to dedicate the first Shabbat of

Chanukah to the members of the *Chevra Kadisha*, the honorary members of the Burial Society, who attended to the specialized preparation of the body prior to interment. The members would be called to the Torah on that Shabbat, and a banquet would be held in their honour.

The association with Chanukah is loose, but it probably derives from the link between light – the primary motif of Chanukah – and the soul, as already indicated in the biblical verse, 'For the lamp of the Lord is the soul of man' (Proverbs 20:27).

LUBAVITCH CUSTOMS

481. Is any particular night of Chanukah favoured in Lubavitch tradition for special treatment?

The fifth light of Chanukah, or as it is called in Yiddish, *der finfter licht*, was always regarded as a special night, and it was on that night that the Chanukah gelt was distributed to the children. The choice of that particular night seems to have been motivated by the mystical consideration that the fourth day of Chanukah corresponds with 28 Kislev. Twenty-eight (*kaf-chet*) in Hebrew is *koach*, 'strength'. That day of Chanukah was thus perceived as having been invested with extra spiritual power, and this attaches to the light that is lit at the climax of that day, namely, the fifth light (though some preferred to give out the *gelt* on the fourth night, coinciding with the initial release of that power).

The late Lubavitcher Rebbe himself gave a simpler explanation of the significance of the fifth day of Chanukah in one of his addresses to children. He pointed out that, until that day, we light on the first side of the Chanukiah, and are only in the first half of the festival. From the fifth night, we have lit the greater part of the Chanukiah, and, since 'everything follows the majority', that is the light which tips the balance towards the completion of the mitzvah, and symbolizes our successful mission to spread the light of Torah in the world.[9]

In more recent years, the Rebbe recommended that all members of the family should receive *gelt* (presumably from each other), and that the children should receive a little on every night of the festival. Lubavitch families always give money, and never presents, since the latter would seem to be aping the Christian practice of Christmas gifts.

482. Do Lubavitch have any variation in the way the lights are lit?

Their custom is to light at the doorway of a main family room, such as a dining room, lounge or morning room, with each male lighting his own Chanukiah. Lubavitch Yeshivah students would light at the doorway of their dormitory rooms. The late Rebbe recommended that, in order to heighten the awareness of the miracle for young children, the Chanukiah should be lit at the doorway of the child's bedroom.[10] However, this recommendation does not seem to have been adopted universally by his followers, perhaps on grounds of safety.

483. Do Lubavitch have any other variations of custom in the lighting of the Chanukiah?

They recommend that oil be used for the lights, but that, for the *Shamash*, a wax candle be employed. The Rebbe explains that, apart from the practical fact that it is not as easy to light the other lights by means of an oil wick as it is with a wax candle, there is also the fact that the latter is secondary in importance to the oil light, which reflects the original Temple practice. For that reason, it is more appropriate to use a wax lamp, of lesser status, to service the primary oil lights with which one fulfils the mitzvah.[11]

484. Why is Lubavitch so eager to install giant Chanukiahs in the centre of towns?

My friend and congregant, Mr Mendy Sudak has expressed it in this way:

> Lubavitch is known for its giant Chanukiahs. Indeed, when this was opposed, either by City Councils or by the *Litvishe* (i.e. non-Chasidic) world, the Rebbe encouraged chasidim to go to great lengths to 'put the case in a forceful and favourable way' and to win the argument, which we always did! In addition to straightforwardly 'publicizing the miracle', the public lighting led to a substantial increase in those attracted to the Lubavitch outreach programme.[12]

It is probably true that in America, a country of immigrants, the notion of a minority group publicly parading and celebrating its peculiar practices is more readily acceptable than, say, in Britain. The *Eiruv* (linked poles, creating a notional enclosure within which one may carry on Shabbat) is a clear example of the difficulties encountered in this regard in London, where opposition to its introduction was so very strong. Indeed, it took almost twelve years of pressure before the local council finally agreed to its installation. This was not helped, of course, by the strident opposition of a number of Jews, who feared that 'it would create a ghetto'.

It was the same with the giant Chanukiah, which occasioned much unease in many Jewish quarters when it made its first appearance. Mr Sudak's comment would indicate, however, that it was always a great attraction among the younger generation that obviously did not possess the same inhibitions as their elders! In truth, it has now ceased to be an issue.

THE MACCABIAH

485. What is the Maccabiah?

The Maccabiah can best be described as the Jewish Olympics, and was conceived as an opportunity to encourage Jews to become involved with sporting activities. This was regarded as necessary in an era when most Jewish youth were afforded little opportunity to enjoy exercise, outdoor activity or professional training in their own countries.

It was the brain child of Joseph Yekutieli, a founder of the Maccabi movement in Palestine, who persuaded Meir Dizengoff, the mayor of Tel Aviv, to build the first sports stadium in the country, and to house the event every four years. Apart from its intrinsic benefit, he also argued that it would bring people to Palestine from all over the world, and would be good for the local economy as well as for encouraging *aliyah* (immigration).

The first Maccabiah was held there in 1932, attracting 400 athletes from eighteen countries, and since that time a further sixteen Maccabiahs have been staged. The event now attracts the participation of over 5,000 athletes from fifty countries competing in over thirty sports.

Among the most notable Maccabiahs was the ninth, which took place in 1973, the year following the massacre of eleven Israeli athletes at the Munich Olympic Games. A capacity crowd at the opening ceremony paid silent tribute to the memory of those murdered. Also memorable was the fourteenth Maccabiah, in 1993, that marked the return of South Africa to international sport after eighty years of political isolation due to that country's Apartheid policies. It was also notable for the participation, for the first time since World War II, of Jewish athletes from Eastern European countries. Their presence was facilitated by the fall of Communism and the freedom of travel and participation in international Jewish events that they were now able to enjoy. The sixteenth Maccabiah took place in 2001, under the dark shadow of the Palestinian *intafada*. The games were reduced from ten to seven days, and thankfully were completed without incident.

486. Which Maccabiah will be remembered as the most eventful?

The fifteenth Maccabiah, which took place in 1997, will sadly remain indelibly engraved on the minds of all who participated and attended. This was because of the collapse of a temporary bridge erected to carry the marching delegations over the River Yarkon into the Ramat Gan Stadium for the opening ceremony. Four Australian athletes were killed and many more were injured. The Australian delegation bravely decided to continue to compete, albeit with their depleted and dispirited members. An investigation concluded that the construction and components of the bridge had been sub-standard, and criminal charges were subsequently brought against the manufacturers.[13]

NOTES

1. See Esther 9:22.
2. See Yom-Tov Levinsky (ed.), *Sefer ha-Moadim*, Chanukah (Tel Aviv, Dvir, 1957), vol.5, pp.246–9.
3. See The Sephardi Sisterhood of Los Angeles, *Cooking the Sephardic Way* (Kansas City: The North American Press of Kansas City, 1971), p.123.
4. See S. Kreuzer (ed.), *Avudraham ha-Shalem* (Jerusalem: Usha Publishing, 1963), p.200.
5. See the illustration of a nineteenth century Moroccan *Ner Tamid*, suspended

from an ornate *hamsa* in *Encyclopaedia Judaica* (Jerusalem: Keter Publishing House, 1971), vol.12, p.965.

6. Mr E. Ezra, personal communication, 20 June 2001.
7. See O. Slapak (ed.) *The Jews of India* (Jerusalem: The Israel Museum, 1995), p.92.
8. See Shirley B. Isenberg, *India's Bene Israel* (Bombay: Popular Prakashan, 1988), pp.6–7.
9. See M.M. Schneersohn, *The Rebbe Speaks to Children* (New York: Tzivos Hashem, 1997), vol. I, p.207.
10. See M Schneersohn, *Sha'arei Halachah u-Minhag* (Jerusalem: Heikhal Menachem, 1993), p.274.
11. Ibid., p.275.
12. Mr Mendy Sudak, personal communication, 15 July 2001.
13. I am grateful to Mr Stuart Lustigman, the British Team Manager, for information on the recent Maccabiahs.

IX
CHANUKAH QUIZ QUESTIONS AND ACTIVITIES FOR THE YOUNGER GENERATION

16

Chanukah Quiz Questions and Activities for the Younger Generation

DATES AND DAYS QUIZ

487. a. What is the Hebrew date of the first day of Chanukah?

(25th Kislev)

b. For how many days does Chanukah last?

(eight)

c. The last day of Chanukah falls some years on 2 Tevet and some years on the 3 Tevet. How is that possible?

(Where the previous month, Kislev, has only 29 days, then the last day of Chanukah will fall on 3 Tevet. Where Kislev has 30 days, the last day of Chanukah will occur on 2 Tevet.)

NUMBER QUIZ

488. a. How many lights do we light, excluding the shammash, during the entire festival?

(thirty six)

b. How many lights do we light, including the shammash, during the entire festival?

(forty four)

c. How many blessings are recited over the Chanukiah during the entire festival?

(Seventeen. On the first night we recite three, since *Shehecheyanu* is added to *lehadlik ner* and *She'asa nisim*. On each of the remaining seven nights we recite just the latter two.)

d. Using the numerical value of the Hebrew letters (alef =1; yod =10, etcetera), what is the total numerical value of the four letters on the *dreidl*?

(Three hundred and fifty-eight. The letters are *nun* [=50], *gimel* [=3], *hey* [=5], and *shin* [=300]).

e. For how long should the Chanukah lights burn each night?

(A half hour into night.)

f. How many sons did Matityahu have?

(Five)

g. How many sons can you name?

(They were Simon, Eliezer, Judah, Yochanan and Yonatan.)

h. How many people are called to the Torah each day of Chanukah?

(Three)

PEOPLE QUIZ

489. a. Who was the wicked leader of the Greek-Syrian empire?

(Antiochus)

b. What was the name of the young Jew who was killed by Matityahu when he volunteered to eat of the pig that the Greeks had brought to Modin?

(Jason)

c. Some pious people refused to defend themselves against the Greek Syrians on the Shabbat, and were easily massacred. What were they called?

(Chasidim)

d. What was the name of the courageous mother who encouraged her seven sons to lay down their lives, rather than worship the Syrian-Greek gods?

(Hannah)

490. a. What title was given to the Judah, the Jewish general?

(Ha-Maccabee).

b. What is the meaning of that title?

(It can mean 'the hammer' or 'hammerer', or it can be a word derived from the initial letters of his battle cry, *Mi Kamokha Ba'eilim Hashem*, 'Who is like You among the mighty, O Lord?')

c. What was the name of the Jewish heroine who slipped into the Syrian camp and cut off the head of the Syrian commander?

(Judith)

d. What was the name of the Syrian commander?

(Holofernes)

TRUE OR FALSE

491. a. Matityahu's first name was Binyamin.

(False. Matityahu was his first and only name.)

b. Modin, where Matityahu lived, is situated to the east of Jerusalem.

(False. It lies north-west of Jerusalem.)

c. The single jar of oil that remained when the Maccabees regained control of the Temple still bore on it the seal of King Solomon.

(False. It bore the seal of the High Priest.)

d. Matityahu was Queen Esther's cousin.

(False. Queen Esther lived about three hundred years before Matityahu.)

e. The Maccabees succeeded in building the Second Temple.

(False. While they did some re-building work, and renewed the altar and other vessels, yet the second Temple had already been rebuilt in the year 517 BCE, that is 350 years earlier.)

f. The Maccabees made themselves kings of Israel, even though they were not of the tribe of Judah, from which Jewish kings are appointed.

(True.)

g. While the lights are burning, we eat an apple dipped in honey

(False. We do that on Rosh Hashanah. On Chanukah we eat latkes and [oily] doughnuts.)

h. The money gifts that children receive are called 'Chanukah belt'.

(False. It is called 'Chanukah *gelt*'.)

i. The Hebrew term for 'the Chanukah miracle' is *Mes Chanukah*.

(False. It is *Nes Chanukah*.)

THE CHANUKIAH QUIZ

492. What is the main difference between the Menorah that was lit in the Temple and the one we use on Chanukah?

The Temple Menorah had seven branches, whereas our Chanukiah has eight branches, to enable us to light it for eight nights on account of the miracle.

493. On which night of Chanukah do we have to add more oil than is used on all the other nights, or use a longer candle?

On the Friday night of Chanukah. That is because we bring Shabbat in about an hour before nightfall. Since the Chanukah lights have to burn for a half hour into the night, there has to be enough oil, or a candle long enough, to burn for one and a half hours on that night.

494. On Friday nights, which do we light first: the Shabbat lights or the Chanukiah?

We have to light the Chanukiah first. This is because, once the Shabbat lights have been lit, it is already Shabbat in the home, and we can no longer light the Chanukiah.

495. Where should the Chanukiah be placed?

In the front window, overlooking the street, so that passers-by can see, and we can publicize the miracle of Chanukah to them.

THE GREEK SYRIANS QUIZ

496. What were the Greeks doing in Syria at that time?

The Greek General, Alexander the Great, had conquered Syria and its surrounding countries in the year 333 BCE. His generals ruled Syria after that time, and they imposed the Greek religion and way of life on a wide area of the Middle East. The struggle against the Jews was when Antiochus, the Greek ruler, invaded Israel and attempted to force the Jews to abandon their religion and adopt the Greek faith and way of life, called Hellenism.

497. What did the Greeks especially forbid the Jews to do?

They forbade the Jews from learning Torah, from circumcising their sons and from keeping the Shabbat and festivals.

CHANUKAH ACTIVITIES WHILE THE CANDLES ARE BURNING

498. How many more words can you make out of the phrase, 'I like Chanukah gelt?'

No answer to this one. While the candles are burning, give all the family a pen and paper and see who makes the most words. Set a time limit, according to age. Give the older teenagers and adults, say, five minutes; the 10–13 year olds, seven minutes; the 8–10 year olds, ten minutes; and the under-eights, until they give up! Obviously the winner is entitled to some extra Chanukah *gelt*!

499. See who can create the funniest limericks out of these openings:

> i. On Chanukah when I was young,
> I found I had the sweetest tongue.
> .....

> ii. I walked past Fagin's gang, so proud,
> My Chanukah *gelt*, jingling loud.
> .....

iii.
> There was a Jewish Greek called Jason,
> Who found some pig in a basin.
> ....

> iv. If I had fought with the Maccabees,
> And ended up on my knees.
> ....

500. Who is the Chanukah Public Speaking Champion?

See who can speak for a minute, without deviation, hesitation or repetition of any key word. A successful challenge allows the challenger to take over the speech, and whoever is still speaking when the minute is up, wins five points. The one to win fifteen points first is the champion. One of the adults in the family should act as the adjudicator and time-keeper.

Here are some suggested topics:
- i. Chanukah *gelt*
- ii. If I was a shammash ...
- iii. If I had met Antiochus on a dark night ...
- iv. Oily Chanukah doughnuts ...
- v. Playing *dreidl* ...
- vi. That miracles still happen these days ...
- vii. My mother's *latkes* ...
- viii. If the Maccabees had lost...
- ix. The Maccabiah ...
- x. If the Temple were rebuilt in our day ...

Bibliography

This reference list is restricted to works actually referred to or quoted in the body of the text or notes to the text. Where no publisher is listed, a private publication – usually that of the author himself – may be assumed. This list does not include the classical rabbinic sources, of Mishnah, Talmud, Midrash and codes of law, that have been freely drawn upon throughout this book.

Abrahams, I. *Jewish Life in the Middle Ages* (Philadelphia: The Jewish Publication Society of America, 1958).

Anav, Zedekiah ben Avraham, *Shibbolei ha-Leket* (Venice: 1546).

Arieti, J.A., 'Nudity in Greek Athletics', *Classical World*, 68 (1975), pp.431–6.

Baer, S., *Seder Avodat Yisrael* (Jerusalem: Schoken. 1937; reproduction of original Roedelheim edition, 1868).

Ben-Sasson, H.H., *A History of the Jewish People* (Cambridge, MA: Harvard University Press, 1976).

Bickerman, E.J., 'The Historical Foundations of Postbiblical Judaism' in *The Jews: Their History, Culture and Religion*, ed. Louis Finkelstein (London: Peter Owen Ltd, 1961).

Braun, S.Z., *She'arim Metzuyanim B'halakhah* (Jerusalem/New York: Feldheim. 1978).

Bright, J., *A History of Israel* (London: SCM Press. 1964).

Cashdan, E., Translation of *The Authorised Daily Prayer Book of the United Hebrew Congregations of the Commonwealth* (London: Singer's Prayer Book Publication Committee, 1992).

Charlesworth, J.H., *The Old Testament Pseudepigrapha* (New York: Doubleday, 1983).

Cohen, J.M., *Blessed Are You* (New Jersey. Jason Aronson, 1993).

— *Prayer and Penitence* (New Jersey: Jason Aronson, 1994).

— *1001 Questions and Answers on Pesach* (New.Jersey: Jason Aronson, 1996).

— *1001 Questions and Answers on Rosh Hashanah and Yom Kippur* (New Jersey: Jason Aronson, 1997).

Dimont, M., *Jews, God and History* (London: W.H.Allen, 1964).

Dubnow, S., *History of the Jews from the Beginning to Early Christianity* (English ed., M. Spiegel) (New York: Thomas Yoseloff, 1967).

Eisenstein, J.D., *Otzar Dinim Uminhagim* (New York: Hebrew Publishing Co.

1938).

Elbogen, I.M., *Ha-tefillah Beyisrael* (Tel Aviv: Dvir. 1988).

Emden, J., *Siddur Bet Ya'akov* (Lemberg: D. Balaban, 1904 edition).

Encyclopaedia Judaica (Jerusalem: Keter Publishing House Ltd, 1971).

Epstein, Rabbi Yechiel M., *Arukh Ha-Shulchan*, 8 vols (Tel Aviv: Yetzu Sifrei Kodesh. undated).

Forms of Prayer for Jewish Worship (London: The Reform Synagogues of Great Britain, 1979), pp.268–9

Frosh, S., *For and Against Psychoanalysis* (London: Routledge, 1997).

Ganzfried, S., *Kitzur Shulchan Arukh* (various editions): *Hilkhot Chanukah*, section 139.

Ginzberg, L., *The Legends of the Jews*, 7 vols (Philadelphia: The Jewish Publication Society of America, 1946).

Graves, R., ed. *Larousse Encyclopedia of Mythology* (London: Paul Hamlyn, 1959).

Greenberg, I., *The Jewish Way* (New York: Summit Books, 1988).

— 'Maccabean spirit can be rekindled.' *Jewish Chronicle*, 7 Dec. 1990, p.29.

Grunewald, M., '*Ha-sevivon u-sevivato*', Y. Levinsky (ed.), in *Sefer Ha-Moadim*, (Tel Aviv: Dvir, 1957), vol.5, p.225.

Hartman, D., *Rabbinic Responses to History as Mirrored in Hanukkah and Purim* (Jerusalem: The Shalom Hartman Institute for Advanced Judaic Studies, undated).

Higger, M. (ed.), *Masechet Soferim* (New York: Hotsa'at D'Bei Rabbanan, 1937).

Humphrey, N., *Soul Searching* (London: Chatto & Windus, 1995).

Idelsohn, A., *Jewish Liturgy and its Development* (New York: Holt, Rinehart and Winston, Inc., 1932).

Isenberg, S.B., *India's Bene Israel* (Bombay: Popular Prakashan. 1988).

Josephus, Flavius, *Antiquities of the Jews* (London: Henry G. Bohn, 1845).

Kahane, A., *Ha-Sefarim Ha-Chitzonim* (Tel Aviv: Masada Publishing, 1960).

Kerkeslager, A., 'Maintaining Jewish Identity in the Greek Gymnasium', *Journal for the Study of Judaism in the Persian, Hellenistic and Roman Period*, xxviii, 1 (Feb. 1997) (Brill, Leiden) pp.12–33.

Klausner, J., *Historiah shel Ha-Bayit Ha-Sheni* (Jerusalem: Ahiasaf, 1959).

Kreuzer, S. (ed.), *Avudraham ha-Shalem* (Jerusalem: Usha Publishing, 1963).

Lauterbach, J.Z., 'The Ceremony of Breaking a Glass at Weddings,' *Hebrew Union College Annual*, v, 2 (1925), pp.351–80.

Levinsky, Y. (ed.), *Sefer ha-Moadim*, vol. 5 (Tel Aviv: Dvir, 1957).

Lichtenstein, Z., 'Megillat Ta'anit,' art. in Hebrew Unopion College Annual (Cincinnati Union of American Hebrew Congregations), VIII–X (1931–2) pp.318–351.

Lurie, Ben Zion, Megillath Ta'anith with Introduction and Notes (Jer., Bailik Institute, 1964).

Maharshak, A., '*Hadlakat ner chanukah bechashmal*' (Jerusalem: Heikhal Shelomo, 5736) pp.172–7.

Oesterley, W.O.E., *A History of Israel* (Oxford: Clarendon Press, 1932).

Rafeld, M., '*Ha-nuscha'ot hashonot shel birkat ner chanukah*', in D. Sperber (ed.),

Minhagei Yisrael (Jerusalem: Mosad HaRav Kook, 1995).

Raphael, C., *The Springs of Jewish Life* (London: Chatto & Windus, 1982).

Rapoport-Albert, A. and Zipperstein, S.J., *Jewish History: Essays in Honour of Chimen Abramsky* (London: Peter Halban, 1988).

Sacks, J., 'Chanukah Address to Rabbinical Council of the United Synagogue, UK', Dec. 1998.

Schauss, H., *Guide to Jewish Holy Days* (New York: Schoken Books, 1962).

Schneersohn, M.M., *The Rebbe Speaks to Children* (New York: Tzivos Hashem, 1997), vol.1.

Sephardi Sisterhood of Los Angeles, *Cooking the Sephardic Way* (Kansas City: The North American Press of Kansas City, 1971).

Shanah B'Shanah (Jerusalem: Annual of Helkhal Shelomo, Chief Rabbinical Centre, 5736), pp.172–7.

Slapak, O., *The Jews of India* (Jerusalem: The Israel Museum, 1995).

Sperber, D., *Minhagei Yisrael* (Jerusalem: Mosad HaRav Kook, 1995), vol.5.

Tcherikover, A., *Ha-Yehudim ve-ha-Yevanim be-Tekufah ha-Helenistit* (Tel Aviv: Dvir, 1963).

Tukachinsky, N.A., *Gesher Ha-Chayyim*, 2 vols (Jerusalem, 1960).

Urbach, E.E., *The Halakhah: Its Sources and Development* (Jerusalem: Yad la-Talmud, 1986).

Waxman, M., *A History of Jewish Literature* (New York: Thomas Yoseloff, 1938).

Weinberger, L.J., *Jewish Hymnography: A Literary History* (London: The Littman Library of Jewish Civilisation, 1998.

Wouk, H., *This Is My God* (New York: Doubleday & Company, Inc., 1959).

Zeitlin, S., *Megillat Ta'anit* (Philadelphia: Dropsie College for Hebrew and Cognate Learning, 1922).

Zimmels, H.J., *Ashkenazim and Sephardim* (London: Oxford University Press, 1958).

Index

Numbers refer to questions, not to pages